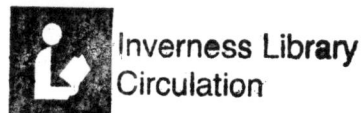 

You Never Fail Until You Stop Trying

The Story of a Pioneer Woman Chemist

by

Nell I. Mondy

DORRANCE PUBLISHING CO., INC.
PITTSBURGH, PENNSYLVANIA 15222

All Rights Reserved
Copyright © 2001 by Nell I. Mondy
No part of this book may be reproduced or transmitted
in any form or by any means, electronic or mechanical,
including photocopying, recording, or by any information
storage or retrieval system without permission in writing
from the publisher.

ISBN # 0-8059-4628-4
Printed in the United States of America

First Printing

For information or to order additional books, please write:
Dorrance Publishing Co., Inc.
643 Smithfield Street
Pittsburgh, Pennsylvania 15222
U.S.A.
1-800-788-7654
Or visit our web site and on-line catalog at *www.dorrancepublishing.com*.

DEDICATION

To my mother and my grandmother
and to my students
whom I call my "Crown Jewels"
because they designated me
"The Potato Queen."

Purpose

As a participant of the Faculty Lecture Series at Cornell University's student union I was invited to lecture on my fifty years of experience as a pioneer woman chemist. The enthusiastic response from the students to this lecture inspired me to write this book.

I decided to write this book with the hope of encouraging today's young women to pursue science as a career option. It was more difficult for a woman to succeed in the field of chemistry when I was starting out than it is today, but the process still remains challenging. The need for hard work and strong drive is stressed throughout the book. The book's appeal is not limited to young women entering the male-dominated fields of science; rather, I hope that every person who has encountered these difficult challenges and obstacles in their lives will find inspiration in these pages.

Contents

Acknowledgments ix

Prologue x

The Early Years:
  1921-1939 1

Becoming a Chemist
  Ouachita College: 1939-1943 16

Graduate Study in the Lone Star State
  Texas University; Austin, Texas: 1943-1945 30

First Year at Cornell
  Research Associate, Biochemistry and Nutrition: 1945-1946 40

Educating New York World War II Veterans
  Sampson College: 1946-1948 48

Return to Cornell: Food Chemistry
  Department of Food and Nutrition: 1948-1951 53

Cornell Ph.D. Degree
  Sigma Xi Fellow: 1951-1953 58

Scotland: First Phase of Food International
  United States Department of Agriculture: 1960-1961 65

Food Behind the Iron Curtain
  Poland, Czechoslovakia: 1966 78

Looking at the Food Industry
  The R.T. French Company: 1966-1967 87

In the Land of Shrimp and Seminoles
   Florida State University: 1969-1970 97

Around the World in Thirty Days
   Japan, Korea, Hong Kong, India, Iran, Turkey: 1978 102

Protecting United States Food Quality
   Environmental Protection Agency: 1979-1980 115

A Journey to South America
   Peru, Bolivia, Chile: 1982 119

Food Congress in the Emerald Isle
   1983 130

Nigeria: Yams and SoyMilk
   1983-84 133

Sharing Science with Africa
   Ivory Coast: 1984 154

Food Around the World
   Spain, Soviet Union, Finland, Taiwan, Thailand,
   Singapore, China, Philippine Islands: 1987 160

Teaching Researchers in Indonesia
   Gadjah Mada University: 1989 171

Adventure on Paradise Island: Mauritius
   African Potato Association: 1990 180

Potatoes Down Under
   Australia, New Zealand: 1991 185

Research
   Microbes, Rats, Potatoes 190

Philosophy of Teaching 206
   I. University Teaching 208
   II. Educating the Public 223

Summing It Up 228

Acknowledgments

It would be impossible for me to thank all the people who have welcomed me, tolerated me, and cared for me wherever I have gone in my years of travel. It would be equally impossible to thank all those who had a part in shaping the life recorded here, but I especially want to thank my mother, grandmother, teachers, mentors, and most of all, the students.

Specifically, I want to thank, for their support, criticism and help with this manuscript, Dr. Ben Elrod, Dr. Andrew Westmoreland, Marguerite Palmer, Margaret Wright, Mary Madearis, and Louise Buckelew. For their able assistance in its preparation I thank, Valerie Adamcyk, Steven Gardiner, Rhoda Morrow, Russell Underwood, and Ann Perna.

Prologue

My mother liked to tell stories, particularly parables that applied to everyday life. One parable was particularly meaningful to me during my life as a chemist. The story involved two common birds, a blue jay and a woodpecker. Mother often called me her little redheaded woodpecker because of the color of my hair. The birds, outside in the bitter cold, peered through a window at a cozy room heated with a nice warm fire.

Determined to get inside to avoid freezing, the birds decided to peck a hole in the wall. After expending a great amount of energy, they discovered they had made very little progress. Discouraged, the blue jay cried, "I can't! I can't!" and quit pecking so he soon froze to death. But the determined woodpecker kept pecking and saying all the while, "I think I can! I think I can!" Although never able to enter the house, his constant effort kept him warm, and he survived. The moral of the story is, "You never fail until you stop trying."

When I was quite young, my mother would sometimes ask me, "Nell, if you had all the feathers you could carry, could you carry just one more?" My answer: "Certainly."

On many occasions I may have undertaken more than I should have, but I have had fun in responding to many challenges.

These words "YOU NEVER FAIL UNTIL YOU STOP TRYING" are printed on a wooden plaque which hangs in my office, offering encouragement to me and my students. During my trying times I remember this parable.

THE EARLY YEARS:
1921-1939

My grandmother's family fled to Arkansas during the Civil War, and Mother was born there in the small town of Warm Springs. The family was originally from Missouri which was a "border" state hotly contested by both sides. Families were often split along political lines, and relatives of mine fought on both sides of the war.

My grandmother Frances "*Fan*" and her younger sister, Lucy, were the youngest of fifteen children of Jesse and Elizabeth Pratt when the Civil War broke out. With the men away fighting, they remained on the plantation in the care of their mother, Elizabeth Pratt, and the few slaves the family owned. It was a trying time for all; the house was often raided by both Confederate and Union soldiers seeking food and supplies.

The children were taught to hide the family's few remaining valuables from the raiders. When the soldiers came, my grandmother slipped two tall brass candlesticks into the woodpile behind the house. One of those candlesticks remains in the home of my cousin; sadly, the other has been lost.

During another raid, a Union soldier slung one of my great grandmother's homemade quilts over the back of his horse. My grandmother, who was very young, was shocked. Her mother's exquisite quilts were family treasures and were also used as covers to protect against the cold winter weather. She couldn't bear to see them stolen. When the soldier returned from the house with more loot, he found my grandmother sitting on the quilt. Not having the heart to move the brave little girl, he left it there.

Today I own that quilt. It serves as a special reminder of my grandmother's strength of character even at a very young age. Several of my great-grandmother's quilts survived the war, and each one reveals something of her personality and her strong belief in God and family. A woven quilt was made from the wool of sheep raised on the farm. My great-grandmother spun and dyed her own threads which she then used to weave parts of our family history into a lovely spread. It depicts a family Christmas tree with Santa distributing presents to the young people. My grandmother was later able to identify all the children represented. The spread also depicts written scripture verses. As a child, I was embarrassed by the printing because all of the n's were backward, but antique dealers have since told me that this quirk makes the spread even more valuable.

My great-grandmother was very religious. Mother once told me she could quote the entire New Testament from memory, and Mother often commented that her grandmother was the most brilliant woman she had ever known. Like my grandmother and me, my great-grandmother had red hair. Although she was not traditionally pretty, she was a woman of integrity and intelligence. Her husband, Jesse Pratt, in addition to being a Baptist minister, was also a plantation owner. The church he established in Ironton, Missouri is still active today.

The family was forced to leave Missouri toward the end of the war when Union soldiers came to the house. This time they had not come to raid but to burn. They told my great-grandmother that she had only thirty minutes to clear the house of valuables before the house would be destroyed. She, with the help of the children and slaves, loaded all that could be carried into an ox-drawn wagon. Together they drove into Northern Arkansas, away from the fighting, to start a new life. The town in which they settled was Warm Springs.

After the war ended, the slaves were free to go, but instead they chose to stay with the family which treated them well. There seemed to be a great affection between the family and their slaves. A slave girl named Cille saved my grandmother's life. My great-grandmother stored lard in barrels to preserve fat she had rendered from the hogs. She buried these in the ground to lessen the effects of oxidation. One day while playing, my grandmother knocked the cover off one of the barrels and fell in. Feeling herself sink, she cried out, but her mother thought she was only being playful. Cille recognized that something was wrong and went to her aid immediately, pulling her to safety. Cille stayed with the family in Arkansas until she died.

Although the family was happy together in Warm Springs, the divisions created by the war remained problematic. My grandmother and her sister Lucy were political opposites. Too young to remember many of the hardships the family had endured during the war, Lucy became a staunch Republican, while my grandmother remained a true Southern Democrat. I remember one conversation they had on the porch when I was a child. Aunt Lucy had loaned Grandmother a copy of Lincoln's biography which she had enjoyed. Lucy said, "Fan, did you read that book I gave you?"

Grandmother did not answer.

"I said, did you read that book I gave you?" Still, grandmother did not respond.

"Fan," Lucy said, impatient now. "Did you read that book . . . that I gave you?"

Finally, Grandmother said, "Hm. Yes, I read it. Imagine—putting Lincoln equal to God."

Despite their differences, Grandmother and Aunt Lucy remained close. By listening to their discussions, I developed a deeper understanding of politics and realized the importance of seeing both sides of an issue.

My grandmother's first husband, Mr. Hufstedler, with whom she had three children, died prematurely. Her second marriage was to my grandfather, Jasper N. Carroll, a farmer and a Civil War veteran endowed with a healthy pension. He was a widower with three children of his own. Together they had three more children, of whom Mother was next to the youngest. The family later moved from Warm Springs to Pocahontas, Arkansas.

Mother grew up in Warm Springs but after moving to Pocahontas, she met and married my father Daley D. Mondy. Though she received little formal schooling, she managed to cultivate a career in journalism and worked as a typecaster and later as a writer on the local weekly newspaper. She and my father, a successful teacher and restauranteur, were each in their thirties and well-established before they married. As was the custom in those days, Mother quit her job to become a full-time homemaker. Shortly after I was born, my father discovered that he had tuberculosis. There was no cure for the disease at that time. Although he sought help at the Woodman Sanitarium in Colorado Springs, Colorado, he died when I was two years old.

We remained in Pocahontas, Arkansas, a small town near the Missouri border with a population of about twenty-five hundred. It was, and still is, a beautiful place, marked by hills and lowlands and surrounded by five rivers, brimming with fish.

In many ways, Pocahontas was a typical Southern town, complete with its own traditions and heritage. We had a cotton gin and two factories, one for canning and the other for making handles for rakes and hoes. In the hills, where the wealthier residents lived, there was a family shoe store that dated back three generations and two corner drug stores that served sodas and ice cream cones for a nickel.

The main churches in Pocahontas—Catholic, Baptist, Methodist, and Church of Christ—served as centers for the town's social life with youth groups, socials, and services many nights during the week. I gave my first speech at the First Baptist Church in Pocahontas. The values I learned there and the faith that was instilled in me have provided guidance throughout my life.

One lesson I learned in church occurred during a musical performance. I often played the clarinet; during one solo, my instrument squeaked horribly. As a perfectionist, even at that early age, I was mortified. I remember crying afterward but my band director reassured me that: "Sometimes I squeak on the clarinet. Everybody squeaks once in a while."

My mother was a religious woman, and through the church she worked to help the less fortunate of our town who were concentrated in the lowlands. During the 1920s and 1930s, there were no dams, and often the rivers would overflow their banks, flooding the low-lying areas and leaving behind deposits of rich soil. These lands were owned by the wealthier people of the town and were rented to the less fortunate. The residents of the lowlands were known as the "bottoms people." They were white sharecroppers mostly and worked the fertile soybean and cotton fields. My mother had always been concerned for the bottoms people whose homes were sometimes destroyed by the flooding. In addition to distributing food and clothing to the needy, Mother taught Sunday school in one of the lowland homes. She constantly stressed that no one is destined for poverty, and that with hard work and ambition, any American can improve his or her lot in life.

Often Mother took me with her when she visited the homes in that area. In one rather poorly constructed house she told me, "Look how clean it is," and showed me around inside. It was clean. The cotton drapes were plain but neat, and the furniture was cheap but well maintained. "Being poor doesn't mean you need to be filthy," she said, "as long as you have pride in yourself." At that time, it was considered a disgrace to be poor. People had a passion to advance, to "pull themselves up by their own bootstraps," without charity or pity.

Thirty years later, mother revisited Pocahontas, and she found that many of her former students had advanced. She was pleased by their words of gratitude for the example she had set, offering them a helping hand rather than simply a handout.

What makes my mother's work with the poor more remarkable is that she raised me as a single parent. My only impressions of my father came from stories told to me by my grandmother, mother, and other relatives. After Father's death, Mother and I moved into Grandmother's home. My grandmother cared for me while Mother resumed work at the newspaper.

By all accounts, my father was an intelligent and honorable man with a good head for business and a talent for mathematics. He was twice elected tax assessor for the county, and Mother had memories of his calculating long columns of figures in his head long before the days of calculators. He rarely made mistakes. Father had been a favorite among the entire Mondy family, and his death at such a young age saddened all. As a result, they turned much of their love and affection toward me. My aunts and uncles were especially attentive.

Although I was very young when he died, I still remember my father's funeral very clearly. It had a profound effect on me for many years to come. The night before the service, father's casket remained in our living room, as was the custom in the South at that time. The next day, men rolled the casket from the living room. I remember asking, "Where are you taking my daddy?" It was not until the actual funeral at the church that I fully began to realize what had happened. When the choir began to sing, I began to cry and Grandmother had to take me from the church. I was unable to enjoy choir music for many years afterward, perhaps due to this horrible experience.

I never felt let down by Mother raising me as a single parent. When fathers were requested to attend school functions, Mother attended. She was always there for me. Some of the other children in class came from broken homes in which the parents were separated, but I never felt I was one of them, for my father had not chosen to leave but left us through death. Although I had no father figure in the home, I had a good sense of who my father was and I was proud of his accomplishments.

With her training at the newspaper, Mother was lucky, for in those days, there was no Social Security, no public assistance for widows, and most women lacked the education necessary to secure a good job. Although we were never rich, we were considered middle class. Along with Mother's salary from the newspaper, we had rent from the rental properties Father had left us, and Grandmother's savings, which lasted until the banks failed in 1929. We got by very well.

One early crisis occurred before I started school. I contracted malarial fever and almost died because the doctor failed for many weeks to diagnose the problem. It was a relatively rare ailment, and at the time mine was the only case in the community. My condition gradually deteriorated until my death seemed imminent. I wanted to die to relieve the terrible suffering. When the doctor finally diagnosed the disease, he began treating me with quinine. Although it was a very unpleasant treatment, I soon improved. My Aunt Lucy declared that I looked like death itself, for I was just skin and bones.

Now I have a better sense of how exhausted my mother must have been during those years. She worked at the newspaper office during the day, tutored me at night, and prepared her Sunday school lessons. She always taught a Sunday school class. She also tended a large garden in which she grew many varieties of fruits and vegetables. Frequently she won special awards for her gardening ability. In fact she grew more than enough for us to eat and shared vegetables and flowers with the neighbors. At times I was even allowed to open a little vegetable stand near our house. I remember sometimes feeling abused regarding the work I had to do helping in the garden. Canning and preserving the produce seemed endless. Although I was never very good at gardening, the experience was beneficial in my later research with roots and tubers, especially the potato.

During the depression years, Mother was determined that we would have good food, so she got a Jersey cow which we named "Sally Ann Becky Mariah Jane Mondy." We just called her "Sal" for short. Sal became a real pet of the family and loved Mother dearly. She would moo incessantly when she spotted Mother, even at a distance. Sal was a very intelligent cow and learned how to manage her own water supply. We had town water piped to the barn where Sal was housed. Early on Sal learned how to turn on the water by rubbing her head on the faucet. She would stick her huge head under the stream of water to cool off. It was funny at first, but town water was expensive, and Sal's little trick ended up costing us.

One night during one of the many Pocahontas droughts, Mother woke up and heard rain. She went back to sleep, content that the drought had ended. The next morning she discovered that the "rain" had been of Sal's doing. Sal had turned on the water faucet and had overflowed her drinking kettle, causing a flood in the lot. We paid dearly for the "rain" and Sal's fun that night.

I remember my early summers in Pocahontas quite well. There were no electric refrigerators at that time, only ice boxes. Every morning the children would wait outside for the arrival of the iceman who filled the iceboxes people used for their perishables. He would give us chips from the ice blocks he cut, and we sucked the chips like candy or rubbed them against our foreheads to keep cool.

My Uncle Tom Carroll had ten children and they lived next door, so I always had plenty of playmates. My favorite was Bill, the cousin closest to my age. We climbed trees together, went bird hunting, and did a lot of the things little boys do like building tree houses. Sometimes we did things that interest little girls like making mudpies and cooking them in our toy stove. I've often thought my childhood friendship with Bill helped me later in my work relationships with men in my chemistry profession. I learned early how to cooperate and be inventive.

Mother was compassionate and supportive, and, along with my grandmother, taught me many things before I started school. She had no formal training in science, but she had an inquisitive mind and a great appreciation of nature. In addition to being a superior gardener, she knew the names of most of the birds, insects, flowers, and vegetables that grew around our house, and she made a point of teaching them to me. As a gardener and as a cook, she experimented constantly: first proposing a hypothesis, then testing it, and finally drawing meaningful conclusions.

She liked to tell stories, particularly parables that could be applied to everyday life. One was particularly meaningful to me, and I thought of it often in my later struggles as a chemist. Two birds, a blue jay and a woodpecker (Mother often called me her redheaded woodpecker) were outside in the bitter cold when they saw a house. Peering in through a window, they discovered that the house contained a nice, warm fire, and they were determined to get inside to avoid freezing. They decided to peck a hole in the wall, but after expending a large amount of energy, they had made little progress. Discouraged, the blue jay cried, "*I can't! I can't!*" He quit, and soon froze to death. The determined woodpecker said, "*I think I can! I think I can!*" and kept pecking. Although he was never able to enter the house, his constant effort kept him warm, and he survived.

The moral of this story is *"You never fail until you stop trying."* The motto hangs in my office still, offering encouragement to me and my students.

When I was six years old, the Great Depression hit us very hard. Mother had gone to her office carrying some gladiolas for her desk and was greeted at the door by the mayor. (It was a small town, and everyone knew everyone.) He said, "Ethel, I'm not sure you'll want those flowers when you hear the news." The town's bank had closed the night before, taking with it Mother's salary and that month's rent money paid to her by our tenants, both of which she had deposited only the day before. Grandmother's savings were also gone. Suddenly we had no cash savings. That night we cracked open my piggy bank and lived on the ten dollars it contained until the end of the month. Our tenants had been hit as well, and Mother accepted for rent whatever they were able to provide. One tenant was a carpenter, and another was a plumber; so they bartered their services for rent.

Times became difficult, but Mother still had her job and we never lacked food. In addition to the food we grew in the garden, we routinely received fish from one uncle, an avid fisherman, and beef and pork from another uncle, a farmer. I still remember the unpleasant job of canning the beef and pork, a necessary undertaking since electric freezers were unknown at that time.

I did not require much food anyway. Since the malarial fever, I had been underweight and averse to all kinds of food. I didn't even like the sight of food. When it became clear my lack of interest in eating was not the result of stubbornness, Mother took me to our doctor who recommended that I begin drinking more whole milk. However, I did not like whole milk or anything else high in fat. Mother resorted to paying me five cents for every glass I drank, which worked to a limited extent. Finally, the doctor gave her some drops to put in the milk. We called it his "nine-drop medicine," and I am convinced now that the drops contained some combination of B vitamins, perhaps thiamin, which had recently been discovered. Whatever it was, it brought back my appetite.

When I was eleven years old, Mother decided I should learn how to manage money. Rather than providing me with a standard allowance, she allocated to me a piece of rental property, a very large house. She told me that it would be my job to make sure the house was rented, to arrange and pay for the up-keep, and to pay the taxes and insurance. Whatever was left would be my allowance. I wasn't too happy with this arrangement, but when I complained, my mother simply said, "You'll never learn a day younger." So we proceeded with the arrangement.

I was not left totally to my own devices; I knew that I had Mother as a back-up in case anything went seriously wrong and that I would never be out on a limb without any money. Finally, I saw running this property as a challenge and decided I would cooperate.

Since the house occupied most of an entire town block, it was not fully adaptable as a rental house. It was more like a big family home. I managed to rent it to the Athy family, wealthy owners of a trucking firm who had a reputation for not paying their rent. I took a chance on them, and when the rent did not come on time, I approached their door, stating emphatically, "I need the rent, because that's my allowance." They must have believed me because they always paid me.

Mother was good about giving me the names of workmen who could do the plumbing or other jobs at the house, but she made certain to stand in the background while I made the actual arrangements. I also learned to pay the taxes and the insurance.

I found that I always had some money left over. I had enough so that in my junior year in high school, I was able to buy a typewriter in addition to paying my other usual expenses. In those days, not every class taught in high school was free. Basics such as reading, writing, and arithmetic were free, but elective courses such as typing and shorthand cost extra. I was able to pay for typing lessons, and they were a very good investment.

With the money I earned managing the house, I was able to put aside savings each month for my college education. Mother would match whatever amount I saved and it was called "The College Fund." When I entered Ouachita College, (pronounced *wash-e-taw*), in Arkadelphia, Arkansas in 1939, I had saved enough money to cover my expenses for my freshman year.

I also bought my clothes and paid for clarinet lessons. When Mother knew that I wanted a new clarinet but that I didn't want to spend the money that I was saving for college, she gave me a new clarinet for my birthday. On a few occasions, she came to my rescue, but for the most part she stayed in the background when it came to my finances. She never gave me money just because I had run low on funds. I never completely ran out of money—I was thrifty and always had something stashed away. I was never in debt, and was able to pay my way through my entire education, including the Ph.D. I won scholarships and fellowships, which were always helpful, and I never needed to take out a loan.

I kept the rental house until my senior year at Ouachita College. By this time I knew that I was moving to Austin, Texas, and it would be difficult for me to keep the house rented. I sold the house and invested the money. I valued the experience of managing the big house; it had given me a feeling of security and taught me at an early age how to manage money and what was involved in owning a piece of property. I am grateful that Mother encouraged me. Over the years, I have continued to manage rental property. At one time, I managed five rental properties in three different states. As I grow older it becomes more of a chore but I still enjoy using the knowledge I gained in my youth.

A few years after the Depression began, I learned to drive a car. Mother owned one of the first automobiles in the county, an early model Chevrolet we nicknamed "Hoopy." When I was eight years old, I sat next to her and learned to pedal the gas and to steer. Learning to change gears came later. We drove to a large field in the countryside where she taught me to shift.

By the time I was twelve, I was driving everywhere on my own and even had a driver's license. At that time there were few requirements and no tests to obtain a license; it was like getting a license to fish or hunt. Even so twelve was younger than average for a new driver. One of the reasons I learned to drive was to help run errands for Mother. Also because she was so busy working, I needed to be independent. By this time, Grandmother's severe arthritis limited her walking, and I ran many errands for her. In later years, when Grandmother became ill, either Mother or I was always with her.

Pocahontas was an unusual Southern town. Because of its German heritage, the town had a large Catholic population. Their center of worship was a place called Catholic Hill where the church and convent were located. A nun at the convent, Sister Rose, was one of the best musicians in Pocahontas. Every week, from junior high on, I would made the trek up to Catholic Hill to take clarinet lessons from her.

It never seemed strange to me that Protestants and Catholics from different backgrounds could get along so well in one small town. I took for granted the long German names of my neighbors, such as Spinneweber and Blissenbaugh. Once, after discussing our upbringing, my college roommate asked me, somewhat puzzled, "Don't people in Pocahontas have any good old English names?" Actually John Smith lived just across the street.

One thing I never understood about Pocahontas was the relative absence of blacks, who chose to be called *colored* in those days. There were only a few, and they were well respected.

Pocahontas was not a completely isolated community. Tucked in the northeast corner of the state, it was close to both the Missouri and Tennessee borders. Memphis was just 100 miles to the east, and St. Louis was close enough for us to receive radio broadcasts from KMOX, the most popular radio station.

Television was still a quarter of a century away, so the best source of news was the *Pocahontas Star-Herald*, the weekly newspaper for which my mother worked. The *Star-Herald* served not just Pocahontas but outlying towns as well. As a local news writer, my mother was a local celebrity of sorts. She seemed pleased with her job and never seemed bitter about the fact that her salary was less than that of her male colleagues. Although she complained occasionally, she was simply thankful to have a steady paycheck.

Pocahontas was not a wealthy town by any means. Only a few citizens could have been considered truly wealthy, including our neighbor, Mr. Clarence Wells. He was such a kind, unassuming man that it was hard to believe he was a millionaire. During times of inclement weather he drove me, along with his son, Preston, to school.

Before the bank folded, my grandmother was also well off. Her house, an old Victorian structure with two verandas, stood on an entire block of land in town. The backyard contained a lush garden and a wood lot. My grandfather had constructed a large, underground tornado shelter, large enough to protect the entire neighborhood. During a tornado watch, neighbors would enter Grandmother's shelter and sit until finally the danger had passed. It became a social gathering. As enjoyable as those gatherings were, they contained an undercurrent of tension. We felt quite safe down below, but we were aware that others were not so fortunate. With their tendency to strike quickly and unexpectedly, demolishing homes and even uprooting large trees, tornadoes were a serious threat. There are few sights in the South as frightening as that of a twister on the horizon: a thin column of ferociously swirling wind backed by dark storm clouds.

Education was very important to my mother. She was largely self-educated and always sought to acquire more knowledge for herself. She encouraged me to get enough education so that I could support myself. We thought I might possibly become a teacher which was an acceptable career for a woman. She took out a special life insurance policy to ensure that if something happened to her, I would have a secure source of income with which to further my education. Nineteen years after I completed my Ph.D. degree at Cornell University, Mother passed away. When the policy payment finally came to me, I was reminded of her devotion. It seemed like such a small amount compared to the sacrifices she had made to see that the premiums were paid. Perhaps because of what had happened to Father, she was always concerned that something might happen to her before I was grown. At one point, she contacted her cousin and his wife, a well-to-do couple with no children of their own, who agreed to adopt me in the event of her death.

Mother sacrificed in order to give me the best educational materials she could afford. Before I began school, she bought a huge *Webster's Unabridged Dictionary* which came to occupy a prominent position in our living room. She also purchased the *World Book Encyclopedia*. When I began school I had access to two good sources of information.

I entered first grade at the age of five. There was no kindergarten in town, so Mother attempted to teach me to write before I entered school. There was a serious problem for I was left-handed and Mother thought that I should write with my right hand. After a few frustrating lessons, I refused to write at all. I preferred to play hopscotch with my friends rather than take lessons at a musty chalkboard. In later years I learned from my Aunt Sarah Carroll that Mother, in desperation, had come to her for advice and had stated, "What can I do? I have only one and she's *dumb*." Amused, Aunt Sarah with her ten children replied that Mother need not worry for children learn at different rates and advised Mother to wait to see how I did in school before panicking.

Upon entering first grade, I realized that I was far behind my classmates, who had all been taught to read and write at home. Immediately I went to work, learning with the help of my teacher, Mrs. Birdie Hulen. By mid-year, Mrs. Hulen thought me qualified to be promoted to the second grade, but Mother decided I should stay with my own age group. I think this was a wise decision. Soon I found that I enjoyed school and considered learning fun. By the end of sixth grade, I had become class valedictorian, an honor I earned again in the ninth and twelfth grades. Included is my sixth grade valedictory speech, which was delivered in 1933 when I was age eleven:

Onward March
Sixth Grade Valedictory Speech

Parents, teachers, friends, and classmates:

If we lend our ears to advice given by men who have gained success and fame, we hear as a clarion call to others who have reached a goal, these stirring words: Onward March.

We, the sixth grade, feel we have reached an attainment as we leave the grammar grades and enter junior high, and, we would like to pause for a moment and flap our young wings and congratulate ourselves upon our advancement, but lo, as quickly as we lose ourselves to such a job the handwriting upon the wall appears to us, and we clearly read these words: Onward March.

In reality we have no time to sing our own praise, for no sooner is one task accomplished than a new one faces us, and if men can onward march in the face of difficulties, surely we feel ready for the pleasant though difficult task of the grades of junior high. Think for a moment of the men who have faced problems when all looked lost. Who has not heard of the stories of Columbus, Washington, Lincoln, and others? But we do not need to go back to the pages of history for examples of brave pressing forward. Today, in these times of depression, hundreds and thousands of parents are onward marching in face of darkest difficulties in order that we, their children, may enjoy what you and I, my classmates, are enjoying today.

No, it is not ours to boast of our attainment, but rather to praise those who have helped us reach our goal. Just here, in the behalf of the sixth grade, I wish to say to all of our parents, "Thank you, thank you many times for helping us onward": to the teachers I want to say "Thank you too, for we shall never forget the patience, love and many kindnesses you've given us."

And classmates, let us enter junior high next year with a greater desire to Onward March, and as Longfellow said:

Let us then be up and doing
With a heart for any fate
Still achieving, still pursuing
Learn to labor and to wait
(Psalm of Life, stanza 9).

The school building itself was quite new when my class first occupied it. It was in excellent condition, and the janitor, Mr. Mitchell, was very proud of it—so proud, in fact, that he virtually terrified the children into keeping it pristine. It was easy to be scared of Mr. Mitchell, for he had suffered a facial stroke, so that his left eye and the left side of his mouth seemed to stretch against the side of his face. I remember at one point thinking that he owned the building. He was very cross with all the children and later, we students were amused at his almost proprietary interest in it.

In high school we were kept busy with numerous clubs and extra-curricular activities. Most of us attended our respective churches. I was never made to feel that I wasn't accepted because of my commitment to academics or my interest in outside activities.

When I was thirteen, I taught a study course to my peers at a Baptist camp in Ravenden Springs, Arkansas. The assignment came from my neighbor, Mrs. Elbert Bly, who became ill and was unable to teach the course. She brought the book to me and asked, "Nell, would you please teach for me?" I agreed, for I had often taught classes in school to my peer group. I studied the book and taught a group of students who were the same age as I.

Most people took me to be older than my actual age. The director of the camp did not inquire concerning my age for he was from another town and assumed that I was an adult teacher. He accepted me as the substitute teacher and later, he told me that if he had known my actual age at the time he probably would have questioned my ability to teach the group. However, he seemed pleased with my teaching.

The camp was held for one or two weeks each year in a very scenic area, Ravenden Springs. Everyone kept very busy with study courses and many kinds of physical activities. I had a wonderful time and was accepted by the other campers. I felt very much at home.

My first date was with a young man named Lowell Gibbs who was editor of the camp newspaper. He was from Corning, Arkansas, a small town located approximately thirty miles from my hometown, Pocahontas. He wasn't handsome but was charming, very intelligent, and admired by many of the young ladies at camp. He chose to date me and nominated me for princess of the camp. I was elected and it was all so exciting!

Soon Lowell and I began to see each other socially in my hometown. I was honored to be dating a fellow older than I, one who was very intelligent and whose background was similar to mine. He was a Baptist; played the clarinet; and his mother, like my mother, was a widow.

When camp was over, Lowell and I still managed to write and visit. We each had cars, but driving to Pocahontas from Corning and back late at night after the date caused his mother to suggest that it would be better if he brought a friend along with him, for a double date. This left me with the task of arranging a date for his friend. The arrangement turned out well, with one slight exception. The girl I secured for Lowell's friend almost always tried to catch Lowell because he was really a lot of fun. Fortunately she never succeeded.

Lowell and I were compatible and enjoyed each other's company. He had already attended Ouachita College and was able to tell me about all the things the school offered. I admired him greatly. He was intelligent, fun to be with, and certainly helped to educate me in many ways.

Unlike most students today, I was fortunate to remain throughout my twelve years of school in Pocahontas with most of the same class, approximately fifty students. Because we were small in number and always together, most of us became close friends, somewhat like an extended family. Although after high school we dispersed into different parts of the United States, we have always managed to stay in touch. In 1989, the reunion for our fiftieth anniversary was attended by virtually all the surviving classmates. It was held at the beautiful home of my cousins, Bill and Ann Carroll. Bill, my cousin and childhood playmate, was battling poor health at that time, but seeing him and Ann, as well as other classmates, brought back all sorts of good memories.

In 1992, when Pocahontas celebrated its Centennial, I was one of the four *and the only woman* selected to receive the Centennial Achievement Award from Pocahontas High School. Other recipients included a Rear Admiral of the US Navy, a Lieutenant General and commander of the Fifth Army of the United States, and a sports hero who had been inducted into the National Football Hall of Fame.

I have always enjoyed competition; perhaps my passion for learning in school was stimulated by a desire to excel in competition with my classmates. My chief academic rival was S. W. Thompson, a nice young man and good friend. Our competition was always friendly; we simply pushed each other to do better. Once, in physics class, I was stuck on a particularly tricky problem. Unable to solve it, I went to sleep thinking about it and I *dreamed* the answer. Such a thing had never happened to me before or since. When our assignments were handed back, I found that I had solved the problem correctly, and S. W. had not. I'm grateful to S. W., because without our amiable rivalry, I may have become lazy in my schoolwork, particularly in high school, where there were so many activities competing for my attention.

At one point, Mother hoped that I would become a professional musician. The problem was that my musical talent was limited and I did not like piano lessons. I started piano lessons at age four, but without much enthusiasm. I did not like to practice, but the thing that kept me going was the spectre of our regular public piano recitals. Recitals made me nervous, and the thought of performing poorly before an audience was enough to make me practice. As unpleasant as they were for me, recitals did help to teach me self-discipline.

One of the activities I enjoyed in high school was the marching band. I considered taking up the saxophone, but it was too expensive, and my mouth was not quite right for the tuba, my second choice, so I settled finally on the clarinet. Being part of the band made music fun because it was something we did together. We played outside instead of in stuffy little rooms. We went on trips and played at sporting events, as well as the famous Cotton Carnival in Memphis, Tennessee. Band was quite an enjoyable experience for me. Our red, white, and blue band uniforms, with blue capes and fancy hats, were very attractive.

Some girls in band had trouble marching, but since I had long legs and naturally took long strides, I never did. For me keeping up with the boys was no problem. At Ouachita College, where I received my BS and BA degrees, I was given a band scholarship, and continued to enjoy the camaraderie and warm social atmosphere of being in a marching band. I played the clarinet until I finished my graduate degrees. After that I was too busy with my studies. I managed to sell the clarinet for more than its initial cost. The clarinet was profitable for me from beginning to end.

Among my other activities in high school was assisting with the high school yearbook, *The Chieftain*. The editor was Raymond Sallee, a fine boy who, despite his leadership skills, was never at the top of the class scholastically. His family was financially well-to-do, but he was never arrogant or ostentatious about his wealth. Some of the students were unable to purchase the yearbook because their families were so poor. Very discreetly Raymond gave those students books and made certain that *The Chieftain* staff members kept quiet about it. He made certain that no one was embarrassed. Raymond was a popular student and was also president of our class. Unfortunately, Raymond lost his life in World War II and our class paid tribute to him at the time his body was returned to Pocahontas for burial. Although I was very busy with my graduate studies at Texas at that time, I returned to Pocahontas to attend the funeral.

Barbara Sallee, Raymond's cousin, was my best friend throughout school. She was a very sociable girl who led the class in various projects. Academics were not her strong suit, and she always struggled to improve in her schoolwork. We complemented each other well: she would instruct me in social graces, and I would tutor her in math and science.

I was blessed with good teachers in high school. I thought Mrs. Birdie Hulen, my first grade teacher, was the most beautiful woman in the world. Because of my high estimation of her, she was finally able to teach me to write with my right hand. Many of my other teachers, such as Mrs. Bertha Mock, Mrs. Alma Spikes, Mrs. Vera Shemwell, Mrs. Vera Price, Mrs. Dorothy Wells, Mr. Sidney Ruby, and Mr. Nixon Shively were excellent teachers as well and instilled in all of us a sense of the importance of education in our lives.

Throughout high school, I was encouraged to become an English teacher. At that time, English was regarded as a subject fit mainly for girls, while science and mathematics were best left to boys. I learned that lesson when students from our school were selected to compete in the state academic contest. Despite my having the highest marks in math class, S. W. Thompson was selected in that category. I was selected for English, which was considered appropriate for females, and I won first place in my category. However, being passed over in my main area of interest bothered me.

When graduation time came, I was named valedictorian and S. W. Thompson was named salutatorian, but not without a bit of intrigue. Valedictorian was an important honor because that person was allowed first choice among the college scholarships made available to our school. It was well known that my first choice would be Ouachita College, a well-known Baptist school in Arkansas. Ouachita was also the choice of another student. Apparently she was quite upset that I would receive the Ouachita scholarship, so one day she slipped into the records office and changed the grades in favor of S. W.

I was surprised when S. W. was announced valedictorian since I knew this was not possible because S. W. and I had always checked each other's grades and mine were higher. I might have let the matter rest had my mother not requested that the school administrators check the grades. They did and soon discovered what had happened. The following day it was announced that I was valedictorian.

At first I was very angry with the girl who had falsely altered the grades, but I decided to drop the anger and substitute pity. My grandmother had taught me the Bible verse which states: "Vengeance is mine. I will repay saith the Lord" (Romans 12:19 KJV). I'm glad that I left the vengeance up to God and went along with my work.

S.W. and my friend Barbara both went to the University of Arkansas, but neither met with success there. Barbara was homesick and eventually dropped out of school, married, and had three sons. Tragically, S. W. drowned in a lake on campus and was never able to realize his great potential.

My cousin Bill was a good student but decided against a college education. He became an accomplished building contractor and constructed many of the finest buildings in Pocahontas, Arkansas, including his palatial home. I was pleased when he married my good friend and classmate, Ann Blankenship who later became editor of the local newspaper, the *Pocahontas Star-Herald*. Ann's grandfather had been editor of the newspaper at the same time my mother was employed there.

While growing up in Pocahontas, I lived among many relatives and friends. Without their support and encouragement I could not have been nearly so successful and happy. In my class which started in the first grade and continued for twelve years were three first cousins—Bill Carroll, Lorell Haynes, and Jessie Ann Mondy. In addition, there were numerous other cousins scattered throughout the other classes in the school. Included in these were Neal, Tommie, Ethel Mae, and Jean Carroll; Harrison, Dewell, Houston, and Jewel Mondy; and Mack Haynes. However, despite my attachments to the days of my childhood, the time had come to move on. I enthusiastically looked forward to new adventures at Ouachita College located in Arkadelphia, Arkansas.

Becoming a Chemist
Ouachita College: 1939-1943

From 1939 to 1943 I attended Ouachita College (now Ouachita Baptist University). The years spent there were among the most enjoyable years of my life. Located in Arkadelphia, Arkansas, a small town near Little Rock in the southwest corner of the state, Ouachita had an attractive campus filled with greenery and stately buildings. It was approximately two hundred and fifty miles from Pocahontas, and although I did not have the resources to return home often, I never felt homesick for long. From the beginning everyone at Ouachita was friendly and gracious and I felt I had made the correct decision in going there.

At Ouachita I became a chemist. Unfortunately, although my high school in Pocahontas offered solid courses in physics, biology, and math, we had no chemistry classes. Unsure of what major I wanted to pursue, I soon became interested in dietetics because I had heard it was a "woman's field" and required knowledge of science. My best friend at Ouachita was going to be a dietician as well. Chemistry was required for dietetic majors, and my friend and I soon found ourselves the only two in a freshman chemistry class of more than one hundred students who had never had chemistry in high school.

I found chemistry challenging and rewarding, and I enjoyed my professor's lectures very much. On the first exam, only a few weeks after classes started, I scored a ninety-nine. Dr. E.A. Provine, chair of the department of chemistry, was impressed and began to watch my work carefully. Several subordinate instructors taught laboratories, but Dr. Provine often visited, sometimes stopping to chat with the students in order to keep in touch. At first I was not aware that he was paying special attention to my work, but it soon became apparent that he was keeping careful track of my progress in both the class and the laboratory.

A young man worked next me in laboratory who had studied high school chemistry, and he gallantly offered to do my experiments for me. I have always been of an independent nature and was determined to do my own work. I thanked him but refused all help in setting up my equipment or conducting my experiments.

Dr. Provine later told me he was impressed with the independence I showed in performing my experiments without the help of others. My grade was based on my own abilities. Later in the semester, Dr. Provine approached me in the laboratory and said, "Miss Mondy"—he always addressed me formally—"may I see you in my office?"

I was frightened and wondered what was wrong. Dr. Provine had always reminded me of a Prussian general (a perfectionist). When I entered his office, he said, "I have been watching your work, and I am impressed with your ability in chemistry. I should like to offer you an assistantship in the chemistry department." As flattered as I was by this compliment, it placed me in a dilemma. I had already agreed to be an assistant in the foods department and in fact was currently serving as an understudy for that position. However, I promised Dr. Provine that I would think about it.

I had never thought of majoring in chemistry, although I had come to enjoy the subject. For weeks I thought about it, contemplating my options. I even wrote to several different schools of home economics to ask which major would be more valuable to me as a dietician: home economics or chemistry.

The answers that came back were interesting. The consensus seemed to be that a good background in chemistry was crucial in order to be a competent dietician. So I chose chemistry. Before making my decision final, I spoke with Professor Gunn in foods. She was very understanding and said "Nell, I'm glad you're doing well in chemistry, and I think it would be beneficial for you to major in it. It's so rare to have a woman in that field." I was the only woman Dr. Provine had ever asked to major in chemistry and, of course, I felt flattered. I accepted the assistantship along with other assistants, Bill Abernathy, Kervin Nichols, and Joe Pipkin.

Because the distance between Pocahontas and Arkadelphia was large, I took the train, which was the most affordable mode of transportation at the time. I brought several potted plants with me. My roommate, Sue Elliff, liked plants, and our room became known as "the greenhouse of Ouachita." Sue, a sophomore, was an understanding and compassionate person, and we got along very well. She was a talented music major, but she disliked science, so I tutored her in science, so in return she helped me enjoy music and took me as her guest to several famous Bach parties. Also I was fortunate to have a cousin, Marguerite Bowers, a well-established senior, who served as my mentor. Marguerite was editor of the Ouachita magazine, *Ripples*.

Our dormitory, Cone Bottoms Hall, was elegant and spacious with three floors and had a lovely beautifully furnished foyer. The parlor on the first floor was used to entertain guests. The residence was arranged in suites consisting of two bedrooms, two dressing rooms, and one full bathroom which was shared by four girls. Sue and I were well acquainted with the girls with whom we shared our suite. We often enjoyed midnight snacks together. Each of us would alternate weeks asking our parents to send snacks, so that no parent was asked more than once per month. After lights out, we would eat in one of the dressing rooms where the light did not show in the hallway. Wonderful friendships developed in this type of setting.

One drawback to keeping such an abundant food supply was that it attracted mice. Mice were not welcome in the dorm, and we were expected to exterminate them ourselves. I was chosen as the chief "mouse catcher" because I knew how to set the trap. Unlike many of the girls, I was never afraid of mice. Due to my mouse catching ability, I became something of a heroine. After a catch had occurred, I would simply open the trap and flush the mouse down the toilet.

The house rules were strict but fair. At eleven o' clock bedroom lights had to be turned out; student monitors checked to make sure. It was permissible to study after hours in either the dressing room or in one of the parlor rooms, provided one did not disturb her roommate or her neighbors. When residents left the dormitory, they had to check out in writing, listing where they were going, with whom, and how long they would be gone. Some girls, not used to such strictly enforced curfews, were bothered by the rules. I never was. I found it comforting that someone knew where I was in case something happened to me, and I never found the rules to be an imposition.

I had many interesting experiences in the dormitory as the only woman majoring in chemistry, and some viewed me in awe. Once I collected my friends' empty face-cream jars and filled them with a special cream I prepared in the chemistry laboratory. I recall combining the ingredients using lanolin and adding citral to provide a pleasant lemon odor. My friends considered the cream very special and honored me with their compliments.

Another of my chemistry assignments was to isolate casein from milk. Upon finding an excess of milk for this purpose, Dr. Provine suggested that I distribute the excess to students in the dormitory. He also permitted me to take chemical beakers to the dormitory in which to serve the milk. Since I had received so much admiration for my face cream preparation in an earlier experiment, I jokingly told my friends that I had synthesized the milk in the chemistry laboratory. As they sipped the milk from chemical beakers some expressed their approval and declared it even better than cow's milk. However, others claimed that it did not taste exactly like milk. Being honest, I could no longer withhold the truth, so I explained the situation and we all laughed. My friends' confidence in my ability to synthesize compounds was reflected in their willingness to consume my products.

Because it was a Baptist school, smoking and drinking were officially frowned upon. Smoking was extremely popular among naive, young women in the U.S. at that time, but it did not interest me. Some young women considered it dignified or sophisticated to smoke, but when I was pressured to smoke, I always asked myself, *What good would it do?* I could never think of a positive response, so I never took up the habit. Because smoking was so popular, one was sometimes made to feel "square" if she objected to others smoking. I often ended up breathing second-hand smoke in order to avoid offending others.

The rules in Cone Bottoms Hall were enforced by Mrs. Winburn, the hall matron. She was the widow of a famous minister and was a warm, intelligent woman who enjoyed working with young people. I always enjoyed our talks together; she seemed interested in me and the other young women. The dormitory had an elected student government whose members helped Mrs. Winburn with various tasks around the dormitory, and I was pleased to be elected president of women's government one year.

I enjoyed meeting the other girls who lived in the dormitory. Many of our meetings took place in the basement laundry room because in those days there were no drip-dry or wash-and-wear outfits. The fashionable fabrics were silk, cotton, and linen, all of which wrinkled easily and required constant care. Many of the girls were from households with maids and were not accustomed to doing their own work. Few knew how to press delicate garments such as the popular rayon, silk, or linen skirts. As a result, many pieces of clothing were scorched. Fortunately, Mother had made a point of teaching me how to care for my clothing, so I soon began teaching some of the other girls what I knew. They were impressed and enthusiastic learners, and I made many friends.

There were many blacks in Arkadelphia, several of whom worked at Ouachita. I had not known many blacks before, for very few lived in Pocahontas. At that time, long before desegregation, there were no black faculty or students, and the blacks at Ouachita held service positions. The polite word at that time was not "black" or "African-American," but "colored," and the colored people who worked at the college were generally quite popular with the students. Two who became a part of my everyday life were Henry, the janitor of the chemistry building, and "Mary the Maid," who worked in the dormitory.

Since I had such a heavy teaching responsibility during the week, I often chose to conduct my advanced chemistry experiments, such as organic preparations and organic qualitative analysis, on the weekends when there were few students around the laboratory. One day Henry, who made a point of checking in on me, entered the lab and found me crying. Alarmed, Henry asked "What's wrong, Miss Nell?" I assured Henry that nothing was wrong; I was synthesizing a chemical called a lacromator, or "tearjerker." Henry remained unconvinced until a few minutes later, when his eyes began to water as well.

Henry was old enough to be my grandfather and thought I was someone special since I was the only woman in chemistry. He wanted to make sure that I was well protected. After I had given my first lecture as a senior instructor, Henry found me alone in a large lecture room, sitting at the lecture desk with my head in my hands. "What's wrong, Miss Nell?" he inquired.

I said, "Henry, I studied for hours and hours for this lecture but could not fill up the entire sixty minutes. What will I do?"

"Miss Nell," Henry replied, "tomorrow you will probably have more to say than you can get said."

As it happened, Henry was right. My first lecture had been on the history of chemistry—a subject about which I had great respect but little enthusiasm. The choice of this material for the first lecture was a sad mistake. When I began to teach chemical reactions, I never found myself at a loss for words. There was always more to be said than time in which to say it.

The other colored person with whom I became well acquainted at Ouachita was Mary the Maid who worked in Cone Bottoms Hall. She was a large woman who kept the dormitory spotless, cleaning the suites and changing the linens. She had a wonderful sense of humor and a laugh you could hear from blocks away. A very religious woman, she often spoke to us of the sermon she had heard the previous Sunday at her church. The churches were still segregated at that time, as was Ouachita, but Mary didn't feel discrimination at Ouachita because the students all liked to talk and spend time with her. She felt like she belonged to the Ouachita family.

Once I asked Mary if she knew how to pray the "Chinese prayer." She replied that she did not but was interested to learn. "All right then," I said, and asked her to get down on her knees, with her elbows on the floor. "Repeat after me," I said. "Dear Lord, if I know my heart . . . ."

"Dear Lord, if I know my heart," said Mary.

"—if I know my mind—"

"—if I know my mind—" repeated Mary.

"—I know that I—"

"—I know that I—"

"Stick up behind."

In her awkward position on the floor, Mary roared with laughter, knowing she had been tricked.

When I returned to Ouachita in 1960 to receive the Distinguished Alumna Award, Mary showed up in her finest attire to greet me. The first thing she asked was if I still prayed the Chinese prayer. Her laughter resounded throughout the entire building. She never forgot me. Many years have passed since I was a student living in Cone Bottoms Hall, and Mary has since died, but I shall never forget Mary the Maid and the fun we had together.

The food in our dining hall, under the supervision of Professor Patricia Gunn, was very good. I came to enjoy the atmosphere of the dining hall which ran according to strict regulations. Rather than serving ourselves cafeteria-style, as is now the general custom, students—men and women—sat family-style at tables of eight. Each table was "led" by a host and a hostess selected by Professor Gunn. Being chosen was not only an honor, but also a responsibility, for Professor Gunn had set down a long list of "suggestions" regarding the conduct of hosts. Sunday noon and Wednesday evenings were special occasions when an effort was made to have everyone wait until all were served before beginning to eat and remain at the table until all had finished. On those special nights, when music frequently accompanied our meals, students were required to dress for the occasion and were not admitted in the dining hall in sloppy clothes. I sometimes found this dress-up rule inconvenient, especially when I had to work late at the chemistry laboratory. If a host or hostess's conduct was considered subpar, the management would feel free to dismiss them from their place of honor and fill the place with someone more desirable. This rarely happened, but those of us who served took the admonition seriously and did our best. Many lasting friendships developed, some even leading to marriage. For example, Dr. and Mrs. Joe Pipkin, my former classmates, recently told me that they had met at my table.

I served as hostess during my sophomore, junior, and senior years, which was unusual. I enjoyed being a hostess and took pains to make sure no one at my table felt left out of the dinner conversation. This was important, because no one was allowed to leave the dining hall until the bell rang. At Ouachita we lived by bells which some might have found restrictive. I appreciated the discipline I learned there and found that I enjoyed the structure that the college provided. My only regret was that students who served as waiters and waitresses were only allowed to eat breakfast at the table they served. Many of them missed out on the fellowship the rest of us enjoyed.

I believe that today's colleges and universities have lost a great deal with their modern, cafeteria-style dining halls. Although I understand why the change has taken place, particularly at large universities, I am pleased that I had access to a system that emphasized etiquette and order, rather than today's impersonal "eat-and-run" approach.

Still things became awkward at times. One year a young man with a speech impediment was assigned to my table. I often found it difficult to understand him but did my best to be pleasant and helpful. Because of his impediment, he was accustomed to being ignored and developed a crush on me. One day he shyly asked me a question I did not quite understand. Not wanting to seem rude, I smiled and said yes. Apparently he had been offering me his dessert. He promptly pushed it in front of me, encouraged that he had succeeded in winning my affections.

Because of my busy schedule, I often found it necessary to turn down dates which was difficult for me because I hated to offend anyone. I was often taken to be older than I was and therefore attracted upperclassmen. I participated in numerous activities and was acquainted with many of my fellow classmates. My dark auburn hair attracted attention, and I was informed that the fellows had even voted me "the girl with the nicest hair."

I spent much time caring for my hair. Once this led to a humorous, though regrettable, situation. A young man, in whom I did not have much interest, called to ask for a date. Wanting to be honest, I told him that I could not go out because I had to shampoo my hair. Later I realized that it sounded stupid and inconsiderate even though I had told the truth. On another night, I might have accepted. Occasionally I dated boys to whom I was not especially attracted because I felt that I learned a great deal by going out and getting acquainted with different fellows. I never lacked for dates to special occasions, but I did not want to become seriously involved before finishing my education.

Some of the girls at Ouachita had a more predatory approach to dating. It was customary in those days for young women to marry by the time they received their bachelors' degrees. Then they would become housewives and leave the educational system and workplace for good. As a result, some girls felt as though they had to get married by the end of their senior year. A few pushed their boyfriends very hard. I recall one girl who threatened to commit suicide if the boy she was dating left her. It was an unpleasant tactic, but it seemed to work for her; they married not long after.

Many weddings took place toward the end of our senior year. Some students got married even earlier as juniors. Junior women who married typically did not return as seniors. One reason for this was that pregnant women were expected to stay at home. This was generally true at that time, and I have always considered this a ridiculous custom.

Despite the prevailing attitudes of the day, the idea of marriage at that time did not appeal to me, for I had seen too many intelligent women with great professional potential sitting in coffee klatches discussing what sort of detergent to use on baby diapers. I had nothing against settling down and raising a family, but neither did I long to be dependent on having a husband and giving up my career. I had a deep-seated conviction that I should develop my mind and pursue an education beyond the bachelor's degree, and I knew that marriage would interfere with these goals. I did not want to sit at home when I knew there was so much more for me to explore.

At the present time, many women have both a husband and a career, but the world has changed considerably since the 1940s. In those days, I could not see breaking through the barrier that existed for women: choosing between either raising a family or having a meaningful professional career. A common notion was that it was unwise to invest scholarships and fellowships on female students who would give up the academic field for homemaking. I was reminded of the statement that "one cannot have cake and eat it too." I felt that a choice had to be made between one lifestyle or the other, and I chose a career.

I had nothing against marriage, and thought I might marry eventually. I had offers, but when I weighed them against the likelihood that I would not be able to advance in my studies, I always declined. When I recently returned for my fiftieth reunion at Ouachita, I found that I was one of only a few students who had never married. It was a pleasure to be surrounded by some of my old boyfriends and to hear what had happened in their lives. Most were very successful. Everyone was cordial and warm, which was how I had wanted them to be—like old friends.

As in high school, I involved myself from the beginning in a number of extracurricular activities at Ouachita. My freshman year, I was elected secretary of the class and I held a band scholarship and played at various events such as basketball and football games, concerts, and even the famous Cotton Carnival in Memphis. We raised money to go to the Cotton Carnival by holding concerts.

Traveling with the band was great fun. We traveled by train, in our special band car, or by bus, and many of us became close friends. After a band concert, we usually held a party or went roller-skating, a popular pastime in the South in those days. One night, feeling rushed, I did not change from my concert dress—which was black taffeta with a flowing skirt—before joining my friends at the skating rink. While skating I tangled in the fabric, fell, and the skirt flew up. To my embarrassment, the rink resounded with cheers. From that point on, I made certain to dress more appropriately for skating.

I participated in a number of church activities with the Baptist Young People's Union (BYPU). Our Bible discussions on Sunday nights were particularly helpful. My other activities included membership in the chemistry club, home economics club, and I was elected president of the Ouachita Women's Council. In my senior year, I was elected vice president of the entire student government—very unusual for a female. Serving as vice president was a good experience, because it taught me how to plan, organize, and coordinate campus activities. One of my responsibilities as vice president was to arrange for outside speakers for our campus. Another was to include the dormitory regulations for women in the women's handbook.

As a junior and again as a senior, I was voted "most intellectual girl" and "most versatile girl" in Ouachita's campus *Who's Who*. I was also selected by the faculty in both my junior and senior years to be listed in *Who's Who in American Colleges and Universities*. I greatly cherished these honors.

During the time I was president of the Women's Council, an issue arose of concern to the young women of Ouachita. Some believed the administration was too rigid. As leader of Women's Council, I took our concerns to Dr. J. R. Grant, the college president. After carefully listening to our arguments, Dr. Grant explained to me cogently the reasons for his position on the matter. He convinced me that he was right, so I was faced with the difficulty of explaining my reversal of opinion to my constituents. The incident taught me a valuable lesson: It is crucial to keep an open mind in listening to opposing arguments, and never become so determined that you cannot change your mind. Fortunately, the council membership agreed with me and accepted my decision.

My numerous campus activities kept me busy, and I always felt a part of campus life. This was fortunate, since I did not have enough money to return home frequently. I usually returned to Pocahontas only for Christmas holidays and summer vacation. Vacations in Pocahontas were very enjoyable, since I was able to see my family and childhood friends. Most of my time, however, was spent working in order to save money for my college expenses. One of the jobs involved measuring aerial photographs of farms using a micrometer to determine the field size. From these measurements I calculated the number of acres within a farm. The only problem was that I had to work at night since the room was unavailable during the day. I was joined by friends who were also earning money for college education. The job paid well, and eventually my biological clock adjusted to the night work.

Another summer I worked for the county library directing the children's story hour. The children were attentive and it was a great pleasure to tell the stories. My popularity as a storyteller was evident in my neighborhood. The six-year-old twins next door would run to my car when I returned home and ask for a story. They even cried when I left for Ouachita in the fall for they would miss my stories.

Back at Ouachita, my reputation as a chemistry scholar grew, and young women in the dormitory began to ask me to tutor them before their exams. I was happy to oblige, so the night before an important examination, we would reserve a room off the parlor where late night-lights were permitted, and I would tutor them as a group. It was good experience for me, because I enjoyed helping, and because preparing tutoring lessons helped *me* to learn. At first I tutored for free, but at the suggestion of Dr. Provine, the chair of the chemistry department, each person began to pay ten cents per hour for the long tutoring sessions. This was quite a bargain for them, as I later discovered when I became an official tutor in organic chemistry at Texas University where the rates were much higher.

Years later, in 1986, I returned to Ouachita to receive Ouachita's Centennial Achievement Award on the 100th anniversary of the university's founding. Each recipient of the award was asked to provide a brief statement titled "What Ouachita Means to Me." In it I thanked good teachers and friends and quoted a statement which had been enclosed with my Ouachita diploma:

Price of Success: *One must not*

(1) steal, cheat, or lie,
(2) be afraid of work, people, or self,
(3) give way to worry or anger,
(4) be ruled by envy, jealousy, or hatred,
(5) depend on diplomas or friends.

Instead one must

(1) work (there is no substitute),
(2) make worthy plans and carry them out,
(3) be true to self, employer, and society,
(4) cooperate efficiently and cheerfully,
(5) trust in self, others, and God.

These guidelines have been very helpful to me throughout my life. A posted copy appears on the bulletin board in my office.

The Centennial was a wonderful occasion, attended by former President Jimmy Carter who gave the convocation address. Also attending was Bill Clinton, Governor of Arkansas, who later became President of the United States. Following the ceremony, I was asked by a former classmate if I had really been as happy as I looked while I was a student at Ouachita. I replied, "Yes." It was a very happy time in my life. I was successful and had so much energy that I felt certain I could change the world. Of course there were also sad times, particularly those related to the war.

I worked hard as a chemistry major. During my three-and-a-half years at Ouachita, I spent endless hours preparing solutions, grading papers, and in teaching laboratories. By the time I reached my senior year, I had become chief supervisor of all general chemistry laboratories and even gave lectures, something I always enjoyed.

I also taught organic chemistry to the home economics students. The organic chemistry course for home economics carried four credit hours less than the eight-hour organic chemistry taught for chemistry majors. Dr. Provine felt that because of my interest in home economics, I would be ideal to teach the four-hour course. "You are more aware of what home economics students need to know in organic chemistry," he told me.

In preparing to teach the course, I selected material that was most appropriate for dietetics. This was a wise decision because most of the girls had disliked organic chemistry. Professor Gunn had frequently complained to Dr. Provine that her students didn't like chemistry. Dr. Provine would reply that his instructors disliked teaching home economics students. A feud arose between the departments, and I wanted to help solve the problem.

Before I took over the course, the students were taught much about hydrocarbons and acetylene generators. However, instructors did not start to discuss proteins, carbohydrates, and fats until a short time before the end of the term. They failed to emphasize the things that were most important to home economics! I decided to do things differently. I taught hydrocarbons but spent less time on hydrocarbons such as acetylene. Instead I related them to nutrition by noting that some vitamins, such as vitamin A, are hydrocarbons. The girls became interested. When I discussed carbohydrates and lipids, I brought in illustrations appropriate for foods.

One day the president of Ouachita, Dr. J. R. Grant, called me to his office and said that he had heard favorable comments about my teaching. He was impressed that I had been able to transform the organic chemistry course for home economics majors into something that the students really enjoyed.

As I neared completion of my B.S. degree, Dr. Provine asked me to continue as a full-time faculty member. At Dr. Grant's request, I stayed on for another semester plus a summer and was appointed Assistant Professor of Chemistry. I lectured in general chemistry as well as organic chemistry. At the time of my retirement from Cornell University in 1992, I received letters from professors at Ouachita Baptist University who recalled some of the statements made by Dr. Provine about my teaching.

Dr. Ben Elrod, Ouachita Baptist University President, 1992
"It is my unique privilege to write a tribute to Dr. Nell Mondy on the occasion of her retirement. Dr. Mondy completed her undergraduate work at Ouachita Baptist University in 1943. As you would expect, she graduated summa cum laude and was outstanding in all of her academic pursuits. Academic and professional notoriety have not dimmed Dr. Mondy's remembrance of her alma mater. Her interest in the University and the students who attend here was demonstrated in a tangible way by her creation of an endowed scholarship fund for science students. The University chose to name that fund in honor of Dr. Mondy and her highly regarded mentor at Ouachita, the late Dr. E. A. Provine. Dr. Provine was a professor in our Chemistry Department for forty-one years, serving as chairman for many of those years."

Dr. Wilbur Everett, Natural Sciences Division Chair, 1992
"It is a pleasure to write you this letter on the occasion of your retirement at Cornell. You have meant a great deal to both your alma mater and to me. First I would like to attempt to speak for someone who can no longer speak for himself. I first came to know of you from Dr. E. A. Provine who was a mentor to both of us. Dr. Provine, I am persuaded, was prouder of you than any other of his many students. He often spoke of you in glowing terms, of your ability as a student, of the great job you did when you taught briefly at Ouachita. If my memory serves me correctly, he spoke of the one semester organic course you taught for home economics majors and others. He spoke of how highly your students praised your teaching. He also talked of your success in graduate school at Texas, of your well earned reputation as the expert in the chemistry and biochemistry of the potato and of your success as a teacher at Cornell."

Dr. Joe F. Nix, W.D., Alice Burch Professor of Chemistry and Nutrition, 1992
"I attended high school in Arkadelphia then enrolled in Ouachita

College. The Chairman of the Department of Chemistry was Dr. E. A. Provine, the same professor under whom Dr. Mondy studied a few years earlier. While attending Ouachita, Dr. Provine continually told us about Dr. Mondy and her accomplishments. Many people may not appreciate the fact that many of us who came from "small town Arkansas" had very few role models. The fact that Dr. Mondy had graduated from Ouachita and had established herself as a leader in her area of research provided us with that role model."

Joe Jeffers, Professor and Chair of Department of Chemistry, 1992
"I am delighted to be able to write to you on the occasion of your retirement to express my appreciation for all you have done for us here at Ouachita. Your greatest gift to us has been your success as a world renowned nutritional scientist. We, of course, never pass an opportunity to boast of your success as a success for Ouachita. We are also grateful that you have not forgotten us. Your support of our students through the Nell I. Mondy—E.A. Provine Scholarship Award has been an encouragement to us and our students. It provides a pattern that we hope the recipients will not only appreciate but will emulate. The recipients through the years have beamed with admiration as they found out about the lady behind the award. We look forward to the newest program, the Nell Mondy Lecture Series. It will provide us, students and faculty, with the kind of stimulation that is critical to good teaching. I wish you the best of luck as you enter retirement."

My B.S. degree was awarded in three and a half years because I always carried nineteen to twenty-one credit hours per semester. After graduation, along with my full teaching load, I took a few courses that I thought would be helpful for graduate work. At the end of the summer, I had enough credits to be awarded a B.A. degree as well. By carefully planning my schedule and by carrying more credit hours, I was prepared to go in several directions. I was qualified to teach either home economics or chemistry in high school, apply for a dietetic internship, apply for medical school, or apply for graduate school training. I chose the latter route. Although I hadn't planned on getting two degrees, it was nice to have earned them. Besides my chemistry major, I minored in education, math, zoology, and home economics, and completed all requirements for pre-med. I never applied to medical schools, but I think I would have been accepted for my grades were good. I graduated *summa cum laude* in chemistry and chose to pursue graduate work in that field.

With Dr. Provine's help, I applied to three well-known southern schools, Louisiana State University, Oklahoma University, and Texas University. I had many credit hours in organic chemistry because in addition to the usual eight hours required for chemistry majors, I took courses in advanced organic, organic preparations, and organic qualitative analysis. These latter courses are usually taken in graduate school.

I was offered an assistantship in organic chemistry at each of the three Universities. I preferred Texas University, but that position paid the least so I wrote and explained the situation. In a short time, I received an offer from Dr. R. J. Williams, director of the Biochemical Institute, who offered me a much higher salary, because in addition to state funds, he had funding from the Clayton Foundation. The Biochemical Institute was widely known for its B vitamin research, so I accepted the offer from Texas and entered graduate school in September 1943.

Dr. Williams' letter was exciting because despite my background in organic chemistry, biochemistry was where I really wanted to work. Working with the B vitamins, I reasoned, would allow me to blend my interest in food and nutrition with chemistry. The job was ideal, for in addition to the large stipend, I was studying the area I loved.

In my lifetime I have been fortunate in many respects. I learned that good fortune most often appears when people take the initiative and apply themselves diligently to the task at hand. The reason I had choices regarding graduate schools was that I graduated *summa cum laude* with an almost straight-A average. Grades are important. I encourage any young woman who is interested in chemistry to make certain that her grades are high.

Dr. Mondy and her former teacher, Dr. E.A. Provine Ouachita Baptist
University, Arkadelphia, AR, 1960
At which time, Dr. Mondy received the Distinguished Alumna Award.
Photo taken in front of Chemistry Building

Graduate Study in the Lone Star State
Texas University; Austin, Texas: 1943-1945

I entered graduate school at the University of Texas in September of 1943. Mother decided to rent our home in Pocahontas and accompany me to Texas. In Austin we moved into a small house in a nice location on Thirtieth Street at the corner of San Jacinto Avenue. It was a lovely white frame house with green shutters, a long front yard, and a cobblestone walk that led to the street. Since it was only a few blocks from the chemistry building, I could walk to work.

It was nice to be within walking distance of the campus and college town. Before World War II, Mother and I had owned an automobile, but during the war it was patriotic to sell one's car in order to avoid gas consumption, so we sold ours. I often worked at night, but I never felt afraid walking to and from the laboratory, for the streets of Austin were quite safe.

When I arrived at Texas University, Dr. Roger J. Williams, who had been responsible for increasing my assistantship pay, decided to make good use of my time. He put me in charge of a number of projects. One of these had to do with the Texas School for the Deaf. Dr. Williams had theorized that the composition of people's saliva greatly affected the number of cavities they developed. The problem was deciding how to test his hypothesis. He needed accurate records on the background of his subjects in order to carry out his experiments. He chose the School for the Deaf in Austin which had extensive student records, and I was selected as his chief assistant.

The study was quite enjoyable and productive. We wore white laboratory coats when we visited the School for the Deaf, and the students thought we were dentists preparing to work on their teeth. When this rumor circulated, the student body suddenly disappeared. Later we spotted many of them hidden behind trees, frantically communicating in sign language. When Dr. Williams and I convinced them that we were not going to hurt them, that we simply wanted to look at their teeth and collect some saliva, they were eager to cooperate and came forward from all directions. The study went well, and Dr. Williams published our results in a popular journal.

As Dr. Williams' respect for my work increased he asked me to take charge of the department's stock cultures for microbiology. At that time, most methods for analyzing the B vitamins involved microorganisms. Therefore, it was important that these strains of microorganisms be kept free from contamination. To ensure their purity, the stock cultures had to be carefully transferred to fresh medium each week.

I was pleased to accept the assignment because it indicated that Dr. Williams had confidence in my work. However, the job was not easy. Austin can get very hot. I had to turn off all the fans in order to transfer the stock cultures. In those days very few buildings had air-conditioning. Some stores and churches did, but homes and automobiles did not. Biochemistry had only one air-conditioned laboratory, and it was too small, so I considered this operation to be a "hot job."

As I started looking for a problem to address for my masters thesis, I began to observe the work of Dr. Esmond E. Snell, a young Ph.D. on the biochemistry faculty who had recently discovered two new B vitamins: pyridoxal and pyridoxamine. He seemed to appreciate my work and asked me to be his first graduate student. I was pleased to work with him, and I'm sure Dr. Snell was pleased to have a graduate student. That meant he could become a member of the Texas University Graduate Faculty. At Texas having graduate students was important for advancement. Later I joked that it was I who was responsible for his advancement from assistant professor to associate professor.

Working under Dr. Snell, I conducted the first human study on pyridoxal and pyridoxamine. Dr. Snell was anxious to know the effect of these vitamins on the human body and was interested in developing accurate microbiological assays for them. He personally ingested quantities of pyridoxal and pyridoxamine and brought bottles of urine for me to analyze. Under Dr. Snell's guidance I performed numerous studies on these B6 vitamins, and part of my masters thesis was later published in the *Journal of Biological Chemistry*.

As much as I enjoyed my research at the University of Texas, I never adjusted to the Texas weather. The sun was unbearably hot and always seemed too close overhead. Since I lived near the chemistry building, at the beginning of the year I decided I would spend my lunch breaks at home. Unfortunately, I found that the short walk home in the mid-day heat caused nausea so that I could not eat. I chose instead to eat my lunch in the chemistry building which was filled with various chemical odors. I could tolerate the bad odors better than I could tolerate the sun.

It was convenient to live close to the chemistry building, and I always enjoyed my cool morning walks to campus with Dr. R. J. Williams. His home was near mine, and we took the same route to work, Speedway, with fig trees lining the street. We were permitted to pick the nice ripe figs, and as we walked we discussed famous scientists and their projects. It never seemed strange to be on such friendly terms with Dr. Williams, for at Texas, the professors did not put themselves on pedestals. The students felt free to discuss various topics with them. Dr. Williams was always supportive of me, as was his lovely wife. Mrs. Williams was very helpful to my family at the time of my mother's illness. She went to the hospital to be with Mother when I was working in the laboratory and was very helpful when Mother returned home.

Because I had taken so much organic chemistry as an undergraduate, my advisor at Texas placed me in a course filled with Ph.D. students. Although I had excellent grades and a solid background in organic chemistry (20 semester hours including advanced organic, organic preparations and organic qualitative analysis) from Ouachita, I felt as though I had been thrown to the lions. It was my first year of graduate study toward a master's degree, and competing with students who were finishing their Ph.D. degree was not easy.

Dr. Henze, who taught the course, was a good lecturer but very demanding. I worked hard, but I was not the top student. This deflated my ego; until that time I had always been at the top of my class. Looking back now, I believe the experience was good for me, for I began to realize that I couldn't be the best all of the time. I passed the course and learned a lot of organic chemistry. However, I still think that my advisor's decision to place me in such a course during my first semester of graduate study was a mistake. I had only recently arrived in Austin and needed time to adjust. In my career of directing graduate students at Cornell, I was careful not to place them in such a situation, even if they had an excellent undergraduate record.

Although I had never taken biochemistry as an undergraduate, I did very well, and also excelled in my other courses that first semester. I had no problem earning an A in biochemistry.

At Ouachita I had been the only woman who majored in chemistry, but in Texas there were a few other women in the biochemistry department. Margaret Eppright, who was older than I, was an excellent chemist. She had taught for many years before returning to graduate school to work toward her Ph.D.

Another student I became friends with, Lorene Rogers, had an unusual background. She had majored in English as an undergraduate and married a chemist. Her husband was killed at a young age in a chemical explosion at his company. Perhaps Lorene felt that she should take his place in the world, and instead of proceeding in her chosen field of English, she returned to the University of Texas and started anew as an undergraduate in chemistry. After receiving her B.S., she went on for graduate work and obtained a Ph.D. in biochemistry. She was a lovely person and very helpful to Mother and me. She and Margaret were close and when Mother and I left Austin, Margaret and Lorene saw us off at the train station.

After Margaret and Lorene received their degrees, they took jobs teaching chemistry at the same small school in Texas, but both were unhappy there. Eventually both women returned to the University of Texas. Margaret took a position in the Department of Home Economics and later became chair of nutrition. Lorene returned to assist Dr. R. J Williams at the Biochemical Institute. She was an excellent manager and served in that capacity for a number of years. Later she became dean of the graduate school and then vice president of the university. Eventually Lorene was installed as the President of the University of Texas, the first woman to hold that office.

Years later, when I returned to Texas to participate in National Food Science meetings I had the pleasure of visiting Lorene while she was president. Her office was at the top of the university's clock tower. It was good to see the special furnishings that are part of the president's office, such as the extensive rare book collection and the gardens outside. The day before I arrived, she had told the Board of Trustees that she wanted to return to a professor's life for a few years before retiring in full. She chuckled as she told me, "You know, Nell, I'm the only president of the University of Texas who has ever been allowed to retire. The rest were fired." I greatly appreciated having Lorene as a friend, and I am proud of her accomplishments.

Beverly Guiard, who served as a technician for Dr. Esmond Snell, was also working toward a Ph.D. under Dr. Williams. Beverly was an excellent chemist and a hard worker. She thought very highly of Dr. Snell and after receiving her degree she continued to work for Dr. Snell for the rest of her professional career. She followed him to the University of California at Berkeley, where he became chair of the Department of Biochemistry. Joan Ravel was beginning her graduate study under Dr. William Shive. After receiving her Ph.D. degree she continued working in the department and eventually advanced to full professor.

There were men doing graduate study in biochemistry but many were drafted for World War II. The honorary chemistry society, Phi Lambda Epsilon, was not open to women although the female students generally had high grades. However, the women students had their own honorary in chemistry, Iota Sigma Pi. Since my grades were high I was initiated into Iota Sigma Pi early in my graduate career. I served as secretary, arranging for dinner meetings and many programs. The women biochemists were joined by women in home economics who also held Ph.D. degrees with a background in chemistry. Together we formed a sisterhood of women chemists. However, many of us wondered what opportunities would be open to us as women chemists, for at that time, a woman, no matter how intelligent, could not reasonably expect to become a tenured faculty member in the chemistry department. The most she could expect was to become a technical assistant or research associate.

At that point, I was not worried about the future for I was young and had done well in chemistry everywhere I had been. I was beginning to receive many job offers. In those days it was rare to find a woman with excellent grades and a strong background in both organic and biochemistry, so I felt no worries about the future. I liked chemistry and was determined to make it my profession.

Not long after I entered the University of Texas, I was approached by members of the organic chemistry department and asked if I would be willing to be a tutor in organic chemistry. Since I was an assistant in biochemistry, it was appropriate for me to tutor in another department. I had excellent training in organic chemistry at Ouachita College. Tutoring paid well, and I agreed to the listing. I had many medical expenses at that time, and the extra money was quite useful.

Many students approached me and soon I found that I had more students than I could handle. In the evenings, and on weekends, tutoring took up all my extra time. I tutored people of all ages. One of them, an older nurse, had returned to the University of Texas to continue her education. She became one of my star pupils and appreciated my help and showered me with gifts in addition to the usual tutoring fee.

Many of my students were young and beautiful. Never have I seen as many lovely, well-dressed women as at Texas University. In fact young men would lurk outside my house waiting for the tutoring session to end. The young women were beautiful, but usually not interested in their studies. However, I did my best and managed to help them through their chemistry courses. I worked hard at tutoring, adapting the material to the needs of each individual student. The experience was valuable, because in teaching I also learned.

Tutoring was quite lucrative, and I decided that I could afford a few luxuries such as tennis and horseback riding lessons. Every afternoon the women equestrian students rode through the open fields until sunset. Watching a lush Texas sunset on horseback in the wide-open fields was an exhilarating experience.

World War II started in 1941 while I was at Ouachita. It was a very difficult time for me in many ways. Many of my former classmates and friends were drafted and headed off to war. It was a helpless feeling to watch them leave not knowing if or when they would return. Often they were not even allowed to reveal where they were going. Mother and I vowed to do our best to aid the war effort at home.

The entire time I was in Austin, from the fall of 1943 to the summer of 1945, the United States was at war. By 1943 the war effort in America was in full swing. There were few women in the armed forces at that time, but many worked in factories previously staffed by men.

During this time I met Erwin Kelley, a student in biochemistry. As the war effort accelerated one of the professors in the chemistry department,

Dr. Watt, took leave from Texas University to work on a military project at the University of Chicago. As the project grew larger and the need for more highly trained scientists arose Dr. Watt began to recruit chemistry students from Texas to help with the project. Erwin was one of those selected. However, he was required to take basic training in the United States army before beginning his special assignment in Chicago. In his letters to me Erwin was free to discuss his basic training in which he found himself doing KP duty on Christmas Day, etc.

Following basic training Erwin went to Chicago to work with Dr. Watt. After that he was never allowed to discuss any of his work with anyone not connected to the project. It was difficult not to be able to mention anything connected with his work—not even to a friend who had chemistry training. After the atom bomb was dropped and the men who worked on the project were able to speak publicly about it Erwin wrote me, "We felt greatly relieved to have the project made public so that we are released from much of the secrecy and can talk freely to friends about our army station instead of trying to avoid, always awkwardly, questions about our assignments."

On the home front, Americans made many sacrifices; many types of goods were rationed. Stamps were issued for scarce items such as meat, sugar, and coffee. Mother and I did not care for coffee, but we both had a sweet tooth and missed having sugar. Fortunately we had a friend, Dr. Lucille Hac, who wanted coffee, so we traded our coffee stamps for her sugar stamps. Such bartering became quite common in those days.

I have memories of the ways we made small sacrifices to help the larger effort. Bananas are one of my favorite foods and were very difficult to acquire. Mother was a friendly person and became a good friend of the grocer, and he sometimes put aside bananas for mother. Instead of giving the bananas to me she often chose to give them to Dr. Hatch who had several small children. I was happy to forego the bananas knowing that the children needed them more than I did.

Another kind of ration stamp that was precious to me was the shoe stamp. I walked to work each day and stood most of the day in the laboratory, so I needed good shoes. Unfortunately, many of the shoes made during the war were of poor quality, and I had great difficulty finding comfortable shoes. I used all of my shoe stamps, my mother's, and the shoe stamps from three elderly neighbors. Finally, I found a pair with *crepe* soles, and with these I could stand in the laboratory without excruciating foot pain. The shoes were so precious that I kept them in my laboratory desk and used them only when I was working in the laboratory. I knew that if I wore them all the time they would soon wear out.

I kept many mementos of that period of American history including a War Ration Book and the Junior Hostess card provided to me to assist with the entertainment of soldiers. I also kept coupons which entitled one to secure shoes, coffee, sugar, and other goods.

During this time many young men were sacrificing their lives for the country; our food sacrifices seemed minute. One of those brave casualties was Raymond Sallee, the president of my high school class at Pocahontas, AR. Letters I received from the boys overseas indicated that they were scared and lonely at times, for they had left behind the company of friends and family. I did my best to cheer them during these trying times and was glad they could rely on my friendship and support.

My friends who were in the army often arranged to visit me while on leave or stopping over in Texas. We shared a meal together before they had to return to their service. It was good to see them but always sad when they left because I realized I might not have the chance to see them again.

A good friend, Dr. Bill Daily, had graduated from Ouachita before my arrival there and was in medical school in Little Rock, Arkansas. One summer while I was a student at Ouachita, he returned to teach human physiology, and I had the privilege of being his student. Since it was not appropriate for a teacher to date his student, we became close friends only after the class was over and after he returned to medical school. He invited me to his graduation from medical school and shortly thereafter he was sent overseas. His V-12 letters to me revealed important aspects of the war. Bill was unhappy with the circumstances he endured, although he tried to be brave. Sometimes parts of his letters were censored when he attempted to relate to me the details of his plight. However, he tried extremely hard to be brave and was awarded the Legion of Merit for "Outstanding Service in the Philippines."

Another war casualty was George Grant, the eldest son of Dr. J. R. Grant, President of Ouachita. Mother and I were deeply saddened by George's death and expressed our sympathies to Dr. and Mrs. Grant. Dr. Grant wrote that he was grateful for our "good letter of comfort and cheer." George was exemplary of many of the young men who lost their lives in the war, his brave, final words to his family were, "If I don't come back, don't worry. Just remember that I gave my life to help build a better world." I agreed with Dr. Grant, who said "If we could only know that his life would really help build a better world, his loss would not be so hard to bear."

Thomas Gray was another fellow classmate from Ouachita with whom I communicated. After the war ended, he took advantage of an opportunity for soldiers to take classes and continue their schooling in England. In a letter dated October 1945 Thomas wrote: "For GI's, this is really an excellent opportunity to get back in the groove before returning to the civilian school. Excellent professors have been imported from the states." Thus, there were some opportunities for the soldiers which were positive.

During my days in Austin, a young Japanese-American man named Hyato Kihara worked in the biochemistry laboratory as a dishwasher. He was an American citizen because he had been born in California, but during the war his father and mother were taken to an interment camp along with thousands of other Japanese-Americans. They were removed from their homes and businesses in California and placed in a camp because of their Japanese heritage. This was done on the baseless suspicion that they might be Japanese sympathizers.

Hy, as he was known, later enlisted with the U.S. army. Before leaving for duty in the service, he visited his parents at the interment camp, and they told him that the U.S. was his country and encouraged him to be loyal and proud. Hy was an intelligent student, and we often had friendly discussions. One day when I entered the laboratory I found all of my associates laughing. Hy had mischievously put on my crepe-soled shoes. And because his feet were so small, they fit him perfectly.

I felt sympathy for Hy because with his intelligence and ability he should have been able to acquire an assistantship in biochemistry. However, we were at war with Japan and the Japanese were not allowed to receive assistantships. At that time, I was offered a job in the physiology department. I thanked the department but declined, saying that tutoring in organic chemistry plus my assistantship duties with Dr. Williams did not leave time for me to take on extra work. I recommended Hy, who had an excellent background. Because of my recommendation he was hired in the physiology department at a higher salary than he received as a dishwasher.

Hy's mother appreciated what I had done for him and presented me with a pin made of small seashells arranged in the shape of a dogwood blossom. She made it while in internment camp. I was impressed that she was so grateful to me for helping her son. I still keep the pin and prize it highly because I realize the difficult circumstances under which it was made.

After the war, Hy contacted Dr. Esmond Snell, who had by that time moved to the University of Wisconsin. Hy was accepted for graduate work at Wisconsin. Later, when Dr. Snell became chair of the Department of Biochemistry at the University of California at Berkeley, Hy followed him. There he finished his Ph.D. and accepted an important position in the medical school.

Hy and I corresponded for many years. After receiving his Ph.D., he brought his lovely Japanese bride to Ithaca to meet me and later I visited his family in California. It was a pleasure to see the progress that Hy had made.

Among my other good friends at the University of Texas were Edith Chu from mainland China and Yen Lu from Hawaii; both held postdoctoral positions. Before going to Texas, my contact with the Chinese had been limited, and I found both of these women delightful.

When Edith and Yen went to chemistry meetings in New York City, they would buy Chinese food that was unavailable in Texas. Upon their return, they served Mother and me special Chinese dinners.

When Edith first arrived at the Institute, she listed her birth date. I marked that date on my calendar, and the next year I organized a surprise birthday party for her. As it happened, she was doubly surprised, because the date she had listed was calculated on the Chinese year, which is not the same each year. Knowing Edith and Yen and learning about their interests and backgrounds enlightened me about other cultures.

Because the University of Texas was the chief laboratory in the United States for the analysis of B vitamins, important scholars came from other universities to learn our methods. One of these was from Cornell University. While I was teaching her methods, she said, "Nell, you have exactly the training that Dr. Maynard appreciates." Dr. L.A. Maynard was the Director of the School of Nutrition and the Chair of the Department of Biochemistry at Cornell University.

She wrote Dr. Maynard about my background and he asked to see my credentials. Shortly after receiving them he offered me a full-time position as Research Associate in Biochemistry and Nutrition at Cornell University. Dr. Maynard, in addition to being the Director of the School of Nutrition and the Chair of the Department of Biochemistry, was also Director of the Federal Nutrition Laboratory located in Ithaca, N.Y. I accepted his offer and agreed to start work at Cornell University September 1, 1945. I completed my master's degree in biochemistry at Texas and worked there full-time until September.

The largest religious denomination in Texas was Baptist, as was apparent by the proliferation of large Baptist churches in Austin. I attended University Baptist Church because it was close to campus, but also because the minister, Dr. Blake Smith, was a graduate of Ouachita College and was well known among Baptists. Despite my heavy workload as a graduate student, I was active in many church activities. Mother was also involved with the church and the local Red Cross.

While I was a student at the University of Texas, the president, Dr. Rainey, who was progressive, sought to improve education for blacks. Most universities in the South were not integrated until many years later after a bitter and divisive debate over civil rights. Many Texans were not ready to take the first step towards integration, and the Board of Regents voted to fire Dr. Rainey for his progressive ideas.

The minister of the University Baptist Church strongly supported Dr. Rainey's position. He was a popular lecturer and was frequently invited to speak on radio broadcasts. Both the faculty and students of the university also supported Dr. Rainey and initiated a march from the campus to the state capitol building to show their support. Students carried banners, and some brought their young children. Later, when other southern universities were embroiled in conflicts over integration, Texas was peaceful, having achieved integration earlier. Although Dr. Rainey was not reinstated as president, progress was made and the university was integrated thereafter. I was proud to have played a part in history.

Writing my thesis was time consuming; I would compose a first draft, then rewrite, and then rewrite again. I sometimes revised chapters of my thesis as many as five times before presenting them to my chairman, Dr. Snell. He was always supportive of my writing and usually added only a few comments. I appreciated his input, for I had always been very impressed with the quantity and quality of his writing. He published many scientific papers and won several awards during the time I worked with him. One of the many awards was the Eli Lily Award granted to the most outstanding young scientist. One day I said to him, "Dr. Snell, I think it is wonderful that you write so well. It seems to be so easy for you."

He looked at me, smiled, and said, "Don't ever think that, Nell. I write and then rewrite and rewrite again." After this I felt better about my efforts in scientific writing.

When the work on my thesis was finally complete all that was left was to have it typed. For a fee the secretary in the biochemistry department had typed the theses of other students, so I hired her as well. To my surprise, she was a poorer typist than I was and made many mistakes. I did not want typing errors in my thesis, so using the special typewriter in the biochemistry building, I set about correcting her mistakes. To use this typewriter, I would have to go to the biochemistry building at odd times, either early in the morning or late at night. I spent hours retyping what I had paid her to type, but I wanted the thesis to be correct.

Before I finished work on my masters degree, Dr. Williams, Director of the Biochemical Institute, invited me to stay on at Texas. When he heard that Cornell had offered me a full-time position as a research associate in biochemistry and nutrition, he was disappointed because he had hoped that I would continue my studies for the Ph.D. at Texas. By then, however, I had become interested in seeing other parts of the country and was curious to discover what Cornell was like. I was also interested in the work of Dr. Leonard A. Maynard, the chair of biochemistry and nutrition, who blended my two special interests.

I also had financial reasons for choosing a full-time position. Although my assistantship at Texas had paid well, Mother's medical expenses had put a drain on my finances. Mother had no insurance policy of her own and was not covered by my policy. She had undergone two major surgeries for which we were financially responsible. We were never in debt, but neither were we able to establish any sort of savings. I thought a full-time job would be helpful.

When Dr. Williams heard I was considering work at Cornell, he offered me a full-time position at Texas at a higher salary than Cornell was offering. I thanked Dr. Williams for his kindness but told him that I wanted to try Cornell.

The temperature in Austin hovered at 105 degrees for more than a week the summer before I left. One could have fried an egg on the pavement or sidewalk. Although I grew up in the South, I have never cared for hot weather. One factor that influenced me to go to Cornell was the cooler climate in upstate New York. I had only rarely seen snowfall in Arkansas, and in Texas we had only one snow in seven years. After the many hot days, I was ready for a change to a cooler climate.

First Year at Cornell

Research Associate, Biochemistry and Nutrition: 1945-1946

On a sunny day in May of 1945, I received my master's degree in biochemistry from the University of Texas at Austin. I worked there full-time in the Biochemical Institute until late August. Then I said goodbye to Texas and joined the faculty of Cornell University in Ithaca, New York, as a research associate in biochemistry and nutrition.

It was a busy summer for I had suddenly gone from being a student to a full-time research associate. I had been hired by Dr. L. A. Maynard, an impressive scholar, who at that time was chair of the Department of Biochemistry, Director of the Graduate School of Nutrition, and Director of the Federal Nutrition Laboratory. I worked at the Federal Nutrition Laboratory with Dr. Willis A. Gortner and Dr. Walter L Nelson, two well-known biochemists.

After several days and nights of train travel from Austin, Texas, Mother and I reached the Lehigh Valley Station in Ithaca, New York. Because World War II had just ended, all modes of transportation were crowded with soldiers. Since mother and I could not secure a sleeper, we had to sit throughout the entire trip and we were exhausted when we finally arrived in Ithaca.

Though we were happy to have reached our destination, we had a momentary temperature shock when we stepped off the train in late August. After the 105-degree temperatures in Austin, Ithaca's cool, damp, northern climate was a chilly surprise. We spent our first night at the famous old Ithaca Hotel on State Street and tucked ourselves under numerous blankets to get warm. It was wonderful to sleep lying down again.

Professor Maynard had promised to help us to find appropriate living accommodations, and he was very gracious to us upon our arrival in Ithaca. When I called his office to report our arrival, the secretary responded that Dr. Maynard was located in Fernow. Since at the time I was unfamiliar with the Cornell campus and had never heard of Fernow Hall, I thought she said "inferno." For a moment I wondered what situation was to be my fate.

Dr. Maynard gave us a list of available places to rent and provided us with two secretaries and a car to aid us in our search. Apartments were extremely scarce in 1945 because there had been little housing construction during the war. As we soon discovered, Ithaca was overcrowded and housing was expensive. Our choices were further restricted by the fact that Mother had just had major surgery in Austin and required a first-floor apartment. We were astonished to find that many of the places for rent were on the third or fourth floors of huge houses, and most of them were located so near to the street that they had almost no front yard. The apartments we visited were expensive, and many were not very nice.

At the end of our day of searching, Mother and I were tired and discouraged. Homesickness began to settle in, and Mother mentioned the possibility of returning to Texas. However, I had committed to work at Cornell for a year, and I felt obligated to fulfill that commitment. We knew we had each other for support, and decided to make the best of our situation.

We finally settled on an apartment at 222 Eddy Street, a large brick house divided into railroad-style apartments. We rented one from an elderly woman who would be spending the winter in Florida and wanted to sublet her apartment for the season. We did not really like the place, but we were resigned to the fact that we could find nothing better. We were comforted, though, that our lease ran only until May, and we hoped that we would find a better apartment by then.

The apartment had a living room, bedroom, dining room, and kitchen. They were lined up one room in front of the other, so that to reach the kitchen, we had to pass through all the other rooms. A gas stove in the kitchen was the chief source of heat for the apartment since the hot-air furnace did not function properly. We had high hopes for the stove, but it quickly proved inadequate against the harsh Ithaca winter. Heat rarely penetrated into all rooms of the apartment because the stove was not meant to serve as the main heating source. One afternoon, as Mother was entertaining some friends in the living room, she fired the kitchen stove up as high as possible so her friends would not be left shivering. She had baked some lovely meringue pies for the occasion (Mother was famous for her wonderful pies), but when she went back to the kitchen, she realized that she'd turned the stove up too high. The pies had liquefied in the kitchen's mounting heat; all she had left was a delicious-smelling meringue soup.

The house's hot-air furnace was ancient and in need of repair, and we soon discovered it emitted sulfur dioxide fumes. We had no way of knowing how much of the sulfur dioxide was accompanied by carbon monoxide, a poisonous gas which has no odor. Because of the fumes, we were afraid to sleep with our windows closed. Even in sub-zero weather in the middle of winter, we kept our windows open for fear that we might be asphyxiated during the night. It was a miserable winter, and both Mother and I longed for the warmth of Texas.

Our apartment was a lesson in endurance; not only was it cold and filled with fumes, but it was also visually unattractive. A curious clause in the lease stipulated that we must leave everything in the apartment exactly as our Florida-bound landlady had left it. Unfortunately, this applied especially to her paintings. She was an amateur artist and the paintings were not pleasing to us. However, we lived up to our word and tried to get accustomed to the "art."

The apartment did have one redeeming feature: its location on Eddy Street in Collegetown, a section of Ithaca just off the Cornell campus that was lined with shops and restaurants and always bustled with people. We could always escape from the uncomfortable apartment into the lively streets.

Walking about my new hometown, I soon became accustomed to the hills. Collegetown and Cornell are set at the top of a steep hill, East Hill, that looked mountainous to me when I first arrived. When I looked up Buffalo Street from downtown on Aurora Street, I was certain that no car could climb it in the winter, and I wondered how professors and students ever made it to class.

Even though I did not have to commute up the steep hill that separated Cornell from downtown Ithaca, transportation was still difficult. From Eddy Street, I could take a bus to campus as far as the Andrew Dickson White House which was then the home of Cornell's president, Edmund E. Day. However, from there I had to walk one mile to reach the Federal Nutrition Laboratory where I worked. I was not accustomed to the cold weather or to such long walks. I also had no stockings to keep my legs warm. Nylon had been used for parachutes and other supplies in the war effort which made nylon stockings very scarce, and pantsuits had not yet become popular. The lack of stockings had not been a problem in the mild Texas weather, but in Ithaca, it became an immediate concern.

In the months following the end of World War II, nylons gradually began reappearing at downtown department stores in Ithaca such as JC Penney and Montgomery Ward. I hurried from work and stood in long lines that had formed for the stockings, but they were gone long before I reached the head of the line. It was discouraging! I realized that because Mother and I were new residents of Ithaca and had not yet gotten to know Ithaca merchants, we were going to have a hard time acquiring scarce items. Mother was especially concerned for my health in the cold Ithaca climate. She wrote to relatives throughout the United States, telling them of my plight and subtly soliciting their assistance. My cousin Versa, who lived in Chicago, was the first to send a pair of nylon stockings. The day they arrived will long be remembered. More stockings arrived from sympathetic relatives from other parts of the country, and before long I had an ample supply, warm legs, and a feeling of gratitude toward my generous relatives.

Although my long walks to the Federal Nutrition Laboratory were warmer, the fundamental issue remained: There was no bus service to that section of campus. I looked into the situation but was told that the city could not furnish Cornell with the needed bus service. I knew that some solution had to be found.

Not one to remain complacent, I prepared a petition requesting bus service up Tower Road. Soon the sheet was filled with signatures and was presented to the Ithaca Transit Company. Dr. Willis A Gortner, my colleague at the Nutrition Laboratory, wrote a thoughtful letter to the *Ithaca Journal* explaining the need for more bus service. Surprisingly our efforts succeeded. A special bus was scheduled to serve Tower Road in the early morning, although no buses were added for the afternoon. I still had to walk a mile after work in order to catch a bus home, but something had been accomplished. Dr. Gortner had given up his car during the war effort, and he often rode the morning bus with me. We were pleased to see the bus full of riders, knowing that we had helped.

Getting to know a new city also meant finding a church. Religion had played an active role in my early years, so when I came to Ithaca, I looked for the local Baptist church. Coming from Texas where the Baptists were the largest denomination, I expected to see several Baptist churches. To my surprise, I was told that there were only a few, and we attempted to locate one in DeWitt Park. Since we had given up our car during World War II, Mother and I took a bus to downtown Ithaca and looked about the park. We saw a large church and smiled at each other. "That must be the Baptist church," we said, but it turned out to be the Presbyterian Church. We went farther down the street and saw another big church. 'This must be it," we said, but again we were disappointed. It was the Methodist church.

We were determined to find it. We went back home and asked our neighbor again: "Where is the Baptist church?" On our first Sunday we had attended the interdenominational Sage Chapel on the Cornell campus. It was pleasant, but we wanted a family church with which we were more familiar. So, with new instructions, we boarded the bus to try again. Somewhere in the park was the Baptist church, and we were going to find it.

As we got off the bus, we saw a woman carrying a bouquet of flowers, and we asked her if she knew the location of the Baptist church. She replied that she would take us since she was going there, too. We were relieved as she accompanied us to a lovely little church nestled in the park. It was very small and so far back from the road that we had missed it the first time. At the church service we were warmly received and felt immediately at home.

Mother joined a Sunday school class, the Philathea, composed of women her age. It was a large class, and its members were very active in all church activities. Mother was friendly and outgoing so people were always drawn to her; she made friends wherever she went, and this church was no exception. Mother's marked Southern accent endeared her to the ladies in her class, and they confided to me later that they often asked her questions just to hear her Southern accent. Mother was a Bible scholar, and in a few months she became the substitute teacher for the class. When the regular teacher retired, Mother was appointed teacher and held that position for approximately twenty years.

However, there was no Sunday school class for people my age, only a class of undergraduates who were younger than I or a class much older, the "Town and Gown," made up of well-established business and university professionals who were fifteen to twenty years older than I was. I approached the minister, Dr. A. H. Boutwell, and asked if a class could be formed for my age group. He thought it was a wonderful idea and helped to organize it.

Along with Reverend Boutwell and Dr. John D. W. Fetter, the University minister, several people showed interest in joining the class and within a short time it was named the "Friendship Class." It became the largest class in the church and was very active for many years. Friendships formed among the members of this class have continued to this day. There are many in Ithaca who still consider themselves the Friendship Class, and whenever former members return to Ithaca the class reunites to greet them.

During the early weeks at church, I attracted the attention of a young World War II veteran, Lieutenant Royal Gilkey who had recently returned from the Air Force to his Ithaca home. Shortly after we met at church, he asked for a date. I politely turned him down. I was not interested in dating at that time because I was so homesick for Texas, but he was persistent and later appeared at my house to invite me to join him for a ride in the country to see the fall foliage. I decided to join him. He was very happy to be home after returning from the Air Force, and he was especially attracted to my Southern accent and dark-red auburn hair.

We got along very well and he introduced me to several of his Cornell friends in the Law School. He was intelligent, courteous, and fun to be with, as well as an excellent dancer who attempted to teach me some new steps. We became good friends and had many enjoyable times together before he left for graduate study at Columbia University. I was not interested in marriage because my academic career meant a lot to me. Still he enriched my life and he told me that I enriched his as well.

During my first few months at Cornell, I was extremely homesick, but I persevered. Fortunately, the people at work were friendly and kind. Many teased me good-naturedly about my Texas accent. This was the first time that I became aware of an accent, but I rather enjoyed the teasing and the attention it brought.

Adjusting to the northern climate was difficult, and I was cold much of the time. In early September I wore a sweater and jacket beneath my laboratory coat. 'What will you do when winter comes?" my colleagues asked. "I don't know," I replied, "but I am going to be comfortable now." Although I put on a brave front with regard to the impending winter, I was actually quite concerned. I had heard horror stories about the harsh Ithaca winters and began to worry that I had made a serious mistake in coming to Cornell. How could I live in a place where the weather could be so treacherous?

My mind was taken off the weather, however, when at the age of twenty-three I was assigned my own private chemistry laboratory at Cornell. My ego soared; it was quite an honor at my age to have my own laboratory at such a prestigious university. Unfortunately, my ego was soon deflated when I learned that I would work with perchloric acid, a dangerous and explosive chemical. My first week in Ithaca I met a young man whose face was badly pitted with scars from an accident with perchloric acid at the Federal Nutrition Laboratory. I was worried and a bit nervous but reassured myself that I had worked with dangerous chemicals before and had no problems. I believed that I could do it again.

One of my assignments was to determine the availability of iron in frozen vegetables, particularly in green peas. It was a difficult topic; in fact, studies are still being conducted on the availability of iron in many food products. I worked hard and put together a bibliography that has been used for many years by others such as Dr. Will Gortner who later joined the Program Staff of the United States Department of Agriculture (USDA) in Beltsville, Maryland. Although my work was productive, pipetting acid slurries of peas was not a pleasant task. When green peas are put in acid, they turn brownish because the green chlorophyll of the pea is converted to pheophytin, an ugly brown shade similar to the color of feces. For many years after working on that project I did not eat peas.

In spite of this, I enjoyed my work at the Federal Nutrition Laboratory and liked my coworkers. Women were definitely in the minority at the laboratory and the seminars on Friday afternoons were blended with a social hour, so I quickly became acquainted with the different people at the laboratory. I soon felt very much a part of everything. Shortly after my arrival I was appointed social chairman of the seminar which meant I was responsible for planning the social activities following the seminar.

The first snowfall came in early November, and I was surprised to learn that my colleagues did not know how to make snow ice cream. My recipe for snow ice cream consisted of a concentrated solution of milk, sugar, eggs, and vanilla mixed with snow until the ingredients take on the consistency of ice cream. The ice crystals were somewhat larger than those in commercial ice cream, but it was a delicious treat and a big success. I had less success with my table decorations consisting of little carved snowmen as centerpieces. I had not realized how quickly they would melt in the warm seminar room; snow was still a novelty for me. Everyone laughed at my rapidly diminishing centerpieces.

Despite the many unfortunate things I encountered in Ithaca from the inferior apartment to the long walks in the cold, my first year at Cornell was enriched by the warm kindness of my colleagues at the laboratory. By midyear my homesickness was gone, and I began to appreciate the beauty of the Cornell campus which I had overlooked before. Even in winter, with the snow piled high, Cornell is a beautiful place. Surrounded by lakes, waterfalls, and deep gorges, the campus is unique and lovely.

I began attending lectures and concerts, and I was invited to join Sigma Delta Epsilon, a national honorary organization for graduate women conducting research in the natural sciences. The Alpha Chapter had been established at Cornell in 1921. Although professional women in science at Cornell were few in number, I found them to be excellent mentors.

Another highlight was receiving an invitation to a dinner in honor of five Cornell recipients of the Nobel Prize. The dinner was held in the Grand Ballroom of the Waldorf Astoria Hotel in New York City and was in special tribute to the most recent winner, Dr. J. B. Sumner, Professor of Biochemistry. Also honored were Dr. Peter Debye, Professor of Chemistry; Dr. John R. Mott, a peace prize recipient; Dr. Isidor Rabi, a 1919 graduate of Cornell who won the Nobel Prize for Physics in 1944; and Pearl S. Buck who received an M.A. from Cornell in 1925 and won the Nobel Prize for Literature in 1938.

I traveled to New York City with a friend, Frances Volz, on the Lehigh Valley train, also known as the "Leaky Valley," which provided an unbelievably rough and rocky ride. Fran was acquainted with New York City, and was eager to show me around. Our first stop was the subway. We purchased our tokens, and I boarded when the train arrived. As I turned around, I saw the doors closing before Fran could join me. Suddenly we were separated, and the train went rattling on its way. I knew nothing about subways but I had sense enough to get off at the next stop where Fran found me. "You've only been here an hour, and you've already had a New York adventure," she laughed.

I was quite impressed by the opulence of the Waldorf Astoria and by the preparations that had been made for the dinner. The menu included crabmeat royal with red caviar, Key West turtle soup, and sirloin of beef *chasseur*. I felt like royalty as I mingled with Nobel Prize winners. The dinner was also attended by Cornell President Edmund Ezra Day who served as toastmaster.

Dr. J. B. Sumner, professor of biochemistry, had received the Nobel Prize for crystallizing the enzyme urease. He had prepared crystalline urease from the jackbean as early as 1926, but the award was delayed because of a dispute with a German scientist. In his speech, Dr. Sumner acknowledged the assistance of his former graduate student, Dr. Viola Graham who had performed many of the actual experiments. Several scientists think that she should have shared the prize. He did not use her first name; he referred to her by only her initials so that she was not identified as a woman. I do not know if this was intentional, but women in biochemistry were scarce and did not receive the same recognition as men. We had chosen our careers in chemistry knowing that we may not be fully recognized. Dr. Graham was an early member of Sigma Delta Epsilon, an honorary for women in the physical sciences, and had designed the key and seal for the organization. I was thrilled to be invited to this elegant event for Nobel prize winners and I was impressed to be in the company of such accomplished individuals.

My fortunes at Cornell were changing for the better. My salary had increased, and Mother and I found a nice house with a yard large enough for flowers and vegetables. On our moving day, May 17, we had a shock when we woke up to find several inches of snow blanketing the ground. Our lovely spring moving day had turned into a wintry adventure. Ithaca weather still had a few surprises for us, but I had mastered my homesickness and fallen in love with Ithaca—its hills, lakes, waterfalls, and beautiful countryside. Although on cloudy days in Ithaca, I sometimes think about the clear, sunny skies of Texas, I am not sorry that I moved here. Living in Ithaca, surrounded by lakes and waterfalls; fields of corn, potatoes, tomatoes, sunflowers, strawberries, and blueberries; orchards abundant in apples, cherries, and peaches; and bountiful lakeside vineyards laden with red, white, and blue grapes, I have found "God's garden."

EDUCATING NY WORLD WAR II VETERANS
SAMPSON COLLEGE: 1946-1948

To educate New York State's war veterans was the goal of New York's Governor Thomas E. Dewey and Cornell's President Edmund Ezra Day in the fall of 1946. Because Cornell and other New York universities could not accommodate all of the veterans, a system of two-year junior colleges was established throughout New York State. This system became the Associated Colleges of Upper New York (ACUNY), the forerunner of the State University of New York (SUNY) system. Veterans were assured that if they did well they could enter Cornell or another New York University at the junior level. Three ACUNY schools were established—the largest was at the former naval base at Sampson, another at Utica, and the third at Plattsburgh near Lake Champlain.

Hearing of ACUNY's need for chemistry teachers, I applied for the job. Although I was a young twenty-four year old, I had teaching experience at both Ouachita College and Texas University. Soon after my interview, a telegram arrived offering me a position in the Department of Chemistry at Sampson at double the salary I was receiving as a research associate at Cornell University. I had already been appointed for my second year as a research associate at Cornell, and I wasn't sure if it would be right to change. After conferring with people at Cornell for advice, I realized that it was an excellent opportunity for me and they thought it appropriate for me to accept.

The newly assembled chemistry faculty numbered more than twenty, and I was the youngest member and the only woman. Several faculty members had Ph.D. degrees and working with them was interesting and challenging because it gave me the opportunity to interact with scholars from different parts of the United States. Among the faculty was Dr. Donald Williamson from Texas, an array of chemists from the New York City area, and a retired naval officer who had taught chemistry.

The buildings on the military base at Sampson were converted to meet classroom requirements. Chemistry was assigned one of the largest buildings on the base and the laboratory was brought up to standard. The chemistry building needed special facilities for equipment and storage, such as an area free of vibration.

Because these buildings had previously serviced the Navy and the Air Force, they had many rest rooms, all of them labeled "Men." At first I went across the street to the language building to use the ladies' rest room, but after a few days, I decided that was enough. I consulted with the buildings' supervisor and mentioned the need for a women's rest room in the Chemistry building. He said, "Pick out the best rest room in the building, and stake your claim by placing a sign on the door." Very soon he promised to have a permanent sign painted. So from then on I enjoyed my own private rest room, with no waiting line since all my students and fellow faculty were male. I felt fortunate to have my own rest room.

Single faculty women were housed in the former officers' quarters which were comfortable. It had windows overlooking beautiful Seneca Lake, the largest of the New York Finger Lakes. My spacious room had previously been shared by two officers and included two huge closets, each almost as large as separate rooms. I used one closet for clothing and the other for food storage, including vegetables. The residents shared a large kitchen area located at the end of the hall. Since my mother had chosen to remain in Ithaca, I traveled to Ithaca on weekends and bought groceries for both of us.

Relatively few women were on the Sampson faculty, so our dormitory was not crowded. I was the only woman in chemistry, and there were only a few from the language department, including an older lady, Mrs. Nora Porter, who mothered all of us. A woman with a marked German accent from the political science department had absolutely no experience in food preparation, so I became her chief cooking advisor. She never quite understood American idioms. Once I told her about a fellow faculty member who tended to look at the world through "rose-colored glasses"—later I heard her speak of "the man who looked at the world through pink eyes."

Teaching general chemistry during my first year at Sampson, I gave four lectures each day on the same material. By the time I finished my fourth lecture I felt like a recording. For my lectures I used an outline in which I checked off point by point the material covered. The technique worked well and my students often scored at the top on the overall departmental exams.

My teaching at Sampson was very enjoyable as both faculty and students were intelligent, friendly, and hard working. All my students were male and most were much older than I, and I did not consider it appropriate to date any of them. I insisted on good discipline, an ideal that was challenged during my first term. Early in the term, two young men in the back row started to whisper while I was lecturing. Stopping my lecture, I quietly looked at the two students until they became embarrassed and stopped talking. I then continued on with the lecture. Earlier I had learned that the best thing to do to maintain discipline was to call attention to the offenders at once and then remain silent until the offenders realized that they had the full attention of their classmates. Quickly word spread among the students that I demanded discipline, and afterwards had no further problems. Dr. Max Hull, the chair of the chemistry department, told me later that my classes were the best disciplined in the entire department.

My southern accent posed a slight problem with teaching at Sampson. Most students were from the New York City area, and sometimes they could not understand my southern accent. When I saw from their faces that they did not understand, I would write the word on the board. To adapt to their needs, I changed my pronunciation and it soon became evident that my accent changed. While visiting the South after a year of teaching at Sampson, my friends observed that I spoke with a "Yankee" accent. When I called my southern friends, Paul and Rosemary Bowlin, Paul answered the phone and after a few minutes I heard him call Rosemary and say, "Rosemary, it's Nell, and she's talking just like a Yankee." At least he didn't say, "damned Yankee."

In addition to lecturing, I offered self-help classes to my students at five o'clock each day to answer any of their questions. Because it was voluntary, I called it a "self-help" class and these classes became very popular. Dr. Hull liked the idea and suggested that other faculty members conduct such classes.

Students often varied in their need for help. One of my students was preparing to take over the operation of his father-in-law's pharmacy and needed chemistry. Although he worked very hard, this young man had limited ability in chemistry. However, he had talent for languages so I encouraged him to move in that direction and allow someone else to handle the pharmacy. He followed my advice and became much happier.

After my first year, Dr. Hull placed me in charge of all general chemistry sections during the summer quarter. This resulted in visits to the other campuses of ACUNY, including the Plattsburgh campus located on Lake Champlain in the Adirondack region. Following my visit to the Plattsburg campus, I was to accompany the vice president of the Associated Colleges back to Sampson. The Adirondack region was unusually hot that summer and resulted in a change in the surface of the asphalt roads, creating an oily film. While we were returning to Sampson, the rain began to fall, making the roads very slippery. My driving companion tried to apply the brakes and the car swerved towards the left guard railing. In an attempt to steer the car to the right he lost complete control of the car and we flipped over. I remember knowing that we were flipping over. It all happened so fast and

I felt a sharp pain underneath my neck, near my shoulder, and my travel companion's head was bleeding. The car had skidded off the highway, rolled over completely onto an embankment, and was completely demolished. Therefore, we were stranded there until other travelers came to our rescue. Later it was discovered that I had a fractured clavicle and broken ribs, while the driver suffered deep facial cuts. He had crashed into the windshield upon impact. At that time seatbelts had not been invented, so it was miraculous that we survived. The accident occurred near Eighth Lake in a sparsely populated area. Fortunately we were discovered by other motorists who took us to the area's only doctor who was ninety years old. There was no hospital in the vicinity so the doctor housed us for the night. I was given some pain medication but it failed to provide me much relief.

The next day my travel companion and I were driven to a hospital in Geneva, New York, which was located near Sampson College. Doctors attempted to set my clavicle, but after three days decided that an "open reduction" (pinning together the fractured bone through an open incision) was necessary. At first the procedure went well, but a few weeks later the doctor attempted to remove the pin before the bone had healed. My arm then had to be placed in a sling for weeks and there was concern that a bone graft might be necessary. Despite my injuries, I continued teaching. When I entered the classroom on my first day back, the students stood and applauded me. My left shoulder had sustained the damage and it was fortunate that I could write on the chalkboard with my right hand (Thanks to the training given me by my teacher in the first grade).

My second year at Sampson went well. I was promoted from instructor to assistant professor and given a nice raise in salary. I think I was the first woman to climb the first rung of the professional ladder in the ACUNY system (later known at SUNY). I taught organic chemistry, my favorite subject, in addition to general chemistry. By this time, Lillian Questiaux had joined our department. Her bachelor's degree was from the University of Chicago and her master's from Columbia University. However, she had no prior teaching experience and was extremely nervous about the prospect of lecturing to veteran students. I attempted to calm her fears and gave advice about the importance of discipline. I felt fortunate to have established discipline early.

It was fun having another woman on the chemistry faculty, and Lillian and I often double-dated with male faculty members. At first she was homesick for city life for she found the Sampson countryside boring. She returned to New York City on weekends, and on Monday mornings she would be so tired that she could hardly teach. I was happy with the lovely Finger Lakes Region and loved living beside the large and beautiful Seneca Lake. I pointed out that there were many interesting things in the country. She finally agreed and eventually came to love the lake country. Years later, after she joined the faculty of the University of Illinois at Chicago, she returned often to visit her beloved Finger Lakes country.

I enjoyed Sampson very much but understood that it was probably a temporary school and might close after the veteran need was met since the ACUNY system had been designed for veterans. After their first two years at Sampson, the students would transfer to Cornell, Columbia, or other New York schools. My work at Sampson with Dr. Max Hull and Dr. Amos Horney, Dean of Liberal Arts of all three ACUNY schools, was very pleasant. Both were very supportive of me but I began to think that it was time to move on. I accepted a position teaching Chemistry in the Department of Food and Nutrition at Cornell University and returned to Cornell in the fall semester of 1948.

Return to Cornell: Food Chemistry
Department of Food and Nutrition: 1948-1951

Toward the end of my second year at Sampson College, a good friend, Leona Jane Bledsoe, a graduate assistant in the College of Home Economics at Cornell University, informed me that her department, Consumer Economics, was looking for a qualified chemist. She told them about my training, and they contacted me. Upon receiving my credentials, they responded immediately by offering me a position.

Meanwhile, I had received a letter from Dr. Catherine Personius, Chair of the Food and Nutrition Department, telling me about a chemistry position in the Department of Food and Nutrition at Cornell. Her department needed someone to teach Food Chemistry, and because my training was in both foods and chemistry, I was offered the job. I weighed the two offers carefully and decided to accept the position in the Department of Food and Nutrition. It was good to return to Cornell.

Cornell University is unique in that it has statutory as well as endowed units. When Home Economics (statutory unit) students took chemistry from the Department of Chemistry, which was housed in the College of Arts and Sciences (endowed unit), they were required to pay accessory tuition. By offering chemistry within the School of Home Economics, the accessory tuition fee was avoided. Dr. Marion Pfund, a Ph.D. graduate in Organic Chemistry from Yale University, was in charge of the chemistry course in the Department of Food and Nutrition. She had developed a hybrid course combining both chemistry and food credit. Because I was qualified to teach both chemistry and foods, I was pursued vigorously. I accepted the offer to work with Dr. Marion Pfund teaching the course in Chemistry and Food Preparation. The course entailed ten credits—six credit hours in chemistry and four credit hours in foods. Despite my training in food at Ouachita, I did not feel as comfortable with the food subject matter as I did with chemistry, so during my first year of teaching the course I spent considerable time developing and writing experiments for both the food laboratory as well as for the chemistry laboratory. It was a pleasure to combine these two areas of my special interest.

At Ouachita College, I had developed a course in Organic Chemistry that incorporated food and nutrition. I realized that home economics students needed chemistry but that it should be applicable to their specific areas of interest. Unfortunately, many chemistry departments were not interested in this combination. It was a delight to find that Cornell University was interested in this approach.

Dr. Pfund was very supportive and placed me in charge of all the chemistry laboratories. It was an interesting challenge to work with her and benefit from her expertise. Not entirely satisfied with my foods background, I audited several food courses at Cornell to improve my knowledge in that area. Fortunately, my chemistry background was excellent and I was able to manage the chemistry part of the course very well.

During my first semester, I was assigned to teach the sections which included hotel students. Previous instructors had experienced difficulty in disciplining the hotel students. My previous experience in teaching male students at Sampson College provided an excellent background, and I had no problem with discipline. The Hotel School at Cornell was still in its infancy under the excellent guidance of Dean H.B. Meek. His extensive knowledge of the field and his bold vision for the future of hotel programs worldwide would soon lift the school to elite status. At this time Statler Hall had not been built, and the Hotel School was housed in the home economics building, Martha Van Rensselaer Hall. When Dean Meek received enough money to move the school from the home economics building to Statler Hall in 1950, he invited some of us in home economics to join the Hotel School faculty. I was tempted because I enjoyed teaching hotel students, but at that time there was very little research support in the Hotel School, and I wanted to be involved in both teaching and research. The Hotel School had no federal support for research, and in order to raise my interest, Professor Meek offered a certain amount of money to be used for research. Although the offer was generous, I decided to stay in home economics where there was federal support for research. However, I agreed to train his teaching staff in food chemistry, and also helped to plan the food chemistry laboratories in the newly erected Statler Hall.

I trained instructors from both the Hotel School and Home Economics. Staff laboratories were conducted for all so that each laboratory instructor was trained in every experiment prior to teaching. In this way, all students in the multiple-sectioned course were exposed to the same material.

Professor H.B. Meek, an outstanding organizer, was a good friend of Dr. L.A. Maynard, another good organizer who chaired the School of Nutrition.

Both men were small in stature but giants in intellect and dedication. At Cornell commencements, these two men always marched together because of their similar short stature. The legacy of Professor Meek's vision is the Hotel School, among the oldest and most prestigious in the U.S. It features its own elegant, student-run hotel on campus. Graduates of the school have taken positions all over the world; and I have had the pleasure of meeting many of them in my travels to such cities as Tokyo, Hong Kong, and New Dehli.

Since I had no disciplinary problems with the male students at Sampson, I applied the same techniques used at Sampson to the Cornell Hotel students. At the end of the term they presented me with a large bouquet of roses indicating their appreciation of me. I enjoyed meeting the many food specialists who came to Cornell to take our food chemistry course. Among them was one of the chefs at the Waldorf Astoria in New York City. He was especially skilled in preparing and decorating fancy foods but wanted to learn more about the chemistry of foods. Our course in food chemistry was unique for no other schools in the country offered courses combining food and chemistry credit. This course enabled students to understand the chemistry of food.

Other opportunities to examine food became available in 1949 and 1950, when I was selected by the Consumer Union, along with two other faculty members, to research and report on two new and exciting developments in the area of food science, namely cake mixes and food mixers.

Prior to that time, most women were closely tied to their homes by the demands that housework and chores placed on them. They had few of the modern conveniences we have today, and operating a household was very time consuming. During World War II, women participated in the war effort and many held important positions outside the home, but when the war ended in 1945, women were expected to return to their former lifestyles as homemakers.

The "food revolution" that occurred shortly following Word War II was crucial to the liberation of women. For centuries the many excessive daily chores in the house kept women at home. The "food revolution" occurred, both in the kitchen and in the workplace, and I am happy to have contributed to it.

With the advent of mixes and mixers, women were suddenly relieved of many of their most time-consuming activities. In order to make a cake it was no longer necessary to buy every single ingredient and carefully measure and mix each. Instead the women could combine prepackaged ingredients, mix them together, and bake. This saved both time and energy.

As researchers in food and nutrition at Cornell University, our job was to evaluate these new products. The first experiments for Consumer Union were carried out with cake mixes. Previously I had developed cake mixes in my food chemistry class at Cornell. Most of these were delicious. Flavor, texture, etc., along with the other traits were evaluated. Baking a good quality cake was important at the time, and I was determined to have our mixes meet the standards of the most exacting housewife. After the investigations were completed, we met individually with a representative from Consumer Union. Our responses were compiled and our scores were reported in *Consumer Reports*. I have high regard for Consumer Union, for their investigations were thorough and the results reported objectively. The magazine is still effective today, a tribute to its success.

The tests for Consumer Union were performed during the Christmas vacation at Cornell. They were rigorous, thorough and demanding, and we took great pride in our work. I was paid well and invested my earnings in a large home freezer. At that time electric freezers were just beginning to appear in American households.

The second year, we tested electric mixers. These were ranked according to specific criteria and were separated into categories of "very good," "good," "fair," and "poor." Each mixer was carefully examined for durability, convenience, performance, and electrical safety. According to their strengths and weaknesses, the brands rated "not acceptable" were considered dangerous. In some cases, the machine's use resulted in flying pieces of metal, and some machines had a severe shock hazard. These were rated "unacceptable" because of potential dangers.

Studying these products was very rewarding. Not only was I participating in a project which would greatly expand the food science area, I was participating in a service that would enhance women's liberation from household chores. Cake and pancake mixes, dehydrated foods, and electric mixers all gave women more free time. My work with Consumer Union was also interesting because it tied in with a former interest of mine: dehydrated potatoes. Before coming to Cornell, I had been interested in dehydrated potato products. In those days, fresh potatoes were stored in the dark and one had to hope that they did not sprout. The space occupied by stored whole potatoes was large and often unsatisfactory.

About this time, the R. T. French Co. in Rochester, NY apparently shared my interest and began to market potato granules. I first used their product while living in the faculty quarters at Sampson College. Although the first powdered potatoes were dark brown in color and lacked good flavor, their convenience led me to use them. In the years that followed, through many stages of research and testing, potato granules greatly improved in color, flavor, and texture and became widely received by the market. In 1966 the R. T. French Co. invited me to be a consultant for their research during my sabbatic leave from Cornell.

Many new products inundated the market during a very small window of time. Students trained in home economics were in great demand because food companies sought their knowledge of food chemistry. Women played crucial roles in the development of these new products. Not only were revolutionary new products appearing in the marketplace, but new uses for them were emerging. A "food revolution" was also taking place in the kitchen. Fresh meat was not always plentiful on the market shelves and many people canned meat at home in order to preserve it. Home Economics students were taught to can meat and vegetables using large pressure cookers. Canning of low acid vegetables such as green beans and asparagus required the use of a pressure canner in order to assure safety from botulism. Deaths from toxins found in improperly canned food were frequently reported and served as a warning.

It was exciting to be a part of the "food revolution." Changes were rapidly occurring. Women were being liberated from domestic chores that consumed much time.

Teaching food chemistry was demanding and required knowledge of both chemistry and food. The Department of Food and Nutrition at Cornell ranked very high throughout the U.S. and attracted many students and faculty from other countries, especially European countries. Dr. Ruth Salinus, from Uppsala, Sweden, chair of the department at the University of Sweden was one who came to study under my tutelage while she was on sabbatic leave. Several years later I visited Ruth while on my sabbatical. It was good to meet her faculty and staff and learn about their work in food chemistry.

Dr. Pfund took a sabbatic leave in the fall semester, 1950, and asked me to be in charge of the entire food chemistry course. I accepted. During that time, I supervised seven laboratory sections, taught all of the instructors, and lectured in the large amphitheater. When Dr. Pfund returned in the spring semester, she asked me to continue lecturing and she sat in the class and took notes. I was delighted with the opportunity. My lectures went well, and Dr. Pfund was so pleased with my performance that she said to me, "You are the very one to take my place. And I plan to retire before long."

In fact I had already decided to pursue my studies further. The next year, 1951, I was accepted as a doctoral candidate in Cornell's Department of Biochemistry. The Ph.D. degree was awarded in 1953.

CORNELL PH.D. DEGREE
SIGMA XI FELLOW: 1951-1953

At the time I was a doctoral student, Cornell required all Ph.D. students to pass proficiency exams in both French and German. Between the spring semester and full-time teaching, and my upcoming summer school studies, I only had a two-week window to prepare for the French examination. A man in Collegetown, Mr. Mattli, ran a service that prepared students for language examinations. I promptly paid him a visit and stated that I had to pass my French examination within two weeks. He looked at me and smiled sadly, shaking his head. "I'm sorry but that can not be done," he told me. Unwilling to accept defeat, I became determined to prove him wrong. So began our business relationship. Mr. Mattli had created a progression of lessons. His ten-minute lessons prepared students for the more advanced fifteen-minute lessons that followed. That afternoon I mastered my first ten-minute lesson and returned for the next, which I also conquered. Surprised, Mr. Mattli decided that I had become proficient enough to attempt more challenging material. By studying diligently and returning to Mr. Mattli on a regular basis, I passed the reading exam after only two weeks of study.

Although this "crash-course" learning allowed me to pass the exam without difficulty, I found soon afterward that the material was not incorporated into my "long-term" memory. My knowledge of French departed almost as quickly as it had entered, and this left me frustrated. When people study something in a very short period of time, they often do not assimilate the information well, and the quickly acquired knowledge is soon lost.

Although I passed both my French and German examinations, I championed the movement to eliminate French and German as Ph.D. requirements at Cornell. The rationale behind eliminating the requirements was that there are so many languages to learn and so much information to gain in graduate study that it is a waste of time to require everyone to learn the same two languages: French and German.

Only once did I have the need for knowledge of these languages. After spending a weekend translating a German article involving an enzyme preparation, I asked Eric, an office-mate and postdoctoral student from Switzerland, to read my translation. He informed me that I had done an excellent job, but I had spent many hours translating that which he could have done in a very short time.

I passed the German exam twice: once in Texas while studying for my master's degree and again at Cornell while working toward my Ph.D. degree. The University of Texas required all masters' candidates to take two years of German or to pass the Ph.D. reading examination. Since I sought the M.A. degree, I decided to sign up for a German course to fulfill this requirement, but the course consisted largely of fairy tales. *This isn't going to help me in science*, I thought, and immediately dropped the course, choosing instead to learn German on my own. I passed the Ph.D. exam and eventually acquired a considerable vocabulary in German.

My German reading exam in Texas was under the chair of the German department. This was a daunting experience, for it included both the written and oral examinations. Although I passed the exam with high marks in Texas, it was not transferable to Cornell, for Cornell would not accept a language reading exam from another university. The best lesson I learned from the language requirements was the meaning of discipline.

Having passed the language exams, I completed my Ph.D. degree in two years. During this time, I was selected for the Cornell Sigma Xi fellowship. At that time there were very few general fellowships offered by Cornell Graduate School. Since there were so few the competition was intense, and I was fortunate to win the Sigma Xi fellowship. Using the fellowship support I was able to work full-time on my own research, and this greatly reduced the time required to finish my degree.

At Cornell my Ph.D. studies involved experimentation with rats. My master's research at Texas University was primarily with microorganisms. However, at Cornell most of my research involved rats as the experimental animal. Although the research was very interesting, I disliked sacrificing rats. My research dealt with enzymes found in rat liver, and I was unable to anesthetize the animals before sacrificing them for this might interfer with the activity of the enzyme under study.

At that time I was the only female graduate student in the biochemistry department and the other Ph.D. students offered to help by sacrificing the rats for me. I thanked them for their offer, but I knew that if I were to get the credit for the research, I had to carry out all of the necessary steps myself.

The first sacrifice was not easy. The rat was decapitated and the liver removed immediately. Prior experience in handling rats had taught me the proper techniques to avoid rat bites. Thick white protective gloves were worn and a swift blow to the head with a hammer stunned the rat. Its head was then placed on the chopping block and I decapitated it using a meat cleaver. The body cavity was opened immediately, the liver removed and placed immediately into buffer solution prior to homogenization. My male colleagues were anxious to see if I could do it. They waited outside and when I left the animal room, they claimed that I was pale, but I knew I had accomplished my task. This operation was repeated numerous times during my research studies.

The research dealt mainly with factors affecting two important enzymes, betaine aldehyde dehydrogenase and choline dehydrogenase. The effects of various chemicals on these enzymes were tested. My coworkers were Dr. Ralph Strength, a post-doctorate, and Roger Christensen, a fellow Ph.D. candidate. A caretaker was hired to clean the rat cages, but the three of us were responsible for supplying the rats with food and water. We shared the responsibilities and rotated the caretaking duties on a weekly basis.

Ralph enjoyed working with rats, and knew how to tame them. He took them from their cage and rubbed their heads and backs and showed me this technique. Roger refused to spend time in taming the rats. If my week to care for the rats followed Ralph's week, the rats were tame and gentle, but if I followed Roger they were wild, and I had difficulty taming them.

Some of my experiments dealt with administering the compound aminopterin—a folic acid antagonist. My task in the experiment was to inject the rat with the compound and observe the rat until it eventually died. I had the unpleasant task of collecting the liver at the time of death.

Rats, like most animals, can become pets. Each rat has its own personality and often exhibits human-like behavior. I remember particularly one rat in my study that always gave me special attention when I entered the room. It would jump up and down in its cage and put its nose out of the bars asking to be petted. I shall never forget the anguish I had when it became necessary for me to sacrifice that rat. Good scientists must be objective and refrain from becoming fond of experimental subjects.

I realize that animal research is needed to study diseases of mankind, but sacrificing animals was always difficult for me. However, my work with rats was very productive and five publications in peer-reviewed journals resulted from my work. One incentive for me to publish my work was a young professor at the University of Wisconsin, Dr. J. N. Williams. We were doing similar experiments and I was determined to publish my results first. Had we not been in competition, I probably would not have published my research as quickly as I did.

My research base was in Savage Hall, the home of the biochemistry department. Several graduate students competed for the limited space and equipment in Savage and some pieces of equipment had to be scheduled days in advance. My name frequently appeared on the schedule board because my research required the use of the Warburg respirometer and took many hours of hard labor. I started early in the morning preparing the solutions, equipment, and rat liver for the enzyme assays. I visited each of Savage Hall's four floors: the rats were located in the basement, while the refrigerator, ultracentrifuge, and other necessary pieces of equipment were located in different rooms on different floors. The exercise kept me in good physical condition, and I maintained a trim figure throughout the course of my research in Savage Hall.

Some of the biochemistry professors working in Savage Hall at the time were Dr. Louise Daniel, chair of my graduate committee and the only female professor; Dr. J.B. Sumner, a Nobel Prize-winner; Dr. L.A. Maynard, Director of Nutrition, and Dr. H.H. Williams, chair of the biochemistry department. In addition, Dr. Leslie Neal, who researched the golden nematod, and Dr. Walter Nelson, who was in charge of the advanced biochemistry laboratory, were important members of the department. I had the privilege of taking the first course in international nutrition given at Cornell by Dr. Maynard.

Dr. Sumner had lost an arm as a young man, a handicap that could have prevented him from pursuing a career in chemistry. However, he had adjusted well to his situation, both personally and professionally. In the laboratory, it was interesting to observe him place a test tube in the upper pocket of his lab coat while pouring another solution into it. He would then remove the test tube, stopper it, and shake it vigorously with one hand. So thoroughly had Dr. Sumner overcome his handicap that he had even become an excellent tennis player. He was a straightforward person who spoke in short concise sentences and he had a good sense of humor. He was especially courteous to me, the only female graduate student in biochemistry. At my first laboratory appearance he made a special visit to the laboratory just to extend a special welcome to me. At this time Dr. Sumner was nearing retirement. He taught two courses: 1) a two-credit lecture course on enzymes, and 2) a three-credit advanced biochemistry laboratory in which he delegated much of the teaching responsibilities to Dr. Walter Nelson.

Dr. Sumner was known for his exam questions which were brief but demanded answers with much discussion. A typical example might be "Discuss urease." or "Discuss anthocyanins." Students were expected to write a one to two-page response. Word spread among the graduate students that Dr. Sumner often used questions from previous examinations, and copies of these old exams circulated among students. The year I took his course I decided to delve deeper into the enzyme literature and did not depend on his old exam questions. This was fortunate because that year, Dr. Sumner created a new examination with new questions. Since I had studied more than just the old exams, I scored at the top of the class.

Dr. Sumner supplied each student with a present: a jack bean on which his initials "JBS" were inscribed. He had used jack beans to crystallize the enzyme urease, and his discovery later won him the Nobel Prize. Students nicknamed him "Jack Bean Sumner."

Dr. Nelson was in charge of the advanced biochemistry laboratory course. I had worked with Dr. Nelson in 1945-46 at the Federal Nutrition Laboratory, and it was a pleasure to work with him again. The course carried three credit hours, but it should have carried much more credit for it required many hours of work. Each section of the course required a written report equivalent to a term paper in length and complexity and involved approximately one section per week.

My first day in the laboratory involved cleaning glassware for I discovered that most of the equipment was not chemically clean. It has always been my custom to ensure that equipment was chemically clean before beginning any experiment. Much time was spent in cleaning glassware before I began my first assignment, the preparation of the enzyme urease. This preparation was tedious, but I was successful on my first attempt. Other classmates tried several times before getting crystals. I attributed my success to the clean glassware. My laboratory partner refused to clean his glassware chemically and was never able to obtain enzyme crystals.

The course required many enzyme preparations, each involving numerous hours of labor. When my partner and I were expected to work together on a preparation, I politely told him, "Don't worry, I'll do it—I have the time." In truth I was concerned that his sloppy work habits would adversely affect our performance; I would carry out the entire preparation myself rather than correct his mistakes. My lengthy reports usually scored A or A+. Although the course was time-consuming and difficult, I learned many valuable lessons which were used later in my own research and in the preparation of manuscripts for publication.

During this period when so much of my time was focused on academics, there were other serious issues surrounding me. I relived the sadness of watching friends leave for a foreign country. My good friend, Dr. John Skory, was not directly involved in the Korean war but was in Korea when the war started. After receiving his Ph.D. in agronomy and statistics, the United States government assigned him to assist Korea in agriculture. He arrived in Seoul just one day before the war started, and his letters to me describing the situation are preserved in the Cornell Archives. As the war escalated, John was flown to Japan, and eventually returned to Ithaca.

After his return, he accepted a position with the American Cancer Society researching the relationship between smoking and cancer. Although a significant, positive correlation between smoking and cancer was established by his group in the early 1950s, the public was not informed of their findings until years later (in the 1960s) because the tobacco companies refused to accept the findings and prevented the research from reaching the public. Many lives could have been saved if the public had been informed of the research findings. It is discouraging to know that special interest groups resist accepting any scientific findings that interfere with the marketability of their products. Both as a scientist and humanitarian, I firmly disagree with this approach. John and his colleagues from the American Cancer Society should have been congratulated on their early findings concerning smoking and cancer, but instead the findings were denied.

Soon after completing my doctorate, I returned to Cornell to teach a ten credit-hour course in food chemistry. The large enrollment of more than one hundred students necessitated the hiring of several instructors to assist me. They were trained to carry out laboratory teaching. Uniformity of teaching was necessary so that all students received the same instruction. Training instructors required much time and left me with little opportunity for research. However, I was determined to continue my own research because I felt that it was important for a teacher to be able to carry out research and interpret the results to students.

Like most Cornell professors at that time, I had a nine-month appointment, meaning that I would teach for nine months, "improve myself" for two months, and take a one-month vacation. In effect this meant that I would be working two months out of the year with no pay. This was one of the arrangements for uncompensated productivity that Cornell had with its faculty. I decided to dedicate the two-month 'improvement period" as well as my month of vacation to my research.

Academic funding was difficult to secure, and because few United States graduate grants were available, I had to make do with the resources around me. About this time, the School of Veterinary Medicine was moving from Ives Hall to its new facility. In making this transition, much of their equipment was left behind. This was a blessing for me, being short of funds and in need of equipment. I was told that I could have the equipment if I moved it to my laboratory in Martha Van Rensselaer Hall (MVR). In this way, I procured a chemical fume hood, a vast array of glassware, some laboratory desks, and a variety of other equipment. At that time MVR Hall was poorly equipped for a chemist because very few chemists were housed in MVR and few had chosen to do research.

Installation of the veterinary school equipment and new laboratory lighting was carried out using my own grant funds. This experience led me to realize the true value of a research facility. I actually created my own laboratory with my meager funds. Later, when other faculty became interested in research and funding became more plentiful, they moved into the laboratories I had established totally unaware of the hard work that had gone into creating the facilities.

Although I had acquired equipment from the veterinary college, my laboratory was not complete. Much equipment had to be specially built, a task undertaken with workers from physics and the Federal Nutrition Laboratory. These men were willing to create special pieces of equipment for me according to my design. They were meticulous in attention to every detail and constructed useful, reliable equipment for my laboratory.

Also needed were specific pieces of laboratory equipment to perform classroom demonstrations. My classes were large, and my lectures were in the amphitheater of MVR Hall, a lecture room spread over two floors.

In such a large room, it was difficult for students in the back rows to see the demonstrations on the lecture desk. It was particularly problematic to demonstrate chemical reactions because the students could not see such things as color changes. For this purpose a novel piece of equipment—a work desk with lights underneath—was designed. My "light desk" increased the visibility of the experiments so that all students could benefit from the demonstrations.

There is documentation that students given demonstrations in addition to lectures have a higher recall of subject matter. My students realized this and expressed their appreciation. My courses were popular with the students, perhaps largely due to the visual nature of my lectures. My teaching was featured in the 1966 yearbook "Cornellian."

Having good tools makes any job easier, and I was extremely grateful to my creative Cornell colleagues for their contributions. I was able to help students understand using meaningful demonstrations. This was something I kept in mind throughout my many years of teaching: If students could apply what they learned in classrooms to their lives, they would be well-disciplined and successful. This idea made teaching very important to me.

Scotland: First Phase of Foods International

United States Department of Agriculture: 1960-1961

One benefit of being a professor is the opportunity to take sabbatic leaves. Sabbaticals are not intended to be vacations from scholarly pursuits, but rather a time for professors to broaden their knowledge through first-hand experience in their areas of study and to focus on their research interests. A professor of English may journey to Oxford to examine medieval manuscripts; a history professor may travel to Greece to study ancient architecture; a physics professor might arrange an extended visit to the labs at NASA. I was fortunate enough to take my sabbatic leaves all over the world where I renewed old friendships and discussed my field's advancements with other scientists. I always returned to Cornell with a fresh perspective and new material for my research.

My first trip abroad in 1960 was on my first sabbatic leave from Cornell. I had been due to take my sabbatic a year earlier but the course I taught, Chemistry and Food Preparation, was difficult for many professors to master. Most of our faculty members did not have the needed chemistry background to teach the course, so the administration asked me to postpone the sabbatic for a year until they could find a substitute teacher for my class.

I was disappointed, but sometimes hardships work out to be blessings. Shortly before my sabbatic was granted in 1960, I was awarded a NATO grant to participate in a food science seminar in Glasgow, Scotland. Of the seven scientists invited from the United States, I was the youngest and the only woman. Most participants were well-established scientists, many of them heads of food science departments, and I was honored to be considered their peer. Had I taken my sabbatic in 1959 as scheduled, I would not have been able to participate in this seminar. I was happy I had been patient and was reminded that "Good things come to those who wait."

I had never been able to travel before because my time was filled with studying for my doctorate and teaching full-time. I had supported my mother throughout my studies, but because of her poor health we had enormous medical bills. By 1960, I had managed to save enough to travel with the NATO grant. Mother was thrilled that I had such a wonderful opportunity and looked forward to seeing the world through my photographs when I returned.

I was excited and a little nervous about the trip; I thought I might feel more comfortable abroad if I could spend some time with old friends. I had many friends in Northern Europe, so I decided to visit the Scandinavian countries before the meetings in Scotland, and then tour the European continent after the conference ended.

I chose to visit Norway first because I had good friends living in Oslo: Dr. Agnar Nygaard, his wife, Gerd, and their two daughters. Agnar had been a post-doctoral student in biochemistry with Dr. J. B. Sumner at Cornell, and his desk had been next to mine in our office in Savage Hall. Working side by side in close quarters, we had gotten to know each other well, and Agnar and his family had visited my home several times. I looked forward to seeing them again, and I was thrilled at the chance to see Norway in the company of Norwegians.

Unfortunately, the NATO grant only covered my expenses with the conference in Scotland. For my excursion to the Scandinavian countries, I was on my own. I certainly did not plan to travel first class, but I again found that hardships could be blessings in disguise. My flight from New York City had been scheduled to depart at 11:00 P.M., but it was delayed and then eventually cancelled. My heart sank, until I learned that I had been rescheduled to fly first class on another airline at 2:00 A.M.

Traveling first class on my first transcontinental flight made me feel like a queen. Though I wanted to sleep, curiosity about the food service kept me awake. I was rewarded with steak served from silver platters and an elaborate dinner service that took two hours. Happy and full, I slept until I was awakened for breakfast, another elaborate affair. Afterward I felt stuffed, but I suppose that too much food is the price to pay for the privilege of being a queen.

On the final leg of my journey from London's Heathrow airport to Norway, I sat next to a woman who was carrying a Norwegian edition of *Time* magazine. She knew a lot about the United States and its politics and was delighted to discover that on my first trip abroad I had chosen to visit Norway first. We chatted throughout the entire flight, and she invited me to meet her husband and visit her home in Oslo. I was fascinated to find that her husband was well known throughout the country, for he had been the "Voice of Norway" during World War II. The woman later called me at Agnar's home and invited me to dinner. She and her husband took me to Holmenkonin Slope which had been a venue in the Olympic Winter Games. I had a delightful time with my new friends, and we kept in touch for many years.

Agnar and his wife, Gerd, met me at the airport in Oslo to drive me back to their home, where they had prepared a wonderful meal. I was so exhausted from the long journey that I needed sleep more than food, so they showed me to my bed, which had a beautiful Norwegian eiderdown. I fell asleep immediately.

When I went down for breakfast the next morning, their youngest daughter was there to greet me. Their elder daughter remembered me and her visits to my home, but I was a stranger to the younger. Gerd had prepared a typical American breakfast of eggs and toast, though the Norwegians usually have a morning meal with cold cuts and special Norwegian bread. The little girl looked at me with wide eyes, amazed by this creature who had invaded her home at night, speaking a foreign language and eating strange foods. I understood her confusion, and once she got over her shyness we became fast friends.

I had come to Oslo to learn about Norway and asked Gerd not to go to the trouble of preparing American foods for me. I wanted to know more about Norwegian foods and customs. The older daughter, who spoke English well, became my guide. Since I had such a short time in Norway, I decided to take a Norwegian tour of Oslo and the countryside for an intimate view of Norway in the company of natives. I was the only American in my tour group of Swedes and Norwegians, but many of the other tourists spoke English, and we had a wonderful time together. Our guide was a Norwegian graduate student who took great interest in me since I, as an American, had chosen a Norwegian tour over an American one.

The tour included a drive through the countryside where we saw goats eating grass from the sod roofs of country houses; we also journeyed to the famous Scandinavian fjords. Part of the tour involved climbing up to a glacier in a jeep, and though I had never been high in the mountains in a jeep before, I was not particularly nervous about the trip at first. The drive up was fine, but as we descended from the glacier, I looked out my window, and saw nothing but empty space. We were so close to the edge of a steep precipice that I could not see the ground below us, and I feared that it would only take a gentle breeze to nudge the jeep off the mountain and send us tumbling into the ravine below. Tense, I sat with my arms folded. I was frightened but kept quiet so as not to distract the driver. The tour guide noticed the change in my formerly relaxed attitude and smiled at me. "Don't worry," he said. "It's safer than the streets of New York." Everyone laughed, and shortly we reached the bottom safely.

After my delightful stay in Norway, I traveled on to Sweden where I stayed with my friend and colleague, Dr. Ruth Salinus. Ruth taught foods at the University of Uppsala. During her sabbatic leave a few years prior, she had come to Cornell to audit my food chemistry course. We had become close friends, and it was wonderful to see her again. She invited friends into her home to meet me, but the women seemed hesitant to speak at first because they thought their English was poor. They laughed when I told them truthfully that their English was certainly better than my Swedish, and from then on we had a fine time. Ruth escorted me on a tour of the beautiful Swedish countryside and showed me the burial places of Swedish kings.

The next stop on my tour of Scandinavia was Finland. I booked myself on an overnight ferry from Stockholm to Turku, Finland. My travels had been great fun so far. Being young and outgoing, I was never afraid to talk to people. I arrived at the Stockholm port a bit early and met a lovely woman and her mother, who were also waiting for the boat. Although her mother spoke only Swedish, the woman's English was clear, and we hit it off right away. She asked me all sorts of questions and occasionally translated my answers for her mother. When the boat finally arrived, I was disappointed to find that the woman would not be boarding; she was only there to bid her mother farewell.

Despite the language barrier, the elderly mother and I got along well. We exchanged coins and stamps, and she kindly arranged for me to share a cabin with a Finnish woman who taught English in Finland who translated for us and the other passengers.

The passengers were interested about my life in the U.S.A. and my cabinmate helped me tell a few stories. I told them some of my favorite tales about my pet parakeet, Billy. When Billy was young, I had taught him to say all sorts of things, from chemistry equations, such as "benzene plus nitric acid yields nitro-benzene," to my phone number and address on College Avenue. I even taught him some scripture verses such as "The Lord is my shepherd, I shall not want," and "Seek ye the Lord while he may be found. Call ye upon Him while He is near." In his old age, he had learned so many things that he began to mix them up. He would say, "The Lord is my benzene, my benzene, my benzene," and "Seek ye the Lord, while he may be found on College Avenue." Once I taught Billy to say "I am a Democrat," because some of my Republican friends were trying to teach their bird to say "I am a Republican." One day, as he was listening to the radio, I found Billy running up and down his pole saying, 'I am a Democrat, I shall not want."

The stories about Billy made me popular on the boat that night. The next morning we arrived safely in Turku where I was met by my friend, Hilkka Halkilahti, a former Cornell student who was well known in the area of home economics. She escorted me through Finland, taking me to various historic locations from the relaxing Finnish saunas to the Department of Biochemistry at the University of Helsinki, as well as to numerous schools of Home Economics. I enjoyed meeting the faculty and students and will always remember the gracious students in their colorful uniforms standing in unison when I was introduced.

As a guest of several home economics deans, I was served delicious food everywhere I went, which was an added bonus of working in the food science area. When I was introduced to a biochemistry professor at the University of Helsinki he said that he wanted to thank me. I wondered why, and he said, "I want to thank you on behalf of the United States." Because the United States had forgiven Finland its war debt, this professor had been allowed funds to equip his laboratory. I was suddenly aware that when I traveled abroad, I was not only representing Cornell University but also the United States; I have always tried to keep this in mind on my visits overseas.

Hilkka was invaluable in guiding me around Finland. The Finnish language was difficult for me, and without her help in translating and introducing me to Finnish scholars, my trip would not have been such a success.

Visiting universities, I learned that Finland requires internships for home economics, which are somewhat similar to U.S. dietetic internships. A Finnish student who chose to major in home economics would study under the supervision of a special advisor for at least a year. Finland had already converted to the metric system, both in the home and in the laboratory. Finnish recipes are provided in metric units, which pleased me, for as a chemist, I have always favored the use of the metric system in the kitchen, and in my book, *Experimental Food Chemistry*, I list metric measurements beside the cups and ounces of the American system.

The last Scandinavian country I visited before departing for Scotland was Denmark. Unlike Norway, Sweden, and Finland, I did not know anyone in Denmark but was able to get around well nevertheless. The Danish people were friendly and seemed to like Americans. Many people spoke English, and I never felt lost as I might have in Finland if I hadn't had an interpreter. As in Norway, I took a guided tour of the Danish capital and the countryside; I saw the statue of the Little Mermaid, Hans Christian Andersen's tragic heroine, as well as the magnificent changing of the guard in Copenhagen Palace.

The rich food in Denmark was superb—so delicious that I must admit I overindulged and gained ten pounds. Throughout my travels in Scandinavia I was served rich foods from open-faced sandwiches to lovely berries from the North Pole in whipped cream and fresh salmon dipped in butter sauce. It was all so delicious but disastrous for the waistline. I had never been concerned about my weight before because I had always been able to lose weight easily, so I considered the extra ten pounds nothing to worry about. I had never had much patience with overweight people, for I thought that reducing was simply a matter of eating less or becoming more active. However, when it came to losing those ten pounds, I found how difficult it can be. I eventually succeeded, but nearly made myself sick because I placed myself on such a rigid diet. I felt terrible, became irritable with people, and was as nervous as a cat. Subsequently, I gained that weight back little by little, perhaps simply as a consequence of aging. But I prefer to blame it all on those Scandinavian countries and those lovely rich foods I remember so well.

My playtime in Scandinavia was over, and the time had come for the main purpose of my trip abroad: the NATO seminar in Glasgow, Scotland, which covered recent advancements in food science. The seminar was hosted by Glasgow's Royal College of Food Technology under the able direction of Dr. John Hawthorne. Food scientists from every NATO country attended the seminar. I remember participants from Scotland, England, South Africa, Switzerland, Germany, and other countries. There were very few women present, but I felt honored to be one of the select few chosen to attend the seminar and looked forward to giving a talk about my research on potato enzymes.

Together the participants formed quite an illustrious group. The English contingent included several Cambridge professors, who were attired in tweed jackets, umbrellas, and walked with an aristocratic swagger. Among the seven Americans in attendance were eminent scholars and chairs of food science departments from all over the United States. Included were Dr. Emil Myrak, chancellor of the University of California at Davis; Dr. George Stewart, chair of the food science department at Davis; Dr. Geddis, a well known cereal chemist at the University of Minnesota; Dr. Irvin Leiner, also affiliated with the University of Minnesota and presently editor of *Agriculture and Food Chemistry;* Dr. Highlands, University of Maine at Orono; G. Robert DiMarco, Rutgers University, and I represented Cornell University.

Another North American representative at the conference was Dr. Joe Hulse, the sole Canadian participant. Always an excellent speaker, Dr. Hulse was reporting to the delegates about the new developments in North American foods, including foods from the United States. He mentioned that a new fried food called "hush puppies" was doing quite well in the North American market. Amused, one Cambridge professor asked how the product had received its peculiar name. Dr. Hulse was stumped. He had never eaten hush puppies before and had no idea where they had gotten their strange name.

As the only delegate from the southern United States, I happily raised my hand to explain. The hush puppy, I said, typically consists of corn meal mixed with onion and other seasonings. It is fried in deep fat, usually in the same oil used to fry fish. Its name derived from the fact that fishermen often took their dogs with them while fishing and camping. At night both man and beast returned to camp hungry. As the fishermen fried their fish, the dogs would bay; to quiet the dogs, the fishermen would feed them this corn meal and onion patty, although hush puppies were certainly fit for human consumption as well. I was pleased to be able to educate this distinguished group of food scientists about a distinctly American food. Years later I reminded Dr. Hulse about the incident. "You know a lot about foods," I told him, "but you sure didn't know about the southern hush puppy."

Although we spent much of our time at the conference listening to the speakers, we also participated in round-table discussions. It was wonderful to sit with these world-class scholars discussing food science. I had always been interested in food and nutrition but had not been passionate about pursuing research in this area. The conference, and these discussions in particular, opened my eyes to food science's wonderful potential around the world.

I was not alone in my enthusiasm. Many participants began to stay up late into the night discussing food science and soon we hit upon an idea that later emerged as the International Food Congress. Two years later the first International Food Congress was held in London, the direct result of the scientists' diligent efforts at the Glasgow conference. Because of my heavy teaching responsibilities at Cornell, I was unable to attend the London Congress in 1962, but I have attended almost every Food Congress held since then. I arranged for another sabbatic to coincide with the second International Food Congress held in Warsaw, Poland in 1966. I have attended congresses in Washington D.C., Kyoto, Dublin, Singapore, and Toronto. Each time I have presented a paper and served on various committees. I recognize the need for international understanding and I enjoy discussing food science perspectives with other scholars.

Although we all took our participation in the Glasgow conference seriously, we also managed to view the beautiful Scottish countryside at the same time. The American delegation arrived in Glasgow several hours before the other NATO delegates. Dr. Hawthorn, the Scottish scientist who was charged with overseeing the conference, decided to take us to a well-known eating place on Loch Loman called Buchannan Arms. It was a beautiful day, and we could see the pink heather blossoms on the mountains nearby. We had a wonderful first meal together, with excellent food and enjoyable company. On another occasion the conference organizers scheduled a high tea for us, but I decided not to go since I had some errands to run. I hadn't realized that dinner was not to be served until nine o'clock, so I was famished by the time we sat to eat again and I never skipped another high tea.

One evening Dr. Geddis decided to order a mixed drink. He asked the waitress for a Scotch and soda. The young Scottish woman was puzzled.

"What did you say?" she asked.

"I asked for a Scotch and soda," Dr. Geddis replied.

The waitress paused a moment and decided to start over. "What do you want?" she asked.

"A Scotch and soda," said Dr. Geddis patiently. "Don't you know it?"

"Do you mean squash?" she offered, trying to be helpful by referring to another drink.

Dr. Geddis shook his head in frustration. What he did not know is that "Scotch" is considered a derogatory reference to a Scotsman. The drink we know as Scotch is simply referred to as whiskey in Scotland. We joined in a good laugh as Dr. Geddis finally got the drink he had sought.

Although we sat for lectures most of the day, we did find time for a few excursions, particularly on Sundays. One Sunday we went to see the countryside with Professor Leach and his wife as our guides. I had come to know the Leaches well because they served as host and hostess for the three women at the conference—(a German woman, an English woman, and I. All of the conference participants were housed at a large suburban estate that had been donated to the Royal University by a wealthy family. The estate was lovely, with spacious rooms and beautiful flower gardens. The women occupied a separate building from the men and our thoughtful hosts did all they could to make sure we had a wonderful time.

On the day of our excursion, various delegates piled onto a bus, eager to view the countryside. Unfortunately the fog was so thick that we could hardly see six inches in front of us. Undeterred Professor Leach proceeded to point out what we would be seeing if not for the fog. At the end of the day, poor Professor Leach had a terrible headache and was almost ill. He suffered from the ailment of a good teacher trying to educate us about Scotland despite the inopportune weather.

On another Sunday, the sun emerged and the natural colors of Scotland shone in their full brilliance. We took a boat trip on calm water, visiting several different villages. In the distance, the heather gave the mountains a lovely purple-blue haze against the deep blue water of the lochs. We also toured various Scottish experiment stations. At the Dairy Research Institute, we watched cows breathing inside individually monitored metabolic units, a fascinating glimpse at modern dairy techniques. We also visited the marine station which was accessible only by boat. Professors who worked there had to send their children to school every morning via boat. This situation was terribly inconvenient on blustery winter days but the marine station itself was in a lovely spot and was generating top quality research.

Among our non-academic activities was a visit to the Edinburgh Festival with its famous performances and exhibits. We had fun taking pictures of the men and children in their kilts and the marvelous Scottish dancing. On the drive over, I noticed that the road ahead of us was covered with tiny bumps called cat's-eyes, which reflect headlights in foggy weather. The cat's-eyes were especially appreciated that night when we returned from Edinburgh to Glasgow. Never had I seen such dense fog before; one could see only inches ahead of the car. Had it not been for those cat's-eyes on the road, I am sure we never would have made it back to Glasgow.

One of the two other women who attended the conference was Dorene Hood, an English woman about my age. Dorene worked for the Seniors Food Company in London and from the very start we got along like sisters. Since we were housed together, we got to know each other well. Each night after the sessions ended, which sometimes would be 10 P.M., we would gather in the kitchen and share the pot of tea that the Leaches prepared for us. I didn't like drinking strong tea late at night, so I carried packets of instant coffee and sprinkled it into a cup of boiling water. Professor Leach was fascinated by my instant coffee, so one night I offered him a cup. He sipped and sipped but did not say anything after he had finished. I watched him for a while and waited, but finally my curiosity got the better of me.

"What do you think about the coffee?" I asked.

Professor Leach paused. Then in his Scottish brogue, he replied, "Well, you know, it does lack the pungency of our tea." He never asked for coffee again.

Dorene shared my tastes and also my sense of humor. During one lecture, a man from Aberdeen in kilts, was addressing the delegates. His accent was so thick that I could not understand anything he said. I listened for a while in frustration, and then finally leaned over to Dorene, who sat next to me at these sessions.

"Dorene," I whispered. "Would you please take notes for me? I don't understand him at all."

Dorene smiled back. "You want me to take notes? That won't do us any good. I can't understand a word he is saying either."

Mr. and Mrs. Leach had accents that were difficult for me to understand at first. One day I wanted some postcards but did not have time to shop for them, so Mrs. Leach got them for me. When she returned, I asked her what I owed her. She responded with a flood of terms I had never heard before. I had heard half penny and even haypenny, but when she said something like haypane I was lost. Finally I held out a handful of money and told her to take whatever she needed.

Mrs. Leach was a dear, sweet lady, and as the weeks passed, I came to understand her accent better. She took quite an interest in a hat I had brought with me from America called a "Whimsey" (a little net hat with bows on it). It had just become popular, and most United States tourists could be identified all over Europe by their Whimseys. A woman could fold the hat and carry it in her purse then remove it when she needed to wear a hat. The Whimseys were attractive and came with nets of different shapes and colors. When I let Mrs. Leach try on my Whimsey, she danced in front of a mirror, admiring herself. Since I still had more traveling before returning to the United States, I didn't want to part with the hat just yet. However, as soon as I returned to New York City I went straight to Macy's and purchased and shipped Whimseys to both Mrs. Leach and Dorene. They were well pleased.

When the three-and-a-half week conference ended, Dorene invited me to come to London and visit in her home. I had planned to visit London before returning to the U.S.A. and here was an opportunity to experience English family life. I accepted her invitation with the condition that she would treat me like one of the family, allowing me to share the chores. Dorene's employer at the Seniors Food Company invited us to lunch and a tour of the processing plant. We ate steak, kidney pie, and apple dumplings. As we were eating, he confided that what he liked most about the United States was our Western movies. I wished I had arrived on a horse wearing a cowboy hat which I could leave with him.

Dorene's husband, Freddy, worked for the British Broadcasting Company (BBC) and took me to visit a production studio while a broadcast was being made. Dorene and Freddy both entertained me like royalty and made my stay very comfortable. Dorene wanted her family to meet me, so on Sunday she invited her brothers and mother over for a typical English meal of Yorkshire pudding, beef, and lots of vegetables. At the table, the conversation centered on Princess Margaret and Queen Elizabeth; it was more interesting to hear the English speak of their Queen than to read news reports in the United States. In the U.S. these stories may sound like fairy tales, but to the English everything concerning the Royal Family was real and important.

The weather was damp and cold, and I practically lived in my suit and topcoat. Dorene immediately noticed that I was not accustomed to the weather and began to turn on the electric heating units in the walls of their house. Accustomed to London's chill, Freddy would sit around the house with only a shirt and perspire while I was bundled in layers of clothes. I insisted that the heat be turned down, and finally we compromised; I wore more coats and Freddy turned down the heat. At night I slept on Dorene's electric blanket with a down comforter on top of me and was very comfortable.

In the morning, Dorene prepared a pot of hot tea and served it to me in bed. She pampered me, but eventually I persuaded her to let me do my share of the housework, and this was a lot of fun. She and I both knew that our terminology for household items was different, but sometimes I would forget. Once I was to take out the garbage but couldn't find the can. "Dorene," I asked, "where is your garbage can?"

"Garbage can?" she asked puzzled. "Oh, we don't have those here. We have dustbins."

It took me a while to straighten out such things as dust bins, lorries, and roundabouts, but I had a marvelous time learning. Dorene, Freddy, and I went on picnics and toured the city. We saw the changing of the guard at Buckingham Palace and visited Hyde Park. I especially liked the area in Hyde Park known as Speaker's Corner where anyone can make a speech about anything. Many people do just that, literally standing on boxes to deliver diatribes on all sorts of subjects to amused passersby. I made a little speech in Speaker's Corner, with Freddy and Dorene as my appreciative audience. The entire trip was enjoyable, seeing London with people native to the country who taught me about their customs and showed me how they lived.

I was sad to leave Europe, but I needed to return to the U.S. to spend the remainder of my sabbatical leave with the United States Department of Agriculture (USDA) in Beltsville, Maryland. My title was Supervisory Food Specialist in the Human Nutrition Research Division of the Food Quality

Laboratory. I worked in the biochemistry section, and my research was especially exciting. At that time, farmers commonly sprayed potato plants with pesticides, and the USDA wanted to know if the pesticides affected the flavor quality of the resulting food.

When I arrived in Beltsville, studies with pentachloronitrobenzene, (PCNB), a chemical used by farmers to prevent potato scab, were under way. The USDA wanted to determine PCNB's effects on potato flavor. However I was interested in learning how the chemical affected the metabolism of the potato plant and its effect on the nutrients stored by the tuber. As an enzyme chemist, I set out to study cytochrome oxidase, an important enzyme in plant metabolism. I also studied polyphenol oxidase, an enzyme that causes potatoes to blacken and phenolic compounds, the substrates for polyphenol oxidase.

My study of the effects of PCNBs on the chemical composition of the potato tuber was well accepted. After completing the research, I summarized the results in a manuscript as is customary at Cornell University. I learned that it was customary for manuscripts from the USDA laboratories to be reviewed by other regional USDA centers in California and Philadelphia. These laboratories would evaluate my manuscript before sending it on to the appropriate journal for publication.

I submitted my manuscript according to USDA rules, and months passed before I heard from them. With each passing day, I grew more anxious and began to wonder if they had disliked my paper. After months of anxiety and frustration, I found that my paper had been reviewed favorably and I was now free to send the paper to the *American Potato Journal*, where it was again peer reviewed and later published. This experience taught me that in working with the government, patience is not only a virtue but a necessity.

Two outstanding women in the food and nutrition area of USDA, Dr. Ruth Leverton and Dr. Hazel Stiebeling, appreciated my background in chemistry and invited me to consider a permanent position in the USDA. I agreed to return to Beltsville for the following summer. Since I had a nine-month appointment at Cornell, my summers were free, and I agreed to continue my working relationship with the USDA for some additional months. However, I decided that I preferred my work at Cornell.

While working in Beltsville, I lived in the lovely home of Mary Slayton in Silver Spring. Mary had retired some years before from the USDA and owned a beautiful house on Highland Drive. I rented a room with cooking privileges. Originally I was supposed to prepare breakfast only, but when Mary found that I could make yeast bread and rolls, she invited me to cook whenever I wished. Mary's home was an ideal place for me. The yard was filled with beautiful flowers and birds and I spent many peaceful evenings in her home.

Mary worried about my safety because she feared that my experience in small town Ithaca was inadequate for the D.C. area. Whenever I ventured out, she warned me to watch my purse, lock my car doors, and never stop and ask strangers for help. She was especially concerned about burglars in her home. My room was on the first floor and with no air-conditioning there was the need to open windows.

One night I had a tremendous scare. Suddenly I was awakened by an awful thump. *Oh, no!* I thought. *Mary was right! The burglars are coming!* I wanted to cover my head, but then I remembered my mother's advice, "Don't let your imagination get the best of you. Find out what is wrong." Frightened as I was, I followed my mother's advice and crept down the hallway to find the source of the noise. Mary who slept upstairs had also heard the noise and was also exploring. Cautiously we peered into the room directly above my bedroom. There sat Mary's huge black cat, Cricket, who had been amusing himself by jumping from a high dresser to the floor. Having located the "burglar" I returned to bed and slept peacefully.

Fortunately Cricket was my only brush with "danger" in D.C. I had enjoyed my work in D.C. very much, and in some ways regret that I didn't take the permanent position the USDA offered me. However I realized that I couldn't tolerate the long daily commute which was necessary to work in the Washington area. Those were the days before the Beltway when the commute to the Beltsville USDA building took approximately an hour. In the summer the trip was exhausting for most cars were not air conditioned at that time. I joined a carpool and found the commute enjoyable with coworkers. However, I did not look forward to driving. One day in particular stands out in my memory. That was the day before Kennedy's inauguration in January 1961. In the afternoon it had begun to snow, but I felt well prepared with my snow tires. However, I discovered that people in D.C. were unaccustomed to driving in snow—an indispensable skill in Ithaca. An incredible traffic jam resulted from the snow. Cars barely moved, and often even stopped and were abandoned. At one point I was stuck for quite a while when I suddenly realized that the car in front of me was abandoned. The driver had abandoned the vehicle because the battery had run down. That night the trip that normally took sixty minutes lasted for almost eight hours. I dared not abandon the car or even stop for food. Fortunately, one of my carpool members had just received grapefruit from Texas that day so she shared the fruit.

We arrived home very late and heard the next day's weather forecast was for more snow. Many friends who had originally planned to attend Kennedy's inauguration decided to stay home, but I refused to let the snow alter my plans. A friend and I took a pot of coffee and went off to witness history. The roads were almost empty because so many frightened people stayed home. Our reserved seats for the inauguration provided an excellent view of the parade and the ceremony. It was such an interesting and joyful occasion. No one realized that Kennedy's administration would end so horribly in such a short time. There was an overwhelming feeling of joy and confidence in the new president. We were proud to be Americans and especially proud that the weather hadn't stopped us from being a part of the celebration.

Another advantage to living in the Washington area is the history that surrounds one there. Many weekends were spent touring the downtown district. There is nothing like Washington D.C. in the springtime for blossoms, especially the famous cherry trees that adorn many streets and waterways. Yet in spite of all its advantages, Washington D.C. was not the place for me. Commuting to work is no problem in Ithaca with its relaxing and pleasant scenery. I also missed Cornell's Mann Library with its magnificent collections and opportunities to attend its seminars on so many topics. For all these reasons, I decided to turn down the USDA's job offer and return to Cornell.

I stayed in touch with my colleagues at Beltsville, and they were anxious to hire my students. Even the undergraduates who had taken my food chemistry course were hired by USDA. My graduate students were much desired, and one of them, Emily Owens, was hired to continue the work on enzymes that I had begun.

My 1960 sabbatic greatly enhanced my own education, and my colleagues at USDA were anxious to learn about the NATO Food Conference in Scotland which I had attended. Frequently I was asked to give seminars and reports on the latest developments in the field of food science. USDA offered invaluable opportunities for research, and I also learned about governmental red tape. When the sabbatic ended, I returned to Cornell to teach the large undergraduate course in food chemistry. I gave three lectures per week and taught one laboratory section. Managing the course was a big job, but I enjoyed teaching. But on some evenings, after classes had ended for the day and the labs were finally quiet, my thoughts would drift back to the pink heather of Scotland; the wonderful friends like Dorene, Ruth, Agnar, Gerd, and Hilkka; and the majestic Norwegian fjords. I also recalled the delicious Scandinavian food. I was glad I had waited for my sabbatic leave. I had been patient, and good things had come to me.

FOOD BEHIND THE IRON CURTAIN
POLAND, CZECHOSLOVAKIA: 1966

My second sabbatic leave was from September 1966 to February 1967. I wanted to step back from the university for a short time to broaden my perspective, so I decided to work as a consultant for the R. T. French Company and participate in the International Food Congress in Warsaw, Poland.

Though I spent most of this sabbatic at R. T. French, I arranged my leave to coincide with the International Food Congress in Warsaw, Poland. I was eager to travel abroad again, and food congresses are always interesting and exciting ways to keep up with advancements in the field. The people at R.T. French were well aware that I was first and foremost a scientist, and they gladly permitted me to take time off.

I wanted to experience Polish life, so my travel agent and I planned my trip to include as much contact as possible with the people of the country. I arranged to travel via train to view the reconstruction of Warsaw which had been almost completely destroyed during World War II. The World Food Congress being held in Warsaw showed courageous ambition on the part of the Polish people since adequate facilities were scarce. The people had wonderfully big hearts and extended warm hospitality to all their visitors.

Instead of flying directly into Warsaw, I chose to ride the train through Germany to see the differences between the east and west sides of the divided country. I boarded the train in what was then West Germany; at the border I would have to secure a transit visa to pass through East Germany. At first I was a bit nervous about traveling through a communist bloc nation as a lone American; my stomach fluttered as I handed over my passport for inspection at the border. But I shouldn't have worried. The East Germans had great respect for professors; when the border guards saw my passport they politely handed me my visa without any problem.

Though my experience was smooth, being stopped at the border was unsettling. When the train stopped in Berlin, the uniformed guards locked the windows and doors, imprisoning us on the train until the border inspection was complete. They looked under all the seats and even checked underneath the train with long spears to insure no one was clinging to the underside.

I followed the American State Department's orders not to take any photographs, but by spending so much time at the checkpoint I formed a good mental picture. I vividly remember the guards patrolling the station with their spears and guns. They watched for attempted escapees as well as for goods illegally transported across the border. On the train I sat with a Polish family that had several pieces of luggage. While the guards were checking everyone's papers and spearing under seats, a large woman in a green uniform, who I assumed to be a Soviet official, entered our car and forced the Polish family to open their suitcases. She found several new shirts and confiscated them on the spot, walking off with an air of authority. Although I couldn't understand the actual words, I understood the shouts of the furious Polish and felt helpless watching how the system worked.

Back in the States I had told my travel agent that I didn't want luxuries. The train had compartments of long benches that faced each other. At first I shared my compartment with the Polish family: a mother, father, and teenage daughter. I exchanged smiles with the friendly parents and shared some of the cookies and sandwiches I had brought. In return they offered me their bottled water, a necessity I had forgotten. The daughter was tired and not as friendly as her parents, but when I motioned for her to put her feet up on my bench, she gave me a shy smile, and I knew then that the whole family had accepted me.

Later a young East German man, who was poorly dressed and seemingly depressed, joined me on my hard bench. He immediately identified me as an American, and moved next to me, saying, "California; sister; Chicken farm." We shared some food and did the best we could to converse in English. He inquired about Jacquelyn Kennedy.

My train journey showed me some disturbing differences in the quality of life between West and East Berlin. A young West Berlin woman in my compartment seemed especially well dressed and financially comfortable compared to the shabby, malnourished young man beside me. We passed from West to East Berlin early on a Sunday morning as church bells were ringing, and the young man motioned me over to the window of the train. He pointed sadly out the window, and said, "West Berlin, cars, bells. East Berlin, no cars, no bells." His poignant words focused my attention on the huge fence which physically and symbolically divided the two Berlins.

I was also saddened by an experience with a Polish priest who sat down next to me at one point on my journey. Although we couldn't converse very well, we communicated by smiling and exchanging food. I opened my well-stocked purse and offered him food and coins as souvenirs. He, in turn, offered me the food he had brought. I'll never forget the little worm-eaten apples in his briefcase; seeing him dressed so shabbily and with such poor food was sobering and upsetting. My efforts to exhibit friendliness and understanding as an unofficial ambassador of the United States helped him smile that day.

I was lucky enough to stay with a family in Warsaw, though this had its share of complications. A native of Poland who held a post-doctoral position in biochemistry at Cornell, Henryka Kurzepa, wanted me to stay with her family in Warsaw, though the communist government made this quite difficult. Henryka wrote to the Polish ambassador to the United States, requesting that I be allowed to stay in the home of her brother, Dr. Stanislaw Kurzepa, and his wife, Zofia. Her brother was the head of pharmacology at the University of Warsaw, but her sister-in-law's job was a real stroke of luck for me: she happened to be the ambassador's dentist. Because of Henryka's efforts and a lot of luck, I received my visa and permission to stay with her family while I attended the food congress.

I later learned that I had been especially fortunate because other Americans attending the congress had to stay together in one hotel so they could be watched at all times. The situation was terribly oppressive, and their hotel rooms were loaded with bedbugs. Apparently the Soviets didn't worry much about standards of cleanliness, especially when it came to American visitors.

Although I was allowed the unique privilege of staying with a Polish family, I knew I was being carefully monitored. I had to register with three police stations at different locations in Warsaw. My host drove me to the first station, and as the huge iron gates in front of the enormous building slowly swung open, I felt a twinge of fear. Several officers interrogated me and had me fill out innumerable forms. As if that weren't enough insurance on me, I had to repeat the ordeal at two smaller stations. I was certainly well documented during my stay in Poland; the authorities always knew where I was at all times.

I had a good experience with the Polish family despite the somewhat cramped quarters. The apartment was so small that their young son had to sleep with his grandparents so that I would have a bed, but the family was extremely warm, friendly, and generous. Their apartment had a lovely balcony from which every morning I would watch the crowds of people hurry to work. Although many buildings in Warsaw still had bullet holes from the war, the newer buildings, such as the opera house, were impressive and well-built.

At that time in Poland, everyone held conversations in a whisper for fear of being heard through apartment walls. In muted voices the family members told me of their frustration at being governed by the Soviets and their hatred of the huge buildings the Soviets had forced the Polish people to construct. They disliked everything about the Soviets but could only express this in secret to a person they trusted. In addition to their political fear, they also had a constant fear of theft. My host had a Volkswagen, and every time he parked it he would remove anything that was detachable, such as the hubcaps and windshield wipers. When he wanted to drive somewhere, he would have to reassemble his car.

My hosts both spoke English, and they acted as my interpreters and tour guides, even taking me to the countryside to meet their parents. Before my trip I had attempted to learn a few Polish words, but language has always been difficult for me. I had practiced my "thank you" and "yes, yes" diligently, but my first opportunity to demonstrate my abilities in speaking Polish revealed that I had none. My reply of, "Yes, yes!" instead of "Thank you" to a compliment elicited much laughter and served as a wonderful relaxing icebreaker. Despite their ever-present distrust of the government and its spies, my hosts were friendly with their neighbors and invited them to the farewell party they threw for me before I left.

As a food scientist, I was deeply disturbed by the food markets in Warsaw. In addition to food shortages, the markets themselves were poorly maintained and unsanitary. Unwrapped meat was always covered with flies, and the vegetables were wilted and in poor condition. But always a trier of new foods, I had fun experimenting in the restaurant that was in the same hall where the congress was being held. Since I did not know the language, I selected at random from the Polish menu. I always managed to get enough to eat, though occasionally waiters would look at me oddly when I inadvertently ordered a meal that consisted entirely of desserts.

One of my favorite memories of Warsaw was lunch with the wives of top government officials. A Polish woman delegate at the Food Congress named Anna asked me to speak at a luncheon meeting of Polish women, wives of communist leaders. With Anna as an interpreter, they were eager to hear an American woman speak. They wanted to learn about my experiences at R. T. French Co. I felt like a real VIP as I stood before my attentive audience explaining about food product development and quality control. The women's response was sobering: They told me that they were worried about food *quantity*, and hoped some day to be concerned with food *quality*. It's all too easy for Americans to take for granted the plenitude of food in our country. After my lecture, the women presented me with a Polish cookbook translated into English. This book started my collection of cookbooks from around the world, and whenever I leaf through the recipes, I always remember the warm, friendly feeling from my meeting with this women's group.

My personal experiences in Poland were undeniably educational on their own, but the purpose of my trip was the International Food Congress. Since World War II had destroyed so much of Warsaw, our first meeting was held in a large, newly-constructed meeting hall. The Poles disliked the hall which was massive like most of the buildings constructed by direction from the Soviets. I suspect it must be difficult to like anything forced upon you by an oppressive and restrictive government. Some other meetings of the congress were held in university buildings that had survived the war.

On the whole, the meetings went well, but we had a few unusual problems. For example, there was no way to darken the university buildings' shadeless rooms for slide presentations. Some presentations were stalled until I suggested hanging sheets to cover the windows. We also had some trouble with translation. Fifty-one countries were represented at the congress, and there were four official languages: German, French, Russian, and English. Although translators were present, I had great difficulty understanding the English translator. However, the people running the meetings were friendly and good-natured, and participants soon forgot about the less-than-perfect conditions.

After the food congress, I decided to join some fellow delegates on a bus tour of food industries in southern Poland. There were three busloads of tour participants: one for Russian speakers; one for English speakers; and one for "other" speakers, such as the German and French delegates. The three buses stayed in close contact as we visited the various food-processing plants. I was fortunate to have a friend from the University of California as a travel companion. Rose Marie Pangborn was a famous professor in the field of food sensory evaluation. We were delighted to be roommates on the tour, as we were close in age, personality, and interests in Polish culture and industry.

Although our entire bus spoke English, we had communication problems because of differing accents. Two of our group's members had marked southern accents. Dr. Ray Dennison, the chair of food science at Florida University, and Dr. William Roberts, the chair of food science at North Carolina, were terribly embarrassed to find that the Polish guides could not understand their English. The same problem arose with the Polish people of the villages we visited. As a former Southerner who could understand the southern accent, I acted as a translator and, thankfully, the Polish guides could understand me.

We toured many different food plants across southern Poland. At the meatpacking plant, we saw ham inspectors in boots and white uniforms stamping high-quality carcasses. At the fish plant, we watched people prepare fish for freezing. In the vegetable-packing plant, we saw many women peeling and freezing cucumbers, a staple of the Polish diet. Because of the language barrier, I could not learn all I wanted to know, but the women were extremely friendly and curious about their visitors; they waved and smiled as we passed by.

Some plants we visited were both fascinating and disturbing. At the bakery, for example, the delicious whole-grain loaves of bread were never wrapped at any stage in the process. This did not bother me much as the crusts seemed too thick for most organisms to penetrate, but our visit to another plant shocked me. At the apple juice-processing plant, workers threw scrawny, wormy apples, peels and cores included, into a huge vat to be turned into juice. After watching that manufacturing process, I could not bring myself to drink apple juice in Poland.

On our tour we were also taken to Krakow, the country's early capital and the pride of its people. Although Warsaw had been nearly destroyed by the Germans during the war, Krakow and its magnificent castle had been spared. The glorious treasures of the castle, including paintings and tapestries that had been shipped to Canada during the war, were returned when the threat was over. Not far from Krakow lies Zakopane, a beautiful resort town near the Tatra mountain range. Our group was treated to an excursion high into the mountains where the fresh air smelled of pine. On another adventure, we took a rafting trip down the river which divides Poland and Czechoslovakia. We were given bagged lunches for this trip, but I had followed my habit of traveling with extra food; my large travel purse always held something to eat. This time, I was especially glad I was prepared. The bagged lunches were so small that all the group members were left hungry, and I saved the day by sharing my Polish cookies.

I think this story has a valuable lesson. Food is not only a necessity but also a means of communication and relating to others, as all human beings understand the importance of food. Food can be an excellent tool for international relations when one is travelling. On a global level, my experience as a food scientist has shown me that the world would be a better place if we focused on providing food instead of weapons. So many wars and tragedies have been due to food, or the lack of it, but food can also bring people together. I may be prejudiced because I'm a food chemist, but I believe food is a wonderful way to share friendship. We all eat, so we're all food specialists.

Food brought people together once again on our trip at a rural Polish potato roast. Though the three tour buses were supposed to arrive in the late afternoon to meet the people of the village and watch them roast their potatoes, the buses had gotten lost and we arrived quite late. I was even later than the others because I had to return to the bus for my jacket to survive the evening chill. Two Russian gentlemen had also been delayed in getting off their bus, and they served as my escorts to the potato roast. The villagers had kept their delicious potatoes cooking under coals underground as they waited for us, and when we were finally gathered together we shared a meal and made new friends. The townspeople who spoke English told me how impressed they were that a woman could travel by herself; they were even more surprised that a woman could be a professor.

Though the two Russian men who had accompanied me to the potato roast had been friendly it was generally difficult to get to know the Russians on the tour. The language barrier was a problem, though some of them spoke English well, but the true impediment seemed to be a sense of isolation and secrecy. The leader of the group was an aloof biochemist who herded his people—especially the women—like sheep. The two Russian women were not allowed to join any other group, though I managed to talk to them when the groups would occasionally come together. They received and read American food science publications and told me about their work in Russian food science. We even traded objects from home: They gave me rubles and pins, and graciously accepted my gifts of American stamps and coins.

A Polaroid camera belonging to a professor from California eventually broke down the barriers with the Russians. I was taking photos for slides but borrowed the Polaroid and asked the two Russian women if they would like a picture of themselves standing beside their group leader. Never have I seen a group of people so grateful for such a simple gift. From then on, I was warmly accepted by the entire Russian delegation. On the last night of the tour, the aloof biochemist actually got up at the banquet and toasted me. I was glad I had gained the Russians' trust and good will.

I wish I could say that my experiences with the French were as positive. When the touring groups would stay at a hotel, we would all dine together. Rose Marie and I were happy to sit near the Russians who were friendly and smiled as they passed the food, but we learned to stay far away from the two Frenchmen in the group. They kept themselves apart and ignored everyone else at the table, even refusing to pass bread along to others. After the first night, Rose Marie and I decided never to sit near the Frenchmen again; over the course of the next few dinners, it became obvious that we were not alone in our opinion. No German, Russian, or Englishman would sit next to the rude Frenchmen, and for the rest of the trip, they sat at a table by themselves.

My encounters with these impolite men did not end when I left Poland. During my subsequent trip to Prague, I had a personal tour from Dr. Parizek, chair of the Institute of Physiology at the Czechoslovak Academy of Sciences. Dr. Parizek was kindly showing me points of interest as we walked across the Charles River Bridge when suddenly one of the Frenchmen from the Polish tour appeared. He saw that I had a knowledgeable escort, and his transformation was incredible. He ran up to me like a long-lost friend, kissed my hand, and treated me like "Lady Mondy." I feigned politeness, but I could not forget how rude and two-faced he had been. Some years later, when I met a young French girl on a plane, I was almost tempted to treat her as the Frenchmen had treated me. The girl spoke little English and was terribly nervous about visiting the United States, so instead of being rude, I took her under my wing, comforted her, and helped her on her way. I knew that I could not hold a nation responsible for the actions of a few citizens, and I hoped that the two rude Frenchmen had learned the importance of kindness.

Despite its few unpleasant experiences, the bus tour was a lovely way to see the countryside and get to know my fellow scientists. Afterwards, we bid each other goodbye and went our separate ways. I then decided to travel to Czechoslovakia. While on a congress tour event in Warsaw, I had ridden the bus with a pleasant Czechoslovakian woman named Dr. Magdalena

Krondl and showed her my list of people in Czechoslovakia who had requested reprints of my research. She knew the people but said they hadn't been permitted to leave the country to attend the congress. In fact, this congress was her first trip out of Czechoslovakia since the Communists had taken over. When Dr. Krondl saw my disappointment with not being able to meet these scientists who were interested in my research, she invited me to visit them at the Academy of Sciences in Prague.

At first I was hesitant to attempt unscheduled travel again. I had already had a harrowing experience in trying to extend my Polish visa for a few days in order to participate in the tour of southern Poland. The police had taken my passport, promising each day to return it at a specific time, and each day had given me an excuse for holding it longer. Fearful that my passport would never be returned, my Polish host took me to the American Embassy where I was delighted to find that the man in charge was a Cornellian. He treated me like family and confided that the Communists like to scare people. He was right, for my passport was returned at the last minute, just in time for the tour of southern Poland.

Later I went to the Czech embassy, which fortunately was more efficient than its Polish counterpart. The Czech officials were friendly, and they issued me a visa to Czechoslovakia without a problem, but getting the train ticket to Prague was infinitely more difficult. In Poland it was not easy to buy a train ticket. I was surprised to learn that my host thought it necessary to leave his work and we spent an entire day going back and forth between the train station and the bank in an attempt to buy one ticket. The rather complicated process involved many long lines which I believe were due mostly to careless workers. The workers were paid no matter how much or how little they worked. There was no competition so they had no motivation. After much waiting and bureaucracy, the ticket was finally purchased near the end of the day.

Before taking me to the train, my hosts gave a party in my honor and when we arrived at the station, I knew immediately that something was wrong for my Polish hosts began speaking in hurried, untranslated Polish tones. For some reason my ticket was not being honored; I was not permitted to board the train. My hostess was a determined woman, and she finally pounded on the train door until they let me board. I soon realized the problem: The only sleeper car going to Prague was filled with Russian men. No one knew quite what to do with one American woman. The conductor kept pointing to my ticket and addressing me in Russian. Since I could not understand, a young man was found to serve as my interpreter. I stated that I could not take another train since it would be too difficult for me to navigate the Polish train system with my limited knowledge of the language. I was firm and clear; I had paid for the ticket and needed to be in Prague the next morning because my friend was to meet me at 7:00 A.M. at the station. The conductor finally agreed I could stay on the train.

My Russian interpreter was twenty years old and related and thought of me as a mother figure, for at this time I was a middle-aged woman. The young man told me that his mother was also a chemist and that he had recently married a young lady he had met at the Black Sea. He was now on his way to a tractor convention, and though he was supposed to share a two-bunk compartment with a friend, he arranged for me to have the compartment. With the help of his dictionary, we conversed for hours and he presented me with an issue of a Russian magazine similar to our *Scientific American*. His knowledge of American history and politics surprised me, for he knew the names of the American presidents and much about the U.S. Constitution. The next morning my new friend bought my breakfast on the train since I had been required to rid myself of all Polish currency before leaving Poland. Then he helped me with my luggage as I departed the train and met my Czech friend, Magdalena Krondl. His kindness was greatly appreciated; what could have been a nightmare turned out to be a very pleasant experience. I felt that international relations between Russia and the U.S.A. had been greatly improved.

I have always been fortunate to find good people who have been very willing to help me. This has made traveling one of the most pleasant and cherished experiences of my life.

My tour of the Academy of Science in Prague was very informative and interesting, but I realized the severe oppression of my Czec friends. When in 1967 the Russian tanks rolled into Prague, my friends escaped to Austria, and I was able to help them find academic positions at the University of Toronto, Canada.

LOOKING AT THE U.S. FOOD INDUSTRY
THE R.T. FRENCH COMPANY: 1966-1967

Dr. Claude Bice, head of research at R.T. French, and Dr. John Fogelberg, the company's chief executive, had contacted me about the possibility of working full-time with them. I was not interested in permanently leaving the university for industry, but I told them that I would spend my upcoming sabbatic with them. I later learned that I was the first professor they had ever hired. They had refused to hire other professors on sabbatic in fear that a temporary employee might give away company secrets. Secrecy was an important issue at R.T. French, as it was with all food companies. I was the first professor to be hired on a temporary basis, and I was glad that they trusted me.

My agreement with R.T. French was that they would teach me aspects of the food industry, particularly product development, and I would provide them with my potato chemistry expertise. I was excited about shifting my attention from university research to the world of big business; I've always liked a challenging new experience. I wanted to learn about the food industry in order to train my students who might enter the food business.

For my first assignment, R.T. French placed me in product development. I was a bit surprised to learn that I would not be working on only one product at a time, but instead on eight different products simultaneously. This taught me careful juggling skills. I worked on products as diverse as Sloppy Joes, sour-cream mix, and Hamburger Helper, but the most interesting product on my lab table was a high-protein spice cookie. R.T. French added their own spices to the protein-rich cookie mix sent from another company. I was asked to determine which spices and in what quantities would improve the cookie's rather unpleasant flavor—a task complicated by the fact that the protein in the cookie seemed to absorb and dampen the spices' flavor.

This research was fun. I consulted my own cookbooks and came across a spice-cookie recipe which I knew was very good. I mixed spices from the recipe into my cookie mix at work, but the cookie was as bland as ever. I added more and more, until I eventually increased the spice level ten-fold. It worked. The cookie was delicious, and the spice flavor was perfect. I invited people around the laboratory to taste the new cookie, and soon they were begging to serve on my taste panel.

I was proud of my results, but then we found one fatal flaw that ultimately prevented the cookie from being placed on the market. When the cookies were fresh they were delicious, but the flavor was lost after some time in storage. We discovered this after subjecting the cookies to a variety of storage conditions, ranging from a room designed to simulate a tropical climate to one that matched the environment of grocery-store shelves. A careful company with high standards, R. T French was not willing to risk having cookies out on the market that would fail to meet the company's standards of quality. This cookie experience not only showed me the interesting effect protein has on spices, but also taught me about the decisions that must be made before a product is placed on the market.

In product development, I learned that instead of experimenting with different individual ingredients to create something new, scientists often make products by combining, blending, or adding to products purchased from other food companies. This was interesting to me because in my university teaching I had always explored the effects of individual ingredients such as flour, salt, or sugar on a product's chemistry; now I had to determine the effect of a pre-blended mix.

At R.T. French I also learned that there are many factors that go into making a good product. One important criterion is mouth-feel, or the texture of a product as it is being consumed. When I was working on a sour-cream mix, my taste panel showed me that mouth-feel is more noticeable than many might believe. I had prepared various types of blends and found that the panel selected the ones that shared the same basic ingredient: coconut oil. Coconut oil gives a wonderful mouth-feel to most foods, something the panel picked up on quickly. The nutritionists worried about the fatty acid composition of the coconut oil, but at that time, the public was not as concerned with nutrition as with flavor and texture. Many products on the market contained coconut oil, and some still do today; in the end, mouth-feel can triumph over good nutrition sense.

As a scientist and academic, I had never been involved in industry, but I learned about the economics of corporate decision-making and marketing when I worked on a fried rice product at R.T. French. The fried rice was delicious and could easily be prepared in minutes by mixing a can of rice with a package of seasoning developed at R.T. French. The rice had a wonderful consistency because the rice was cooked, canned, frozen in the can, and then allowed to return to room temperature. The freezing process caused the rice grains to separate easily, a process that a Canadian rice salesman had discovered accidentally. He had left some canned rice in the trunk of his car overnight in subzero temperatures and found the next morning that the rice had frozen. When it thawed, he saw that the grains separated nicely and secured a patent on this process.

Unfortunately, this Canadian patent added to the cost of R.T. French's fried rice product, causing the company to price the product beyond the reach of most shoppers. The company decided to discontinue it, even though in test marketing consumers had liked the taste and ease of preparation. Although the marketing people were sensitive to quality, I found that they were more interested in cost and the economic side of product development. I was disappointed because I had liked the fried rice, but I understood that the marketing department had to do their job.

R.T. French taught me more than I thought I would ever need to know about keeping secrets. Despite my earlier conversations with Dr. Bice and Dr. Fogelberg, I had not anticipated the level of secrecy in product development. Among other regulations, I was told never to leave my desk unlocked or throw out carbons that might be of use to a competing food company. These instructions, which were carefully followed by all staff members, opened my eyes to the very real threat of industrial espionage. I learned that competitors had been known to place spies in janitorial positions at other companies; these "janitors" would look for useful material on desktops and in trashcans and pass the material back to their employers. I was always careful about what I discarded, although sometimes I wondered what could be in any desk that anyone would want.

Every Friday after work, I would drive the three hour trip from Rochester back to Ithaca to spend the weekend with Mother. One Friday I left the office late and in a hurry. I was almost halfway to Ithaca before I realized that I had not locked my desk at work. For a moment I considered just driving on. "What could a snoop possibly find in my desk?" I asked myself. But my conscience spoke with a louder voice. I have always followed my employer's rules, and with a sigh, I turned around and drove all the way back to Rochester to lock my desk.

To maintain secrecy, workers were also not allowed to bring visitors upstairs to the laboratories and the office. This rule especially applied to me for two reasons. For one, my office adjoined the research laboratory, and company officials worried that a curious visitor might observe something in the laboratory that could be useful to the competition. Also, many of my visitors were consultants from other companies, and so naturally the people at R.T. French were suspicious of them. I didn't mind meeting my visitors in the foyer with its beautiful conference room, but sometimes the level of secrecy was bothersome. At Cornell I never hesitated to bring visitors to my laboratory, and I felt free to discuss my work openly. It was quite an adjustment to realize that I could no longer do these things. Also, when I produced work that I believed should be published, I had to get permission from the company before submitting the results to a journal. I felt constrained by this policy, for on some occasions I was denied permission to publish things that might have been of value to the public.

Of course potatoes found their way into my work at R.T. French. The company wanted me to solve some special problems at their large potato plant in Shelley, Idaho. At the plant, the workers cooked potatoes and processed them into granules for instant-potato mixes. They needed to know if they should peel the potatoes before cooking them. If they left the peels on throughout the process, they could sift out the peel when the potato granules were dry. Leaving the peels on while cooking could reduce processing costs, but the company was not convinced that it was appropriate and wanted me to examine the situation.

In previous research, I had discovered that the potato peel sometimes contained undesirable compounds, including phenols and toxic compounds such as glycoalkaloids. Because of this, I was somewhat skeptical of having the potato cooked with the peel on, even if the peel was sifted out at the end of the granulation process. I put the issue through a series of tests that lasted two months. R.T. French provided me with all the help I needed to complete this assignment with special assistance from the chemists in their quality-control laboratory. This was a wonderful way to work. I used top-flight equipment and had access to several chemists, a full-time food technologist, and a dietician and a test kitchen. If I needed a certain chemical, I only had to write it on a list in the morning and by the afternoon I would have it in my laboratory. Often I found myself wishing that the university could be half as efficient as the food company in providing and replacing chemicals and equipment for important research. At R.T. French I never had the long delays I sometimes encountered at Cornell. In industry achieving profit depends on efficiency, and a good company provides its workers with the proper materials to do their jobs correctly.

In my experiments, I first analyzed granules that had been prepared from unpeeled potatoes, and then I compared them with granules processed from peeled potatoes. Dr. Fogelberg and the members of my taste panel all detected large differences in the flavor: The potatoes that had been processed with the peels on were more bitter and earthy than the others. Also, when granules were recombined with water or milk to simulate mashed potatoes, the peel affected the texture of the mix. I discovered that lipids and other ingredients came out of the peel when the granules were formed, and these interfered with liquid absorption. The result was granules that were not nearly as smooth as those from the peeled potatoes. I also compared the two products side by side, the "peel-on" mashed potatoes were somewhat darker than the others. This was significant to the company because marketing research has shown that consumers prefer white, fluffy mashed potatoes.

Leaving the peel on had unfavorable effects on the taste, texture, and color of the mashed potatoes which were due largely to phenolic and lipid compounds in the peel. When phenols react with oxygen, they can cause potatoes to blacken; if the potato is not peeled, there is time in the processing for a darkening reaction to occur. Phenolic compounds also tend to be bitter, or astringent, which accounts for the off-flavor of the "peel-on" granules. We found that if the potato is cooked with its peel on, the peel releases phenolic compounds in the cooking process that penetrate the potato itself. This was clearly what was happening to the granules, and the phenolic compounds then affected the flavor, color, and texture. To make matters worse, products that result from the oxidation of lipid compounds can be harmful to people's health.

When I pointed out the role of phenols in this process, Dr. Fogelberg and his team checked the conditions at the Idaho processing plant and found that if potatoes were cooked with the peels on, the overall phenolic level in the cooking water rose considerably. Since some of the cooking water is reused in the process, they discovered that reducing the phenolic content of the cooking water greatly improved the quality of the granules. In light of these findings, the R.T. French Company decided to revise their methods and began to check the phenolic level of the cooking water on a regular basis to keep it within an acceptable limit.

Company officials were pleased with my work and told me that they would eventually allow me to publish my findings in scientific journals, but I knew that R.T. French did not want me to publish my work immediately. Competing food companies were studying this problem as well, and R.T. French felt that if my research were made public, other companies would benefit from the work I had done. This does not usually happen at a university. A researcher publishes without regard to who may benefit, and the information is equally available to all.

Years later I had a graduate student repeat my R.T. French experiments using three different varieties of potatoes. I had experimented only on Russet Burbank, or 'Idaho" potatoes, the variety primarily used by R.T. French. My student found that for each variety, the results matched what I'd found with the Russet Burbank. At that time, I was not studying glycoalkaloids or other toxic compounds that we now know exist in the peel. However, it seems likely that because glycoalkaloids contribute to a bitter flavor, perhaps they were also involved in some of the negative flavor reactions we found.

For the company, peeling the potatoes before cooking was more expensive than sifting the peels out afterwards, but given the disadvantages revealed in my studies, R.T. French decided to peel its potatoes first. I was impressed to see that the company was not interested solely in profit, but was also concerned about the welfare of its consumers and the quality of its product.

At R.T. French I had the opportunity to work with the public relations department which had set up a beautiful test kitchen. I worked there with Ms. Rita Dubois who was an expert at attractively preparing and presenting different foods. One day, while I was in the test kitchen preparing outdoor meals with Rita, a television crew arrived and photographed some of the things we were doing. We signed a release giving the crew permission to broadcast the program, and the show found its way onto the air that winter. The night when the TV program aired it was snowing vigorously in Rochester, yet Rita and I were preparing foods for outdoor eating. We laughed at the introduction to the show: "It may be snowing outside, but R.T. French is having a picnic!"

I enjoyed all aspects of my work with R.T. French including product development and marketing, packaging and storage, public relations and working in the test kitchen. By rotating through these different departments, I acquired a solid overview of how the company operated. When I gave a speech in the company's lecture room to an audience of visiting dieticians, I was pleased to see that the crowd was full of familiar faces—students I had taught at Cornell. During my stay at the company, I was featured in the Rochester Times Union, as well as in the R.T. French monthly magazine. The company seemed pleased to have a professor learning first-hand about industry and carrying this knowledge back to the classroom.

However, toward the end of my stay at R.T. French, I began to miss Cornell. I thought about the university's library facilities and the daily seminars on so many different topics which I considered a part of my continuing education. Although R.T. French had an excellent library, particularly for a food company, it could not compare with the Mann Agricultural Library at Cornell. I was pleased to have had a chance to learn about the workings of industry and contribute my expertise while obtaining useful information to help me advise students choosing to enter the food industry. However, I knew I was meant for university teaching and research. After my sabbatical I returned to Cornell, and in 1974 Dr. Claude Bice, from R.T. French, made these comments concerning my work:

> "I have known Dr. Nell Mondy since about 1953. At that time I was Manager of the Technical Research activity at the R.T. French Company in Rochester, New York, and retired last fall as Assistant Research Director to become a consultant to the food field. Throughout this period I had frequent visits with Dr. Mondy at meetings of the Institute of Food Technologists and other food science conferences. On many occasions she was accompanied by several of her students and it was obvious that she had good rapport with them and was a real source of inspiration to them. She did an excellent job of introducing her students to the industrial scene and its opportunities for food research. As a result of these contacts, I hired quite a few of her students and all of them were exceptionally well trained and proved to be superb performers in research and product development. One of these young ladies, hired in 1954, is still at French's and is now a research manager. Several years ago, we

were fortunate to have Dr. Mondy as a staff member for six months during her sabbatical leave from Cornell University. Her enthusiasm, dedication, and ready smile made her a productive and pleasant addition to the research group. She gave inspiration to the young researchers and I believe she got something in return—a practical insight into the complex ingredient systems and problems of today's foods. Dr. Mondy has done a good job of helping to bring the university and industry closer together."

Because of the popularity of my course, Chemistry and Food Preparation, I was chosen by the students to be featured in Cornell's 1966 yearbook, the *Cornellian*. I received a special invitation to attend the dedication which honored selected Cornell faculty.

This special recognition given to me by the students seemed to annoy my department chair. Without discussing the matter with me, she used her authority to remove my course from the curriculum. Strenuous objection to the discontinuation was expressed by both students and faculty who valued the course. I had taught the course for eighteen years and had given much time to its development. The course was popular not only at Cornell but internationally; faculty from universities in Canada, Finland, and Sweden as well as the United States came to audit the course in order to emulate it at their own university. The idea of blending chemistry and food preparation was unique and appreciated by many.

Notification of the course's deletion was *via* letter to me while I was on sabbatic leave at the R.T. French Company. I was surprised since she never discussed the matter with me, and I expressed my concerns in a multi-paged letter, but her only written reply was a paragraph in which she acknowledged the receipt of my letter. The students were also very upset that the course would no longer be taught. They sent a petition carrying many signatures and wrote personal letters requesting that the course be reinstated. All appeals were ignored.

Upon my return to campus from the sabbatic leave I discovered that not only had my course been discontinued, but the chair had demanded that my secretary hand over my typed lecture notes. Since tape recorders were not common and photocopying technology was still in its infancy, my custom had been to leave typed notes with my secretary for the benefit of the students who had been ill. They could "check out" the lecture notes for a brief period in order to help them catch up. These notes were my personal property for they had been drafted on my own time, usually at night, and the confiscation of them was not only a serious breach of professional etiquette but also an act of dishonesty and theft. The chair later used some of the material in her own courses, presenting my work as though it were her own. One of the alternatives I considered was to file a lawsuit, for I felt certain that I'd win, but after careful consideration, I realized that taking legal action would cost valuable time that could better be devoted to research.

However, I was extremely upset by the events and consulted with colleagues in food science. Their unanimous response was: "She's jealous of your accomplishments." My reaction turned to anger, both at her unwarranted interference in my life and at her dishonesty. Anger disrupted my ability to concentrate on work, and I realized that in anger, one accomplishes little. I finally came to grips with the situation and felt pity for her. I knew that I had done nothing wrong, so I decided to work on something constructive. I believed that concentrating on research would be beneficial.

In the past my teaching load and graduate student advising required so much time that I researched little during the school year. Typically I spent the three summer months conducting research. When the chair made negative remarks about my research to the Cornell Experiment Station Director, Dr. Nyle Brady, he was unimpressed. At that time I had eleven publications, five resulting from my Ph.D. work, one from my master's, and five from recent research in peer-reviewed journals, such as the *Journal of Biochemistry*, *Archives of Biochemistry and Biophysics*, *Proceedings of the Society of Experimentation of Biology and Medicine*, and *Food Technology*.

Dr. Brady commented, "When she told me your research wasn't good, I replied that I had read it and it was excellent." (Fortunately he was a biochemist who had taken the time to read my publications.) He pointed out that I was the main one in the department who was publishing, and he had decided to channel research funds directly to me for he feared that if he channeled it through the college, the chair would take the money for herself. He suggested that I enter regional research which would bring me in contact with researchers in other universities. His enthusiastic support was extremely helpful during this frustrating period in my career.

In addition, the chair attempted to prevent my graduate student advising by cutting off funding, but the Field of Food Science supported me and students came to me through this route. One of these students, Elizabeth Petterson Sonoff from Norway, came with her own support from the Kellogg Foundation.

I carried out research projects in cooperation with various departments in the College of Agriculture and Life Science such as plant pathology, plant breeding, and vegetable crops. I also worked with the United States Nutrition Laboratory. These professors were highly complimentary of my performance and enthusiastically supported my advancement. My spirits were boosted by the wonderful support and respect I received from these professors, my former students, and Dr. Brady.

Although my relationship with the department chair was upsetting, she could not prevent me from receiving awards. In 1968, I was elected a Fellow of the American Institute of Chemists and cited for "outstanding contributions to basic food and nutrition research." The award was a prestigious one, for I had been recommended by a council of fifteen outstanding American chemists and chemical engineers, including Dr. Glen T. Seaborg, chairman of the Atomic Energy Commission, and Dr. Henry B.

Hass, director of research for the Kellogg Company. To be selected as a Fellow, one must be considered "an outstanding chemist or chemical engineer and must have completed ten years of progressive experience in the practice of the profession following the receipt of the degree in chemistry or chemical engineering, and must have met requirements satisfactory to the Council of outstanding United States chemists and chemical engineers." I was thrilled to be thought worthy of this prestigious award and eagerly awaited the initiation dinner in Pittsburgh, Pennsylvania. This honor was ignored by my chair, but the recognition was undeniable; in fact the honor was reported in several local and state newspapers. Bolstered by this award, as well as the support of Dr. Brady and other colleagues outside the department, I set about concentrating on research and attempted to overcome the obstructions placed in my way by the chair. Instead of anger and hate, I began to feel pity for this person who in my opinion resorted to such drastic measures in order to boost her own morale. I realized that I was not alone in receiving her wrath—she had refused tenure to two competent young male chemists and denied teaching to an outstanding food chemist, Dr. Thomas Schoch.

When Dr. Schoch joined our department, I was delighted, but it was not long until he too witnessed her incredible behavior. He retired from the food industry after a brilliant career and accepted the position at Cornell because he wanted to teach. He was especially knowledgeable in the area of starch chemistry. I always found it a pleasure to speak with him about food chemistry. Apparently, the chair grew jealous of him and later barred him from teaching his specialty. Dr. Schoch shared his concerns with me, and although I tried to console him, he found this treatment very hard to accept. Teaching had been his sole motivation for coming to Cornell, and he felt that his efforts were not appreciated.

In reviewing this dark period of my life, I now realize that it was a blessing, for it strengthened my character and increased my research productivity. Many opportunities opened to me that would never have been possible had I continued with the heavy teaching load. I have visited, presented papers, and served as a consultant for food companies, research institutes, and universities in forty-seven different countries. From this experience, I understand better what it means to make lemonade when life gives you lemons. Although there was much pain in this part of my life, it has contributed to the person I am today. I chose not to let circumstances in life destroy me but instead to make the best of what life had dealt. Looking at what I have gained from this dark period in my life, I can say that I am thankful because it has given me an inner strength and has taught me the value of perseverance. My motto, *"You never fail until you stop trying,"* helped me and my students.

During this difficult period in my life, Dr. Richard Barnes, Dean of the Graduate School of Nutrition offered understanding and support. In 1964 he appointed a committee to evaluate food science at Cornell and determine the direction the program should take. He selected me to represent the Graduate School of Nutrition and the Department of Food and Nutrition.

Other members of the committee were: R.S. Shellenberger and L.R. Mattick, Food Science of Geneva; R.C. Baker, Poultry Science; J.D. Hartman, Vegetable Crop; R.M. Smock, Pomology; G.H. Wellington, Animal Science; P.A. Buck, Food Science at Ithaca. Dr. Baker served as Chair of the committee and I served as Chair of the sub-committee on curriculum. We surveyed all courses concerned with Food Science on the Cornell campus and made recommendations concerning curriculum development.

Dr. Baker arranged a meeting in Washington, D.C. with representatives from food science departments at Ohio State University, Michigan State University, University of North Carolina and the University of California at Davis. The purpose was to obtain information on Food Science at the various universities. Members of the Cornell committee attending were Baker, Buck, Hartman, Mondy, and Shellenberger. Following this meeting the committee met several times and proposed the establishment of a single department of Food Science at Cornell and emphasized that the Geneva faculty should be integrated into the Cornell department. The proposed new department provided an organization in which members could be attached by joint appointment and food science faculty from colleges outside Agriculture such as the College of Home Economics and the School of Hotel Administration could be included. A single strong department would help promote development of a curriculum better adapted to students needs.

Affiliation would be left to the wishes of each faculty member and effected by negotiation with department heads. Thus the ground work for the Institute of Food Science was laid and in 1967 the Board of Trustees at Cornell approved the establishment of the Institute of Food Science. I was happy to have played a role in its establishment.

IN THE LAND OF SHRIMP AND SEMINOLES
FLORIDA STATE UNIVERSITY: 1969-1970

Ithaca was a wonderful place until the late 1960s. During the winter of 1969, a campus demonstration against racial inequality was carried out by armed students who seized control of Willard Straight Hall, Cornell's student union. There was much unrest on the Cornell campus that year, and students provoked confrontations with faculty, administration, and even the university president, Dr. James A. Perkins. The campus was in an uproar symptomatic of the times, and academic work took a backseat to political posturing by students and faculty. I was disappointed and unhappy to witness these events, for though I supported the right to protest unfair conditions, I believed teaching and research should be the primary objectives of any university. The struggles on campus prevented me from continuing my teaching and research work that I loved.

Cornell was not unique in its unrest. Throughout the country, college students were challenging authority, and these demonstrations often got out of hand. Classes at Cornell were cancelled, and threats of arson forced faculty members to guard academic buildings through the night. In Collegetown, students, drug dealers, and protesters filled the streets; violence was the horrifying result. A drug dealer was killed on Dryden Road in the heart of Collegetown, and I began to fear that the city of Ithaca was no longer a safe place in which to live.

I had been offered positions at many other schools across the country, but Cornell was my home. I had refused offers from schools ranging from Oregon to Maine, and Georgia to Illinois, but in 1969 I began to wonder if there might be a better place for me. I hoped I might find ease from Cornell's unrest on another campus where I could continue my teaching and research without fear of violent interruptions.

At this time Dr. Betty Watts, a nationally recognized food chemist, was retiring from Florida State University. She suggested me as her first choice for her replacement. I admired Dr. Watts very much, and though I wasn't certain that I wanted to leave Ithaca for a place of palm trees and hurricanes, I decided to discuss the matter with Dr. Nyle Brady, the director of the New York State Agricultural Experiment Station at Cornell. Dr. Brady was wonderfully sympathetic. He appreciated my work and understood my frustration of being severely limited on the Cornell campus. He did not want me to resign from Cornell but suggested that instead I take a leave of absence and accept the faculty position in the Department of Food and Nutrition at Florida State University. It seemed appropriate, therefore, that I take a leave without pay. I then began to prepare for the land of sunshine.

Florida turned out to be the perfect place for me. I was a full professor in the Department of Food and Nutrition at Florida State University from the spring of 1969 through the winter of 1970. The university treated me very well. I was given an excellent salary (higher than at Cornell), and I was pleased to discover that Florida had no state income tax. Mother and I settled into a trim brick house which I purchased in Tallahassee with a screened-in porch and an acre of land that boasted magnolias, peach trees, dogwoods, and three precious live oaks, which are very special in Florida. Tallahassee is lovely, with rolling hills and warm weather and many beautiful flowers and trees.

I had a heavy teaching load at Florida State, but I enjoyed teaching food chemistry very much. I was also encouraged to develop my own research program. Dr. Watts had established an excellent program, and she left a good laboratory which was well equipped and filled with enthusiastic students when she retired. My responsibilities included teaching a large undergraduate food chemistry course, a graduate food course, as well as directing graduate students. Since I did not want to abandon my Cornell research, I kept in touch with my Cornell graduate students and returned to Ithaca regularly to make sure that everything stayed on track.

My travel arrangements gave me new meaning for the term "commuter." I flew back and forth between Tallahassee and Ithaca at least once a month. Throughout the week I taught in the sunshine of Florida, and then landed in the snows of Upstate New York over the weekend, trading light dresses for heavy boots and a fur coat. During the winter of 1969, Ithaca had extremely heavy snowfall; the weather was so bad that on one occasion I had to land in Buffalo and take a bus to Ithaca in order to give a Ph.D. exam to one of my students. Often I traveled with luggage that would have startled any nosy baggage handler. More than once I carried suitcases full of NY potatoes back to Florida for my students there. Potatoes are harvested in Florida in the spring, but in New York they are harvested in September and October; so all winter I ferried samples of New York potatoes to Florida to compare the chemical composition of potatoes from each region. It was important for me to work in Florida and to continue some research at Cornell, so I accepted the monetary expense as well as exhaustion that accompanied those journeys.

Everything ran smoothly in Florida because there was little student unrest. At Florida State University, the students and administration maintained good relations. However, on one occasion, two students attempted to take over the podium before the university's president was to speak. The administration, forewarned, had worked out a plan of action and the results were markedly different from that of a similar event at Cornell where the students had successfully wrested control of a public demonstration from the administration. At Florida State, the campus police arrived and physically lifted the students off the stage, and removed them from the premises. This ended the demonstration. All seemed peaceful from that point forward. I was relieved to accomplish my work in a non-threatening environment.

Hearing that I was in Florida, my good friend and colleague Dr. Ray Dennison welcomed me warmly. Chairman of the Food Science Department at the University of Florida at Gainesville, Ray knew my particular interest in potatoes and introduced me to Dr. Dale Hensel and Dr. Peter Weingartner in the Department of Vegetable Crops at the University of Florida. These professors agreed to provide me with varieties of Florida potatoes for my research. These potatoes were grown on the research farm in Hastings, which is closer to Gainesville than to Tallahassee. A special arrangement of potato transport was worked out among us. The Hastings workers delivered the potatoes to Dr. Dennison at Gainesville, who in turn had them loaded on a Greyhound bus bound for Tallahassee. Dr. Dennison notified me when the potatoes were loaded, and I picked them up at the Tallahassee bus station and transported them to my laboratory.

Dr. Dennison also invited me and my students to attend the monthly food science meetings held in Gainesville. This brought together the departments of food science of Florida State and the University of Florida. These meetings were often held on Saturdays, so on conference days I would gather my sleepy students for the 155-mile drive to Gainesville. There we met and shared research with our supposed "university rivals." It was nice to see that the football field was the only place where the Gators and the Seminoles clashed. The schools had a friendly relationship in food science.

While in Florida, I had an interesting opportunity to branch out into areas of research that did not involve potatoes. Dr. Betty Watts introduced me to the Florida State University faculty involved at Marine Research Station near Tallahassee. I learned that shrimp have a polyphenol oxidase enzyme system similar to that of potatoes. I was fascinated to discover that shrimp blacken using the same enzyme system that causes potatoes to blacken. Since I was already familiar with potato blackening, I applied my knowledge of potato enzyme chemistry to shrimp, easily converting my research from one organism to the other. However, I did not stay in Florida long enough to finish the shrimp project, but I was grateful to Dr. Watts for introducing me to another field of research so well-suited to my interests.

My time in Florida was well spent; I enjoyed the change of scenery and especially the students, who rated my teaching highly. However, my mother sorely missed her home in Ithaca. Although she loved the people and the Florida climate, she felt uprooted. In Ithaca Mother had taught the Philathea Sunday School Class at the First Baptist Church for eighteen years, and her friends there missed her very much. They sent cards and letters to Florida telling mother how much she was missed in Ithaca. On more than one occasion I found Mother depressed and homesick. Our Florida neighbors loved Mother with her soft southern accent, and they all pitched in to help her plant a garden in our large back yard. However, the vegetables didn't grow well under the shade of our many lovely trees. Mother was like the plants in her garden—she flourished only in a place that was right for her, and I realized that Ithaca was that place. I was sorry to leave the gracious hospitality shown me by Dr. Helen Cate, Chair of Food and Nutrition, and the other faculty members but it seemed to be the proper thing to do at that time. By this time, the Cornell campus had become peaceful again under the administration of a new president, Dr. Dale Carson. So Mother and I said goodbye to Tallahassee and returned to our home and friends in Ithaca.

Upon my return to Cornell, things were changing. The School of Home Economics had a new dean and our department chair was replaced. Life within the department of Food and Nutrition resumed a more logical course, and I was well received.

During my career, with its ups and downs, I have always been grateful to know that there are good people in the world who are understanding and supportive. Dr. Brady's support had been most helpful to me during an unfortunate situation and I used the experience as a lesson for growth by remembering that *you never fail until you stop trying*.

My return to Ithaca was a happy one. Though I was sad to leave Florida, many opportunities and awards awaited me at Cornell. In October 1973, I was invited by the President and Board of Trustees at Princeton University to attend the presentation of the Rockefeller Public Service Awards. The December award ceremony was held at the Shoreham Hotel in Washington, D.C. The awards were given in recognition of "distinguished service to the United States Government and the American people." Established in 1952 by John D. Rockefeller III and administered by Princeton University, these grants were considered to be the most prestigious annual awards for the nation's federal career employees. I was thrilled and honored to be among those invited.

President Bowen of Princeton University presided at the meeting, and the principle address was eloquently given by the Honorable Earl Warren, Chief Justice of the United States. John D. Rockefeller III's words were also timely and well-chosen. I had the pleasure of meeting Mr. John D.

Rockefeller who graciously welcomed me and thanked me for coming. While attending the award ceremonies, I had the opportunity to meet many famous people and was thrilled to be among their company.

Around the World in Thirty Days
Japan, Korea, Hong Kong, India, Iran, Turkey: 1978

Nineteen seventy-eight was a year that took me around the world. I was invited to lecture at the World Food Congress in Kyoto, Japan, and was also invited to visit India as a guest of the Indian government. I purchased a special around-the-world air ticket (which allowed stopovers in different countries) because I wanted to visit Hong Kong and a few other nations as well. I packed my bags and prepared to see the world in thirty days.

I was concerned about flying into the then newly-constructed Tokyo airport because I had heard that local farmers, upset with the airport's location, had been holding angry protests. This was my first trip to Japan and I did not speak the language. As a country person at heart, I wasn't sure how well I could get around in such a large foreign city.

Two Japanese food companies, S & B Shokuhin Co. and Nihon Kaken Co., served as my hosts while I was in Japan. My former employer, the R.T. French Company, had recommended me as a consultant to both companies. S & B Shokuhin Co. bought dehydrated potatoes from R. T. French and were producing chips similar to Pringles® produced by Proctor and Gamble. Prior to my visit to Japan, Mr. Yashio Hidaka was sent to Ithaca to meet me. Later I learned that these companies were surprised that R.T. French had recommended a woman and they wanted to make certain that I would be capable of performing the duties of a consultant.

As I was boarding my plane at Kennedy Airport in New York, I met a young Italian chemist who had previous experience in Japan. I showed him the three-page itinerary S & B Shokuhin Co. had provided me which, in addition to my speech, included activities such as a tea ceremony and an overnight stay at a mountain resort. My Italian friend was impressed and told me I must be a very important person (VIP) to receive this sort of treatment. I assured him I was not a VIP, but another look at the itinerary left me to wonder what was in store.

The twelve-hour flight seemed interminable, and because we were traveling west across several time zones, the entire trip was in daylight and I was unable to sleep. My companion helped me pass the time by explaining to me about various Japanese customs. When we finally arrived in Tokyo, I was met by a representative of the S&B Shokuhin food company who handed me a neatly typed letter from the company containing specific details of my stay. Because of the civil unrest at the airport with the farmers, the official company representatives were unable to greet me in person but they had sent this man who handed me the letter, took my bags, and ushered me to a waiting limousine for the long drive into Tokyo. The limousine was elegant, with white lace seat covers; I began to suspect that the Italian chemist had been right. I was receiving royal treatment.

I had reserved a simple room at the Imperial Hotel for Japan was an expensive country to visit, and I did not feel I could afford anything elaborate. To my surprise, I was brought to a luxurious suite with a living room, a separate bedroom, and a lovely bath. A note written in English sat beside a bowl of fruit and a bowl of flowers on the living room table. It was an invitation to a welcome banquet the company had planned for me that night. I later discovered that the manager of the Imperial Hotel was a Cornellian. This I think was partially responsible for the wonderful service I received.

I was exhausted from the long, sleepless flight, but my nerves held up well. I had a good time at the banquet. Everyone sat on pillows at a long table set very low to the floor. The waitresses knelt to serve the food (both American and Japanese) and I enjoyed it all. I slept soundly that night in preparation for the next day's trip to Kyoto.

The next morning, I was escorted to the train station by Mr. Hidaka. A ticket was provided for Japan's famous bullet train which traveled over one hundred miles per hour. At the station, we passed a young Japanese man signing autographs for a crowd of excited young women. 'Who is that?" I asked my escort curiously. He looked over at the man who was surrounded by his fans. "Oh, that man is a famous entertainer. I guess you could say that he is our Elvis Presley."

When I boarded the bullet train's luxurious green car, I found that "Elvis" had been assigned a seat across the aisle from me. He must have performed the night before because he looked very tired. He drank some milk and fell asleep immediately. The young waitresses in their pink and white uniforms soon became aware of his presence. They stood together, whispering and pointing at the sleeping young man. When he woke up, each young woman got his autograph on the back of a paper plate. I figured I shouldn't pass up the opportunity to meet the Elvis of Japan, so I also asked him to sign my paper plate which I kept as a souvenir.

The train traveled rapidly through the beautiful countryside to Kyoto. Getting around Japan was much easier with the help of the S & B Company. A convenient shuttle bus ran continually between my hotel and the large congress hall. My room was on the fifth floor, and on my first night there I heard some strange popping sounds outside my window. I got out of bed and pulled back the drapes. Nearby were bright lights and what appeared to be an expanse of grass. After a moment, I realized what I was seeing: Some Japanese men were practicing golf on the roof of the building next door! The grass was Astroturf, and a net suspended over the rooftop caught any stray balls. I later learned that the Japanese are great golf enthusiasts, but because of the country's hilly terrain, there are only a few excellent courses. Many golfers go to great lengths to get in their practice time.

The next morning I was pleased to discover a McDonald's restaurant not far from my hotel. I was relieved because, although I enjoy Japanese food, I did not look forward to uncooked fish for breakfast. Each morning I went to McDonald's, and the young women would curtsy and take turns waiting on me. I enjoyed communicating with the young waitresses, and it was good to have a familiar meal to start the day.

The International Food Congress meetings were held in a large, beautifully decorated conference hall beside which ran a picturesque stream full of exotic fish. The lecture hall was impressive, and each speaker at the congress was provided an interpreter. The day before my lecture I was told that my translator had practiced my speech but was unable to deliver it in the allotted time. I was distressed because I had carefully edited my speech to be exactly on schedule. I was given a typewriter and asked to shorten the speech. I soon met others in the same predicament. A gentleman from India who sat next to me seemed to know even less about Japanese typewriters than I, so we took turns asking for help. Finally, my lecture was edited down to acceptable length, and all went well from there.

Following my lecture I was quickly surrounded by congress participants. Many wanted to discuss the contents of my speech but included in the crowd were a number of Chinese women who were interested in hearing about Cornell. These Chinese women, all Ph.D.s, comprised the Chinese delegation, and they told me that their husbands had studied at Cornell years before the revolution. They were chemists, microbiologists, and physicists; but food science had not yet reached China. Many years later, in 1987, I was a member of a delegation of American food scientists who lectured at several Chinese universities. By this time, most of the universities had instituted Food Science programs, and I was pleased to see the progress China had made in this field.

Several of my former students who had gone on to distinguished careers in their own countries attended the food congress. One was from Norway, another from Sweden, and another from Guatemala. We shared our experiences and stories about our recent endeavors. It is always a pleasure to see my former students and I was happy to learn of their success.

Representatives from S & B Shokuhin Company attended my lecture and escorted me back to Tokyo at the close of the congress. I was not scheduled to speak at the company until Monday and thus anticipated spending the weekend in my suite at the Imperial Hotel. Instead, I was greeted by a pleasant young Japanese woman named Lily Fujikake who spoke fluent English and gave me a guided tour of the city. That weekend marked Japan's equivalent of the U.S. Memorial Day when Japanese families pay homage to relatives who have died. Knowing that I was interested in learning about Japanese culture, Lily took me to a cemetery where we watched family members placing flowers in special vessels located at the area where loved ones' ashes were buried.

Lily and Mr. Hidaka had arranged a special tea ceremony for me. We were joined by the company presidents and their wives for a visit to the home of a teacher of the Japanese tea ceremony. The ceremony, a Zen-influenced ritual in which every movement is meaningful, took nearly three hours to complete. I was fascinated by the intricacies of detail and the order of the activities. My companions kindly explained the many levels of the ritual. The teacher also taught me the Japanese art of flower arrangement.

On Monday, I delivered my lecture to an all-male audience of S & B Shokuhin executives and employees. At that time few, if any, Japanese women occupied management positions. I had planned the speech to last an hour, but because of the time it took for the Japanese interpreter to translate and the many questions from the audience, it took two and a half-hours. Thankfully the audience was interested in what I had to say.

Following my speech, I was escorted to a mountain resort renowned for its natural hot baths. Two limousines of workers from the food company accompanied me; we stayed the night and shared breakfast in the morning. I was given a kimono and slippers to wear before entering my suite at the resort. The suite was beautiful, and I was told that it was often reserved for famous Japanese visitors. Bamboo doors opened into a spacious living room. The bathroom was small but immaculate, and I was provided special slippers when I entered. I was amazed that I had to wear special shoes just to go to the bathroom.

The bed, or futon, lay flat on the floor. I wondered if I would be able to sleep, but I had no need to worry. Never have I spent a more comfortable night. A radio and telephone rested on the floor within reach of the bed. I was taught a few relevant Japanese words in case I needed to call the front desk. I appreciated the help, because I was aware that no other women had been brought along on the excursion. My maid served me tea in the living room where I sat on a cushion at a beautiful low table. The maid did not speak English, but we communicated through gestures and smiles. My interpreter told me later that I was the first American the maid had served and that she was very favorably impressed. I have always tried to make a good impression as an American in my travels abroad.

After I settled in, I was given one of the hot spring baths. The bath was large and located in the center of the room. It was surrounded by a white-tiled floor with a special drain. It looked like a well which was filled with bubbling water. The maid motioned me to disrobe and sit on the stool; she proceeded to wash me all over, rinsing with warm water from the well. When I was thoroughly clean, I climbed into the bath well. The water was clear blue and relaxing, and I felt like falling asleep. When I returned to my bedroom, I dropped into bed. As a nice touch, the maid left the small lamp lit in my room all night to keep me from feeling insecure.

The next morning I had breakfast with the representatives from S & B Shokuhin. The place settings were beautiful, and the food was artistically presented and served. I had ordered Japanese food for breakfast. I found the food tolerable but not particularly to my taste. I had developed a trick to use in foreign countries when I did not want to eat the food but also did not want to offend my hosts: I carried a camera and took pictures of the food. I used this trick at the breakfast, and no one seemed to notice that I was not eating.

One embarrassing incident occurred after breakfast. In Japan, complimenting an object is an invitation for the owner to give it to you. I had forgotten this and during breakfast I had admired a particularly lovely triangular blue bowl. As we were leaving the Inn, the maid rushed out with this beautifully wrapped bowl. I accepted it graciously because not accepting the gift would have been an insult. The bowl is a beautiful souvenir of my visit to Japan, and each time I use it I am reminded of the wonderful hospitality of the Japanese people.

The vice president of the S & B Shokuhin Company, Mr. Masaru Yamasaki, had graduated from the School of Business at Cornell several years prior to my visit. He arranged a Cornell banquet in my honor on my last night in Tokyo and invited other Cornell alumni. Lilly warned me that the wives would not accompany their husbands to the banquet because in Japan it was not customary to have wives present for such an occasion. A special Japanese dancer performed during the banquet, and my host explained the meaning of the different stages of the dance. Following the dance, the performer came to my table and shook my hand. The banquet organizers presented me with an automatic Konica camera and several rolls of film, another example of Japanese hospitality.

I had brought along boxes of recent slides of Cornell University as gifts. The alums were delighted to see recent pictures of their alma mater. It was obvious that all the men had enjoyed Cornell and Ithaca very much. As they reflected on their Cornell days, there was only one time they remembered as being unhappy—Christmas Day. When most students were celebrating with their immediate families, the Japanese men had been lonely. When I returned to Ithaca, I resolved to invite international students to my home and make certain that they were cared for on holidays.

Lily also told me of another Japanese custom—that of calling the Japanese host from the airport just before departing to thank him for his hospitality. Lily was very helpful in keeping me informed on Japanese customs and behavior. She explained to me that Japanese people stared at me because they admired my red hair which was unusual in Japan.

I was overwhelmed by the graciousness of the Japanese people. My new friends took care of every need; they even wrapped and mailed my packages to the United States. I felt honored to be the recipient of such wonderful hospitality. I was sorry to leave Japan, but my schedule took me to Korea, where I had an equally wonderful experience.

Royal treatment in Korea was provided by Ki Yull Lee, Dean of Home Economics at Yonsei University who was formerly a graduate student in Food and Nutrition at Cornell University.

During the course of my career as a professor at Cornell I have had the pleasure of training and working with a number of international students; many have gone on to important positions in their home countries. One of the international students I worked with was Ki Yull Lee. She was an intellectual and industrious student, and I empathized with her being so far from her family in Korea.

Christmas can be a lonely and difficult time for international students at Cornell who cannot return home for the holidays. Students who remain on campus through the Christmas recess are housed together in a single heated dormitory. Knowing that Ki must be feeling alone and isolated, I invited her and her friend to share Christmas with Mother and me. We had a wonderful time together, and Ki got along especially well with Billy, my parakeet. I have a photograph of Ki with Billy perched on her head.

Toward the end of Ki's time in Ithaca, she began to experience personal and financial difficulties and decided to return to Korea to complete her Ph.D. She was worried that she would be unable to afford the trip home, but Dr. Frances Johnson, a wealthy and kind professor in our department, came to her aid and supplemented her travel.

Ki persevered and earned her doctorate in Korea, ultimately becoming Dean of the School of Home Economics at Yonsei University, one of the major educational institutions in South Korea. We corresponded for several years following her departure from Cornell. As time passed, we began to exchange letters less frequently, as often happens when friends are far apart. We eventually lost contact. Years later, when a new student from South Korea arrived in our department, I asked her if she knew of Ki, thinking it unlikely that she would. I was eager for word of my old friend, however, and was delighted when the student responded that Ki was her dean at Yonsei University. She provided Ki's address and soon our correspondence began again.

My Pan American around-the-world ticket did not include South Korea, but I knew that I dare not come so close to Korea without visiting my friend, Ki Yull Lee. So I paid extra to schedule a trip to Seoul following the food congress in Japan. I felt like royalty when I disembarked at the airport in Seoul, for Ki had rolled out the red carpet for my arrival. There were two limousines filled with her faculty on hand to greet me. This was only the first example of the gracious hospitality which Ki showed me throughout my stay in Seoul.

Ki was an excellent hostess even though she had to attend to her duties as dean during my visit. She brought me to Yonsei University where I visited various departments and met with the faculty. I became acquainted with a number of professors there, and Ki held a faculty dinner in my honor. Ki also invited me to be her special guest at the Moon Festival which was being celebrated at that time. The Moon Festival is a special event in Korea, full of bright pageantry, dancing, and important sporting events. During the festivities I sat with the University president and his wife, both delightful people.

Ki had scheduled a full and interesting itinerary and assigned instructors and professors to entertain me when her responsibilities as dean prevented her from doing so. These bright, eager young people escorted me to a number of interesting attractions in Seoul. I especially enjoyed the visit to one of the city's oldest historical museums, a Korean version of our Williamsburg, filled with people in native dress acting out vignettes from daily life at various times in Korea's history. I photographed these lovely women in their traditional Korean dresses and thoroughly enjoyed this opportunity to learn about the history of the country.

I made a point of visiting Seoul National University where Dr. Haymie Choi, a former student of mine at Florida State University, was teaching. Unfortunately, Haymie was in California at the time, but I met her colleagues and saw her nutrition laboratory. It was a pleasure to learn that she was working successfully on the faculty. In subsequent years, Haymie sent several high-quality students to our program at Cornell.

I could not have asked for better treatment than I received during my brief visit to Korea. In addition to her other efforts, Ki had hired members of the local press to cover my visit. The press was never obtrusive, and I was well-photographed throughout my entire visit.

One of the things I enjoyed most about my stay in Korea was the opportunity to sample native foods. Ki's staff was kind enough to take me to a traditional Korean restaurant which in some ways resembled a traditional Japanese restaurant. Before entering, we removed our shoes, lined them up outside the door, and then sat on cushions at a very low table inside. The food was delicious, with many beef dishes served from a central dish on the revolving table. We served our bowls from the central dishes.

In her office, Ki showed me photographs documenting the professional path she had taken in the years after she left Cornell. Not only had she been Korea's National President of Home Economics, but she had also presided over the entire regional district of Far Asian countries, including Japan. She also co-authored a book on Korean foods and presented me with a copy. In return, I gave her a copy of my book on experimental food chemistry which she later translated into Korean. Korean students entering Cornell are aware of my work. Ki showered me with gifts, especially silks and very special Korean dolls to be added to my collection. These dolls adorn a special cabinet in my living room.

Ki had many accomplishments. She had done quality research and had risen to a position of administrative authority in a major university. She was greatly respected by both faculty and students. During my time with her, it was apparent that she had some degree of influence with the Korean government as well. She has received many awards for her service to her country, including an award from the Ministry of Agriculture and Forestry.

I wished for a longer stay in Korea, but soon it was time for my next flight to Hong Kong.

Although I had heard that Hong Kong was a beautiful and interesting city, because of pressure for time, I scheduled a brief stay there. I had reserved a room, but Professor Ericson of Cornell Hotel School informed one of her former students, Mr. Roy Olsson, now manager of Hong Kong's Sheraton Hotel, that I would be visiting the city. When I arrived, Mr. Olsson personally escorted me to the Sheraton where I was treated like a queen and given a beautiful suite filled with fresh fruit and flowers. Mrs. Olsson, Roy's mother, ran an upscale boat service in Hong Kong's historic harbor. She treated me to a tour on one of her boats, where I was served the most delicious Chinese food I have ever tasted.

My brief stay in Hong Kong showed me once again how Cornell's international students take pride in their alma mater and take pleasure in entertaining fellow Cornellians. Throughout my travels, I have met many individuals from different countries who fondly remembered their days at Cornell in Ithaca and graciously extended friendship and assistance to me while I was in their country.

My stay in Hong Kong was short for I had an important agenda ahead of me in India. A group of Indian potato scholars had invited me to tour their research facilities as a guest of the Indian government. The government of India arranged my itinerary and coordinated my transportation to different parts of the country. At every research facility I visited, I was greeted by a host who gave me a tour and told about the research being conducted. Throughout my entire stay, I was treated very well.

My plane arrived in Delhi in the early hours of the morning. Although the sun had not yet risen, the air was hot and muggy, and I dreaded facing the heat of mid-day. I quickly found a taxi to the Oberoi Maiden Hotel where I was greeted by its proprietor, Mr. Prithipal S. Lamba, a former student of the Cornell Hotel School. He had returned to India and was now vice president of operations for the entire Oberoi chain of hotels. I felt secure being under the supervision of a Cornellian, and my stay at the Oberoi was very pleasant.

On the second day in Delhi, a visit to the local research institute was planned. It was an interesting and informative visit. The third day, I was to meet two professors from New Zealand who would accompany me to the

National Dairy Research Institute at Karnal. The New Zealanders, I learned, had come to teach classes in dairy science at Karnal. (New Zealand is noted for its dairy industry.) We had one problem, however. When it came time to meet the New Zealand professors, my taxi driver did not know how to find them for he had not met them and did not know what they looked like. The problem was compounded by the fact that the driver did not speak English, which was unusual, since English is commonly spoken in India as a result of the British occupation.

The New Zealand professors and I were able to spot each other, largely because of our attire. The three of us stood out among the Indians in their turbans and saris. The New Zealanders were jolly fellows, and together we laughed over our harrowing trip to Karnal, as the driver swerved the taxi back and forth between the mobs of people and every possible type of carriage crowding the streets of Delhi.

At the Dairy Research Institute in Karnal, we were assigned rooms in a spacious and well-appointed guesthouse surrounded by beautiful gardens. Although it was not air conditioned, it was quite comfortable. I settled in immediately. Having been warned of the dangers of food contamination, I sampled it carefully. Fortunately, I had developed a habit of carrying food such as cookies, cheese, and bread on trips overseas. I also relied on two food products available almost anywhere: Coca-Cola and bananas. I knew that even if the local water contained contaminants, the strong acidity of Coke would kill them. Bananas have their own natural protection in the form of the peel. The safety of other fruits, such as oranges, can be questionable because in some countries merchants remove the peels prior to selling them, which can lead to contamination.

I had met Dr. Pandey, a professor at the Dairy Research Institute, (NDRI) when he visited Ithaca. He knew one of my graduate students from India, Subash Chandra. Because of his hospitality, as well as that of Dr. K. M. Narayanan, head of the Division of Dairy Chemistry at NDRI, I felt welcome in Karnal. At the Institute I sampled ice cream made from buffalo milk and learned about the process of taking buffalo milk and by dilutions, additions, and deletions, creating safe and nutritious milk for babies.

The Dairy Research Institute was a modern research facility, and both Dr. Pandey and Dr. Narayanan were eager for their school to take its place as a world-class institute. In the foyer of the Institute, I was particularly pleased to see a poster in which lines had been drawn from Karnal to the top schools of the dairy world. One line was drawn to Cornell University which made me proud.

I was fascinated with the people and environment around me at the Institute. Each morning I awoke early and went to a nearby street to take pictures of the people passing by. I saw all sorts of people using many types of transportation, including bicycles, automobiles, rickshaws, three wheelers, ox-drawn carts, and camels pulling heavy wagons. I also took photos of local children in their school uniforms.

After leaving the Dairy Research Institute, I was taken to Chandigarh, the home of Panjab University. The campus was well-planned and beautiful with modern, tastefully arranged buildings. The campus had a man-made lake, a special rock garden, a cactus garden, and many other lovely places to stroll and relax. My host was Dr. D.V. Vadehra, the dean of students. I had known Dr. Vadehra at Cornell years earlier when he was a professor of food science. I stayed in the guesthouse at the university, but this time I had my own private cook, an elderly man who had cooked for the British during their occupation of India. Dr. Vadehra left strict instructions for the cook that he was to protect my health. I appreciated his concern for my health, but he need not have worried because the cook prepared excellent food for me. I was pleased not to have to rely on crackers, bananas, and Coke.

At Panjab University, I presented a lecture for the Department of Biochemistry and also visited many faculty members in their homes, including Dr. Vadehra and his wife, and Dr. N. Nath, chair of the department. I enjoyed this tremendously; the professors were friendly and hospitable, and being entertained in their homes was a special treat. Dr. Vadehra, in keeping with the Indian custom, had returned to India to select a wife. She held an M.D. degree, and, because she did not want to relocate to the United States, he remained in India with her but retained his affection for America. When I visited in their home, I photographed their kitchen thinking that it would be a typical Indian kitchen, but when the photo was developed I noticed that the shelves were stocked with Corningware which Dr. Vadehra had brought to India with him from the U.S.A. I smiled at this reminder of the long reach of American culture. My next visit was to the Central Potato Research Institute at Simla.

I have exchanged letters with people all over the world who have requested reprints of my research, and when I journey to their country, I try to meet them. There were many correspondents from India, including Dr. S.B. Lal, head of the Division of Plant Pathology, and Dr. S. Grewal of the Division of Biochemistry at the Central Potato Research in Simla. The highly trained researchers at Simla had received their education (Ph.D. degrees) from a variety of countries. These researchers had requested reprints of my research since they were researching a similar topic, sprout inhibition. They had adopted my research methods developed for the potato and were excited that I was coming to India and invited me to visit them at the Potato Institute.

It was good to have a chance to meet these long-distance colleagues. Two young professors and their wives arrived in Chandigarh in a taxi to greet me and escort me up the Himalayan Mountains to the Potato Research Institute. Because we had already communicated, I was familiar with some of their research and did not feel like a stranger. I was placed in a guesthouse at the Institute but was not left alone for very long. The wives of the young men continually invited me to their homes for meals. Because they feared that I might not be able to tolerate their spicy food (a well-founded concern) they prepared dishes with minimal spices and then they placed the spices on the table so that they could add seasoning to their own food.

One of the couples had recently returned from a wedding and had brought back cakes and other desserts prepared for the ceremony. I was delighted to learn about the customs and foods served at Indian weddings. The desserts were delicious.

Soon after my arrival at the Institute, I learned that Dr. Grewal and some of the other potato researchers were planning to take me via jeep up to the very top of the mountain where the "seed" potatoes were grown. I was excited because I would have a chance to see the people harvesting the potatoes. My study of potatoes has often taken me to mountaintops.

The Institute itself was located at more than twelve thousand feet above sea level. The air was so rarefied that if I walked for any distance, I became breathless. The young researchers walked slowly and helped me by carrying my purse and briefcase. The next morning I climbed into the jeep and rode even higher up the mountain to see the harvesting of the "seed" potatoes. On the way up, I observed that the land on the sides of the mountain had been terraced for crops by industrious farmers. There were small houses—little more than huts—clinging to the steep slope of the mountainside; they looked as if they might slide off.

The seed potatoes grown at the Institute were special; they were more resistant to viral infection, a useful trait in tropical and subtropical climates. But why grow seed potatoes so high on a mountain? The farmers do so in order to escape harmful vectors such as aphids which are known to infect the potatoes with different viruses. Aphids can live only at certain altitudes, so if farmers plant high enough, the aphids are unable to carry disease to the potatoes.

The people who harvest the seed potatoes carefully prepare and sort the potatoes for shipment to different parts of India. Fascinated, I observed the harvesting, which was done using two age-old methods. One used oxen to plow up the potatoes from the soil. The other method was to dig the potatoes out by hand, using a pronged fork. Without the benefits of modern technology, the farmers had to go a lot of trouble to get the potatoes out of the ground.

I took pictures of the view from the top of the mountain, a panorama of the snow-capped peaks of the Himalayas set back against the deep azure of the Indian sky. From this vantage point, the potatoes in India had the most beautiful view in all the world. The researchers told me later that they especially liked to work there because it was a good place to ski in the winter, and the potato researchers had special skiing privileges. I can understand what a joy it must have been, because the view from the potato fields was spectacular.

Following our visit to the potato fields, I returned to the guesthouse, which was very near the Institute. I was exhausted and fell immediately into bed but I could not sleep. I felt very cold. At first I wondered if I had contracted some local illness. I did not know what was happening to me. I was so cold that I put on all the clothes I had brought, including suits, sweaters, a topcoat, and even my raincoat. I piled four blankets on top of me, but I was still cold. Soon I developed a high fever. It was not until some time later when I traveled in the Andes Mountains that I learned this was simply a reaction to the high altitude. My symptoms disappeared the next day, and I felt much better after my body made the proper adjustment. Despite feeling weak, I was anxious to photograph the sunrise as it came over the mountains. This view from the guesthouse in early morning was spectacular.

All too soon my visit to the Institute came to an end, and Dr. Grewal escorted me back to Chandigarh. From there I returned to Delhi where I took the train to the city of Agra, the home of the Taj Mahal. This magnificent building seemed to have been plucked from the pages of an eastern fairy tale. Its beauty is beyond description.

My stay in India coincided with one of the Hindu holiday festivals. The Indian people were in the midst of an immense celebration which lasted several days and reminded me of Mardi Gras. Figures the size of three-story houses were built and filled with fireworks. When the celebration ended, people rushed up and pierced the sides of these big dolls, setting off enormous fireworks. It was an exciting spectacle, and I wanted to know more about their religion and flamboyant customs, but it was time for me to move on to my next destination: Iran.

I felt sad as I left Delhi because in the aftermath of the celebration, I saw many people lying in the streets. Some of them were sleeping, but many of them were dead. I found it difficult to reconcile the two sides of India that I had seen: its wealth and great natural beauty, and the squalor and sadness of the people in poverty. I was also having problems of my own at this time because I had contracted a viral infection that hit me quite hard during the flight to Tehran, Iran. Fortunately, the Pan Am flight was not full, and the flight attendants permitted me to lie down across a row of unoccupied seats. They brought me plenty of juice and were very attentive. I felt terribly sick and weak, and I was grateful for their kind assistance. As the plane began its descent into Tehran, I watched from the window as the huge city seemed to materialize from the surrounding desert, and for a moment I realized just how far from home I was.

Because of my illness at that time, I have few recollections of my short visit in Iran. It was 1978, only a year before the forces of the Ayatollah Khomeini overthrew the Shah, the country's monarch, and anti-American sentiment was already mounting. My sense of uneasiness, coupled with the virus, persuaded me to reduce my stay in Iran to only twenty-four hours. My only memento of Iran is a lovely and unusual bracelet made of small china squares with paintings of Iranian people which I purchased before flying on to Istanbul, Turkey.

In Istanbul, I discovered that the hotel where I had made reservations was being renovated, and I could not stay there. I was quite flustered because I was still suffering from the lingering effects of the viral infection. However, the cancellation turned out to be a blessing, for I quickly found a room at a small hotel with an extremely friendly and helpful proprietor. Seeing that I was ill, he provided me with a steady supply of home-brewed tea, which was delicious and had some medicinal effect.

I was determined not to let the virus force me to miss seeing Turkey. I did not feel well enough to present a lecture, but I did visit the local university. Thanks to the manager of my hotel, I also took a delightful guided tour of the ancient city, which previously had been named Byzantium and Constantinople.

The slices of roast lamb and other foods of Turkey were delicious, and I also enjoyed the friendly, open people I met. Toward the end of my time there, I took photographs which I treasure. I regret that I visited the country in such poor health; I am sure I could have enjoyed it more if I'd been well. Some time later, I met several food scientists from Turkey at an international meeting in Spain, and we began a scientific correspondence. I have fond memories of Turkey and hope to return some day.

I had wanted to visit Israel and could have done so at no extra cost with my around-the-world ticket. However, I had set a deadline of thirty days for my travels because various responsibilities awaited me in the U.S. I had been elected chair of the Northeast Regional Research Team composed of researchers from Maine, Massachusetts, Maryland, New Jersey, New York, Connecticut, Rhode Island, Michigan, and Georgia, and I wanted to perform well. I was the first woman to hold this position and I took my duties very seriously.

Although I was not fully recovered from the viral infection, I chaired the annual meeting of the Northeast Regional Research Team in Washington, D. C. My concern was that all should go well. I felt a special responsibility to do a good job for the sake of the women who were to follow me. Since that time, other women have been elected to this position, and I am glad to have opened the door for them.

PROTECTING UNITED STATES FOOD QUALITY
ENVIRONMENTAL PROTECTION AGENCY: 1979-1980

In 1978, I was invited to lecture at the World Food Congress in Japan. I had never been to Japan before, and the weeks before my departure were filled with excitement. In the midst of my planning and excitement, I received a call from Dr. Joseph Breen at the Environmental Protection Agency (EPA) in Washington, D.C., asking if I would serve as an EPA consultant. They needed a scientist to study the role of toxic halogenated hydrocarbons in the food chain. Because of my strong background in organic chemistry and my experiences at R. T. French and at the United States Department of Agriculture, I was a logical choice for the position. Dr. Breen felt that my training would be a great asset to the EPA, and I was pleased. I didn't have time to consider anything new just then, so I told him that I would like to discuss the job upon my return from Japan.

Immediately upon my return home from the food congress, Dr. Breen contacted me again to remind me of his offer. I realized that I would soon be eligible for a sabbatic leave from Cornell and the work sounded interesting so the job appealed to me.

From discussing halogenated hydrocarbons in my graduate classes at Cornell, I knew that studying their place in the food chain would be challenging. At Cornell I had been one of the pioneers in toxicology and among the first to call attention to the risks and benefits of certain chemical additives in the food chain. My interest in toxicants in the food chain led me to join other researchers from various departments in establishing the Institute of Toxicology at Cornell in 1980.

My assignment at EPA was to build bridges between the EPA and other government agencies such as the Food and Drug Administration (FDA) and the U.S. Department of Agriculture (USDA). The EPA needed someone to bring these agencies into a closer working relationship and help cut the government waste that comes from research being duplicated in different agencies. The job presented an interesting challenge. I decided to accept the offer. After arranging for a sabbatic leave from Cornell, I spent the spring semester of 1979 working as a consultant at the EPA's main office on M Street in Washington, D.C.

I arrived in Washington at the beginning of February 1979. I did not have to be concerned about finding a place to live in the D.C. area because my friend Lee Batcher, known to me from my previous work at the USDA in 1960, had invited me to stay in her home in College Park, Maryland. Lee and I had become good friends and had several things in common, including our shared interest in food chemistry. I preferred to live in a friend's home instead of maintaining a separate apartment since Washington is known for its high crime rate. Some of my Cornell acquaintances had been seriously hurt and one killed by burglars in Washington apartments.

Lee gave me excellent advice on finding my way around the Washington area. The metro system had been built since my first sabbatic in D.C. in 1960—61, so I decided to use the subways rather than battle parking in the city. I assumed that this would be quite a convenient way to travel, and I congratulated myself on my good fortune. However, my positive feelings dissolved on my very first day of commuting. A tremendous snowstorm hit Washington shortly after my arrival, and many people packed the transit system. The subways were so crowded that it was almost impossible to board. I found myself uncomfortably sandwiched in the crowd, being pushed and shoved, and I feared that the subway might stop running before it reached my destination.

Due to my years of living in Ithaca, I was accustomed to winter driving, and I simply could not understand the Washington psychology regarding snow. The public panicked at every snowflake and then traveling became a nightmare. Fortunately, I reached M Street safely on the metro, but I realized that I needed a better means of commuting. I soon joined a car pool from College Park. Joe worked at the Department of Transportation and preferred to do all the driving, and the three other passengers simply rode along and reimbursed Joe for the travel. This was an ideal arrangement for me since I never enjoyed driving in D.C. traffic. The two other passengers in my car pool both worked at the Food and Drug Administration and were well-informed about food chemistry so we often talked business during the long commute and left the driving to Joe.

At EPA I researched the ways halogenated hydrocarbons enter and move through the environment and also their effects on human health. The Agency had an excellent library and a helpful technical support staff which made my search for information much easier. The work was very interesting and challenging, and I sometimes felt guilty accepting pay for work I enjoyed so much.

The Environmental Protection Agency also worked with the American Cancer Institute and other related agencies to determine the risks vs. benefits of certain chemicals. Sometimes I was asked to serve on review panels, where the "risk/benefit" analysis for certain chemical compounds was under consideration. The panel considered the benefits of each compound as weighed against the potential health risks, and since their decisions impact the health of millions of Americans, they were not taken lightly. Deliberations often lasted several days, and sometimes experts were flown in from various areas of the United States to share their knowledge and expertise. In effect, these proceedings were like a trial for each chemical. If the benefits of a compound did not greatly outweigh its risks, the compound was banned. My friends at the Cancer Institute invited me to attend several informative and interesting meetings and seminars.

At Cornell some of my research had been concerned with the use of the sprout inhibitor, maleic hydrazide, on potatoes. I was very concerned about the toxicity of this compound and carried my concerns to EPA. The chemical appeared to pose a serious health threat, and I was able to convince EPA that this sprout inhibitor would be less dangerous if it were applied to potato plants in a different way. In order to eliminate problems, I prefer to work quietly on matters such as this by working with other chemists who understand the implications. In this way, people can be protected without frightening the public unnecessarily.

At the conclusion of my sabbatic, the EPA invited me to continue as a consultant. Cornell allows professors a certain amount of consulting time each year, and I used this time as well as my vacation time to continue working at EPA. While still carrying a full load of teaching at Cornell, I was able to continue the EPA study. I considered the work to be very interesting and challenging and it was good to find meaningful ways to bring the different government agencies together to solve common problems.

Prior to my assignment at EPA I was aware of the need to address toxics in the environment and had included studies of toxic chemical in my own courses. I joined with other Cornell faculty who also were concerned. Frequently we met over lunch for discussions. My work at EPA confirmed my belief that Cornell should be in the forefront in training students in the field of toxicology. In 1981 Cornell faculty from various disciplines joined together to form the Institute of Comparative and Environmental Toxicology, and Dr. Christopher Wilkinson was appointed as its first director. I was pleased to have been involved with its establishment.

Dr. Mondy as a consultant to EPA, 1980, Washington, D.C.

A Journey to South America
Peru, Bolivia, Chile: 1982

In February, 1982, I was invited to deliver a lecture at an international potato conference in Lima, Peru. The conference, "Research for the Potato in the Year 2000," was organized to celebrate the ten-year anniversary of the International Potato Center (CIP) in Lima. My lecture was on "factors affecting the nutritional quality of potatoes." I had never been to South America and was excited to visit Lima. I looked forward to seeing my friends in the international potato community.

One of my former students, Gustave Olascoga, lived in Lima. Gus was a native of Peru and, along with his mother and sister, ran a pharmacy. I arrived in Lima before most of the other American delegates. My hotel was located in what seemed to be a safe, upscale area of the city, and I decided to explore some of the shops near my hotel. I carried along my camera and took several pictures of the fruit stands, natives, and shops. However, when Gus learned of my expedition, he informed me that I had been lucky to have escaped robbery for that section of Lima was not as safe as it appeared. Gus insisted that I not wear any jewelry, even my watch, when I went out and that I should grip my purse tightly at all times. His advice was sound for during my visit to Peru, two of my friends had the pockets of their coats slashed and purses stolen while walking. I considered myself very fortunate.

Another former student who lived in Lima was Dr. Ulises Moreno-Moscoso. A few years earlier, Ulises had attended several of my potato seminars while a doctoral student in plant physiology at Cornell University. Currently he was Professor of Plant Physiology at the Universidad Agraria, La Molina, which was located adjacent to the International Potato Center. When Ulises discovered that I was in Lima, he invited me to visit his home.

His wife, also a Ph.D., had prepared a lovely meal for me featuring many of the local delicacies. Meeting his young son was an added pleasure.

Another former student, Dr. Maria Scurrah, had worked in my laboratory on the methodology of phenolic compounds while studying toward her doctorate degree at Cornell in plant breeding. She also invited me to her home to meet her family. Maria had married while in Ithaca and I attended her wedding which was held in a Quaker Meeting House because her husband was Catholic and she was Jewish. In Lima, she worked at International Potato Center; I was impressed with the quality of the research she contributed to the center.

During my stay in Lima, I was also entertained at the home of Dr. and Mrs. K. V. Raman. Mrs. Raman was my former secretary at Cornell while her husband pursued his doctorate. Dr. Raman now worked at CIP, and it was a pleasure to renew my acquaintance with them and to meet their two young daughters.

CIP was a well-established center that maintained experimental plots for examining all aspects of potatoes and potato diseases. It also housed stock cultures for the many varieties of potatoes around the world. I enjoyed visiting the potato fields with my colleagues where we met breeders who were searching for special varieties of the potato to clone and blend with U.S. varieties. Researchers from Idaho, Canada, and almost every other potato-growing region of the world were represented at the center. The center had been established largely through the efforts of Dr. Richard Sawyer, a colleague of mine from Cornell University. In my early years of research, Dr. Sawyer had supervised growing research potatoes for me in his former position as head of Cornell's experimental station on Long Island. Dr. Sawyer, currently the director general of CIP, arranged for the president of Peru to address the delegates of the conference. I have regretted not having my camera the night the president spoke to us, for he stood very close to me and I could have gotten a wonderful photo.

Dr. Sawyer's group developed an ingenious method for transporting various potatoes from one country to another at low cost. In the past, "seed potatoes" consisted of tubers or sections of tubers which when planted would regenerate into entire potato plants. Dr. Sawyer experimented with the true seed of the potato which develops in the green berries of the plant. Not only is it much less expensive to ship these small "true seeds" rather than the whole tubers, but it also eliminated the possibility that the tubers might be damaged in transit. Thanks to the researchers at CIP, it is now possible for countries to receive "true seeds" for planting without shipping the whole tuber.

My speech at the conference noted that many forecasters had predicted a pessimistic future for the world food supply. Indeed, the Global 2000 Report postulated that "if present trends continue, the world in 2000 will be more crowded, more polluted, less stable ecologically, and more vulnerable to disruption than the world we live in now." My view was optimistic. I projected that by the year 2000, we would feed the world a nutritious diet—a diet consisting of many varieties of delicious and nutritious potatoes. Potatoes are grown in many areas of the world and yield a much higher food value per acre than grain. They can be stored easily, are palatable, and have a high satiety value—that is, they give a feeling of fullness and satisfaction. Even the most inexperienced cook can prepare potatoes easily and quickly, and there are hundreds of recipes for the cook who desires to dress them up.

Following the one-week conference, I joined a group of potato researchers on a tour of the Lima potato fields and a trip to the Incan city of Machu Pichu. Our first stop was Cuzco, where we spent the night and then boarded the train for Machu Pichu the next morning. The night in Cuzco was very unpleasant for I developed a high fever and felt as if I had contracted influenza. I was concerned that I would be unable to accompany the group to Machu Pichu the next day and I had anticipated the excitement of seeing the spectacular ruins of the Incas. I slept little during the night but did not want to be left behind.

I forced myself to go down for breakfast the next morning. At breakfast I learned that two other people had experienced symptoms similar to mine and concluded that my problem was the altitude. Three years earlier on my trip into the Himalayan Mountains of India, I had experienced the same type of problem. Fortunately the symptoms were temporary; they lasted only a day before abating. Some of our group were so ill from lack of oxygen that they had to abandon the trip to Machu Pichu.

Our train arrived at the foot of the mountain, and we were transferred to another car that would take us to the top. This trip involved many hairpin turns but was very exciting. I was very impressed by what I saw of Machu Pichu which the Incas had built on a mountaintop to escape from the Spaniards. The Incas did a marvelous job adapting to their mountainous environment. We were shown their extensive irrigation and food storage facilities. I was impressed with the extent of their knowledge regarding the cultivation and storage of the potato which they grew on terraced fields on the mountainside. I also observed among the ruins special rooms where potatoes had been stored, suggesting that the Incas were aware that potatoes require a cool, dark environment.

Life must have been difficult in a city at that elevation, but the views from Machu Pichu were spectacular. My altitude sickness subsided, and I could enjoy the many views from the mountaintop. I would have been sorry to miss the opportunity to visit the Incan ruins and to learn of the technical sophistication of this ancient culture. During my travels in South America, I visited the enormous Inca wall around Cuzco. Again, I marveled at the engineering skill required to place the huge sculptured stones side-by-side so that they fit perfectly, as if held together by concrete. At one point I found wild potatoes growing out of cracks in the wall. This did not surprise me because I have long known of the potato's ability to grow wild under difficult conditions.

The weather in Peru's mountains can turn quite cold, even in summer. To preserve the potato for long periods of time in harsh, wintry conditions, Peruvian families produce a substance called *chuño*, using traditional methods developed centuries ago. *Chuño* is made by a freeze-drying process, possible because the high Andean regions experience severe frosts during the summer nights. In the first step of the process, known as *chuñificación*, the potatoes are spread evenly on the ground and allowed to freeze overnight. If the tubers do not freeze completely, they are exposed to additional nights of frost. They are then allowed to thaw during the day, often beneath some covering to protect them from blackening.

This process of freezing and thawing causes the tuber cells to separate and destroys the differential permeability of the cell membrane. As a result, cell sap spreads into the spaces between cells. The people then trample the potatoes to release the moisture and remove the potato skin. The resulting product is immersed in a stream to be washed and is covered for one to three weeks before being left in the sun to dry. The dry *chuño* takes the form of a large solid that looks like starch but retains many of the potato's nutrients. The *chuño* can then be formed into cakes and stored for quite a long time without refrigeration. The white crust that forms gives the product its name, *chuño* blanco, or white *chuño;* it is also known as *tunta* or *moraya*.

A second kind of *chuño*—*chuño negro*, "black *chuño*" is a dark variety that is easier to process than its white counterpart. When *chuño negro* is produced, the potato skins are not removed during trampling. Also, instead of being soaked, the trampled potatoes are immediately left to dry in the sun. The blackening that gives *chuño negro* its name results from the reaction of phenols with oxygen in the presence of an enzyme resulting in the formation of melanin, a dark pigment. If the potatoes are washed first, most of the melanin-forming pigments are eliminated. The result of this washing procedure gives the preferred white product.

As interesting as my excursions to the Incan ruins were, I was not satisfied with seeing only the tourist sites. In my international visits I have always made an effort to go beyond being a tourist in order to discover more about the culture of the natives. According to many scholars, potatoes originated in Peru, and I wanted to speak with a local potato farmer. Many farmers live high in the Andes mountains in homes that are difficult to find and practically inaccessible. In addition, many people are reluctant to interact with an outsider unless they are in the company of a person who is familiar with their language and customs.

My Cornell friend, Betsy Risley, a linguist who had worked with the Native Indians of South America and was very knowledgeable of the Ouechua language, invited me to visit her at the worksite of Wycliffe Bible Translators in Huanco, Peru. These workers lived together in a compound that housed many volunteers. I was anxious to visit Betsy and experience first-hand the natives of Peru.

My plane trip to Huanco was an adventure in itself for the plane was very small, and I was a bit nervous while flying high into the mountains. I wondered if such a small plane could manage to miss the Great Andes range. At times we flew very close to the mountains. My flight was rough, and the landing strip was extremely narrow. I feared that the pilot did not have enough room to land the plane so I closed my eyes and gripped my seat while the experienced pilot landed safely with no difficulties.

The weekend with Betsy was very pleasant. She was fluent in Ouechua, the local language of this area of Peru. In previous years, she had taught Ouechua at Cornell University. Betsy escorted me to many different villages in the area and introduced me to the local people, explaining to them the purpose of my visit. Once they learned who I was, they were friendly and we were able to communicate (with Betsy's help). They seemed pleased when I asked to photograph them.

There were many varieties of potatoes for sale in the village market. The potato is the main food in South America, and potatoes are available in virtually every shape and color imaginable. It was clear to me that the Peruvians were knowledgeable about their potatoes, for the merchants using roof covers in the marketplace made certain that the tubers were not exposed to bright sunlight. Bright light accelerates the formation of toxic compounds, known as glycoalkaloids. I enjoyed visiting the potato market and took several photographs of the market activities. It was fascinating to watch the older ladies of the village making belts and weaving llama wool into blankets.

On Sunday, Betsy took me to a local church high in the mountains. The church had been established many years earlier by a Texas missionary. It was small, neat, and quite comfortable.

Despite the language barrier, I did not feel like an outsider during the service. The congregation sang hymns with familiar melodies even though the words were not familiar to me. Following the service, Betsy introduced me to a nice lady and her young daughter who were members of the church. Betsy, knowing my desire to meet local potato farmers, conveyed this message to the woman.

That afternoon the four of us—Betsy, the woman, her daughter, and I—took a long and tedious bus trip up the side of the mountain to a farmer's home. Little did I know as we wound our way high up the mountainside that this would be one of the most satisfying experiences of my life. The farmer was extremely pleased that an American had come to visit him and his family, and his enthusiasm was contagious. His hospitality was very impressive, and, with Betsy's assistance, I conversed with him about potatoes and his life as a farmer.

The farmer's house lacked several basic amenities. The floor was dirt, and instead of windows, the house had only openings in the mud walls through which many things might enter. While we sat on a couch in the living room, I watched a chicken fly through the window, land on the desk, and then continue its flight out the door opening. There was no door. A guinea pig shuffled in very peacefully in front of me as we sat on the couch.

There were several guinea pigs in other parts of the house. Guinea pigs are a source of meat in Peru, and the farmer was raising them for food. The house had some unusual decorations on the walls. Posters of numerous pin-up girls covered the walls of the living room.

I was relieved when I was offered Coca-Cola, for I knew that Coke is usually safe to drink. Its acidity is such that harmful microorganisms cannot survive in it. Fortunately, he did not offer me food for I might have declined and certainly did not want to embarrass him. In my visits through forty-seven countries, I have been very careful of food and water intake and have never experienced a digestive upset. At times I have survived on bananas and Coca-Cola when I was uncertain as to the safety of the food and water. As stated before, the banana, a nutritious food, has its own protective covering, and cola offers liquid which is often safer than water.

After the refreshments, we went out into the fields to see his potatoes. There I observed (quietly to myself) many fertilizer deficiencies. He was proud of his crop so I delicately told him about the benefits of fertilizer and the beneficial effects of substances like potassium, nitrogen, and boron on potato growth.

The variety of potato he grew was unfamiliar to me, so I asked its name. He told me that it was called "Revolution." I looked at Betsy. "Revolution?" I asked.

"That's what he says," Betsy replied. "Revolution."

I struggled to keep a straight face; it seemed such a strange name for a potato, but then I remembered that Peru had had many revolutions.

Although this farmer lived in Peru, he had never been in contact with the International Potato Center located in Lima. I realized that the center had information that could be useful to him, so I gave him the address and suggested that he make contact. Upon my return to the United States, I wrote the center, urging them to send information to the farmer. I shall long remember my afternoon with the farmer and his family and would like to think that I helped him improve his crop.

It is the personal contacts such as the one I had with the farmer and his family that make my international experiences so special. Traveling with an American tourist group, I would have missed the opportunity to visit the small church high in the mountains and to meet and visit with the people in their own homes in the villages. Many of my travels around the world have been with a friend like Betsy who speaks the local language and introduces me to the true lives of the natives.

During my visit to the compound, Betsy and I visited a nearby hospital. It was small and clean and had attractive flowers growing in beds around the building. She also took me to see local brick making from clay. The hot Peruvian sun was right for drying the clay. Another time, we walked to a stream where women were doing their family wash. They were surrounded by their children who played in the same stream. Later I observed a woman and her daughter planting potatoes with a special hoe that resembled a slender shovel. In Peru potato farmers rarely use a cultivator like a plow; instead they dig holes and then drop in the potato tuber seed pieces.

It was wonderful being around the children of Peru who were open and friendly with Americans. They hovered around me, expecting treats, and I made certain I always had an adequate supply. After my interesting and informative visit to Huanco, I said goodbye to my friends at Wycliffe Bible Translators Compound and flew back to Lima in the small plane that could barely clear the landing strip.

My next stop after Peru was Bolivia where I visited Dr. and Mrs. Robert Kunkel. Dr. Kunkel was on assignment at the Consortium for International Development (CID) in Cochabamba, Bolivia. The Kunkels and I had been friends since their earlier days at Cornell University. Dr. Kunkel had visited at Cornell on sabbatic leave from Colorado State University and became interested in my research on blackspot in potatoes. Later he took a research position to study the blackspot phenomenon at Washington State University. Because of our similar research interests, we kept in touch over the years and enjoyed discussing this topic at various national and international potato meetings.

Unfortunately at this time, Mrs. Kunkel was having difficulty breathing in the high altitude of Bolivia and was definitely handicapped. Because of her illness, a nice Bolivian maid was hired to help with housework. The maid was bilingual and very friendly, and she escorted me on several tours of the city.

On one of the excursions into Cochabamba, I observed an unusual biscuit-like food sold along the sidewalk market. The maid explained that the biscuit was a cooked potato product used by local people as medicine to treat digestive upsets such as vomiting and diarrhea. It was interesting to learn that Bolivians believed the potato was effective in treating these conditions. I had long appreciated this value of the potato. As a child, tea and toast had rarely helped when I had digestive upset, but my mother's white potato soup invariably calmed my stomach. I had even recommended this home remedy to graduate students when they had such digestive ills, and they also experienced similar beneficial results. It was interesting to learn that Bolivians were also aware of this medicinal value of the potato.

One Sunday afternoon, Dr. Kunkel and his wife took me to the famous Women's Monument located high on a hill in Cochabamba. I took pictures of the monument and the impressive view of the city from the hilltop. One of my favorite photos is of two native women sitting with their baskets of small potatoes. They talked and peeled the potatoes while enjoying the park. They seemed to know it is best to peel potatoes before cooking in order to remove the toxic compounds present in the peel. Often I showed my classes this picture to illustrate the importance of peeling potatoes to remove the poisonous glycoalkaloids.

Dr. and Mrs. Kunkel escorted me into the mountains to see the potato fields. We drove along narrow roads to our destination, passing donkeys carrying large sacks of potatoes. I was intrigued to see the area's widespread potato growth. There were potatoes in many places such as on deserted hillsides. We stopped and chatted with a man who lived in the mountainous area. He was friendly and accommodating and showed us his house and his outdoor oven where he baked bread and potatoes.

In a local restaurant, I observed potatoes being cooked in a pit on the soil floor. The potatoes, which were baked from underneath the coals, were very delicious.

Bolivia had been on my original schedule to South America but Chile was included later after I received a very special invitation from Dr. Alberto Plaza. He insisted that I should not visit Bolivia without visiting him in Chile. As a Cornell Ph.D. in plant breeding, he had attended my potato seminars and was now Director of the Area of Production Vegetable Institute in Santiago. This was all the encouragement I needed because I was eager to observe the research being done at his Institute.

Booking an airline reservation to Santiago was time consuming. Actually it took one whole day. I struggled for hours to schedule my flight at a time that would accommodate both me and Dr. Plaza. When the extra trip seemed to be more trouble that it was worth, I remembered my motto: "*You never fail until you stop trying.*" Eventually things worked out; I was on my way to scenic Chile.

I shall always remember the sight of the Chilean coastline from the air as the country came into view—miles of sandy beaches coupled with majestic, snow-capped peaks. Alberto met me at the airport and escorted me to my room in a small, comfortable hotel in the heart of the city. I was happy to stay there, for I had access to many of the city's finest attractions, and I could visit on my own. I often walked around the city, watching the people on the streets. I enjoy meeting, seeing, and smiling at people whenever I travel abroad, and people always respond to me as if they are pleased to have someone genuinely interested in their country. I did not lack for attention in Santiago: Alberto was a gracious host and showed me the city's beauty, but one afternoon while I was alone on the street I noticed soldiers in uniform watching me.

My trip to Chile was during a time of political unrest, and it soon became apparent that a couple of local police officers were studying my public interactions closely. I did not want them to suspect me of seditious behavior, so I approached them and explained the reason for my trip to Chile. Pleased that I had chosen to visit their country, they were very polite and I never had a problem with them.

At the Agricultural Institute, which had been largely funded by sources from the United States, Alberto introduced me to his staff and showed me the laboratories which were clean and well kept. I was impressed with the equipment in the well-planned institute which resembled an American agricultural experiment station. On the day I visited, Alberto and his staff were working primarily on wheat, but they also worked with the potato, so I was taken to the experimental plots where potatoes were being harvested.

I was also invited to visit Brazil, but because of my obligations back at home and Cornell in Ithaca, NY, I returned to the United States. I was sorry to leave South America; I still regret not continuing on to Brazil, but I had a full schedule of activities awaiting me at home. I had purchased a house in December of 1981, just two months before I left for Peru; I postponed renovating it until my return.

Moving into my new home was very time-consuming. Because the moving company would not insure my antique china, I moved the heavy, fragile packages myself, which was quite a painful chore. I also spent an entire month catching up with my university work and household chores. Life was hectic, but I have always welcomed the challenge of new activities.

While I was in the midst of managing my graduate teaching, research, and housing situation, I received a call from President Daniel Grant from Ouachita Baptist University, my alma mater. He asked me to serve as co-chair for the "Ouachita in the Year 2000" fundraising drive. I did not want to give Dan a flat refusal, so I told him I would consider it. After some soul-searching, I decided to help. The assignment did not require me to travel, but I spent weekends on the phone contacting former classmates. We were successful in reaching our fundraising goal, and I enjoyed catching up with old friends despite my overloaded schedule.

When I think back to this time in my life, I see how it highlights my "weakness" for work. When I was child, my mother would ask, "Nell, if you had all the feathers you could carry, could you carry one more?" My answer was always, *Yes, of course*. I never seem to know when to say "no" to work.

Potato Market, Cuzco, Peru, 1982

International Potato Center, Lima, Peru, 1982
Symbol exhibited—Peru Potato God

FOOD CONGRESS IN THE EMERALD ISLE:
1983

In 1983, I was happy to be invited to the sixth World Congress of Food Science and Technology in Dublin, Ireland. I had always wanted to visit Ireland because relatives from Mother's family had emigrated from there many years ago. My regret was that Mother was not alive to accompany me.

Shortly after I arrived in Dublin, a taxi driver glanced at me and said, "Oh, lassie's come home." He had noticed my red hair and thought I was a native. I arrived in Dublin a few days before the conference began and decided to tour some of the country. An Ithaca friend, Mr. Stanley Griffith, was born in Wales and had spoken at great length about its beauty. Intrigued, I decided to travel across the Irish Sea one Sunday to visit Mr. Griffith's homeland. It was a beautiful trip; the sky's blue merged against the horizon with the deeper blue of the ocean. I had heard that the Irish Sea could be tempestuous, but that morning it was lovely and calm.

I arrived in Wales around noon. All along the old cobbled streets, I visited the local people, who were open and especially interested in tourists. Since it was Sunday, I wanted to attend a Welsh church service, but the churches had emptied by the time I arrived. However, I happened to meet someone who had just come from church. Recognizing my desire to attend a Welsh service, she invited me to the next best thing—a piano recital to be held that afternoon in her church. The Welsh people have a reputation as excellent musicians, and the recital confirmed this.

Finally the time came to head back on the early evening boat across the Irish Sea. I discovered that we had been lucky on my trip over that morning, for on the return trip a storm came up suddenly, darkening the sky and sending strong gusts of wind across the water. Enormous waves slapped against the sides of our vessel, causing it to shift and lurch. Before long people were lying on floors, tables, couches, and chairs to ease their nausea. The lines to the restrooms were long, and the people lying down on the floor made it almost impossible to visit the restroom.

In all my travels, I have never been seasick, and fortunately that day was no exception, but I felt sorry for the other passengers who were so ill. Deciding not to let the gloomy mood of the ship get me down, I began taking pictures of the majestic waves and of some of the passengers. I was probably the only one who had a comfortable cruise and I even won a door prize from a drawing based on my boat ticket. My prize was an expensive bottle of Irish whiskey. Being a teetotaler, I do not know much about alcohol in drinks. This particular brand was unfamiliar to me, but other passengers seemed quite impressed with the quality of my prize. I took the precious prize back to my room at Trinity University and placed it on a shelf thinking that I would pass it on to some friend who could enjoy it. I felt some trepidation about bringing the bottle into the dormitory; for I did not want anyone to think I was an alcoholic.

By the end of my stay in Ireland, I had not found a home for the bottle. I did not want to take it back to the States with me and considered it too valuable to simply throw away. The day before I left Dublin, I passed a large liquor store on one of Dublin's main streets. I approached the proprietor and asked him if he would like to make an offer to buy my whiskey. He seemed interested and the price he quoted was generous. With the money I received, I purchased a gold claddash ring which I have kept as a reminder of my wonderful trip to Wales.

I presented a paper at the World Congress and was eager to catch up with old acquaintances and international friends. One person I was especially interested to see was Dr. John Hawthorne from Scotland, the originator of the first World Congress. Plans were made for the first World Congress at the Glasgow meetings in 1960. He had been extremely active in international activities over the years, the Food Congresses in particular. I was pleased to recognize him with others for his many achievements. His lovely wife was there as well, and I enjoyed visiting with both of them. Dr. Joe Hulse, who had been the only Canadian at the Scotland conference in 1960, served as president of the sixth World Congress. It was a pleasure to see and visit with him again as well. In addition to renewing old acquaintances, I made several new ones and saw former Cornell students who had gone on to research at various universities in their home countries. It was a pleasure to catch up with them and to learn of the progress they had made in their careers since leaving Cornell. Perhaps the most interesting Cornellian I met in Dublin was Dr. Paul Ma, director of the Taiwan Food Research Institute. He had graduated from Cornell shortly after the end of the World War I and was anxious to hear more about Cornell and Ithaca. Together with his wife, we had a series of enjoyable visits throughout the conference.

When I was preparing my presentation on potatoes in preparation for my trip to Ireland, several friends half-jokingly asked me how I had the nerve to address the Irish regarding potato research. When I arrived there, I learned, much to my surprise, that very little potato research was being done in Ireland. Actually, Ireland was importing potatoes from other countries. When I inquired about the state of potato research in Ireland, I was told that farmers had sharply scaled back on the amount of potatoes they produced to the point where importing was necessary. Ireland's primary food research in 1983 was in the area of dairy science concerning the effect of different types of grasses on the production and composition of cow's milk. I was disappointed when I ate a locally-grown potato, for the texture was poor and the flavor bland. It seemed a shame that a nation with such a proud history of potato production had fallen behind in both potato production and research and I mentioned my concern.

In the years following the World Food Congress in Dublin, I have been contacted by a number of researchers at Dublin universities who are researching the potato. I am pleased that my efforts at the conference to renew Irish interest in the potato have begun to pay off. I knew that the potato had great potential to fill many needs and that Ireland had the potential to once again be at the head of the industry.

Following the Congress I, along with other food scientists, toured the beautiful emerald isle. We visited castles, cemeteries and many little villages with thatch roofs and mills. In Ireland the name "Carroll," my mother's maiden name, and red hair were very common. As suggested by the taxi driver in Dublin, I felt as if I had come home.

NIGERIA: YAMS AND SOYMILK
1983-1984

Dr. S.K. Hahn, the head of the Root and Tuber Division of the International Institute of Tropical Agriculture (IITA) in Ibadan, Nigeria, visited Cornell in the mid-1970s and asked to meet me. He was familiar with my research on potatoes and he seemed surprised upon discovering that "N. I. Mondy" was a woman. He brought pictures of IITA and invited me to Nigeria to work with him on yams. He believed that chemical research similar to that I had done on the white potato would be helpful on yams.

Arrangements were made for me to work at IITA as a visiting scientist but unfortunately my trip had to be delayed. After taking the necessary shots for my visit to Africa, my health deteriorated since I had serious reactions to the vaccination shots. I was ill for several months, but finally in 1983, I took a three-month leave from Cornell to work in the Root and Tuber Division of IITA. Despite the delay, Dr. Hahn seemed delighted to have me.

I left the United States on my birthday, October 27, and arrived in Nigeria a few days later. It was an interesting and exciting trip, and we passed over several African countries, stopping only to refuel. In Liberia we were told to exit the plane and wait in the airport while the plane was checked. I enjoy taking photographs and I saw several lovely potential shots. After digging into my bag for my camera, I quickly focused to take a picture of a Liberian jet. Suddenly a Liberian soldier touched my arm and politely explained that all photographs were forbidden. I apologized and quickly placed the camera back in my bag.

Never have I seen roaches as large as those at the Liberian airport. Quite impressed by their size, I wondered if they would be as large in Ibadan, where I would be staying for three months. Tired of the long wait in the airport and frustrated by the restriction against taking photos, I did some exploring. I discovered a large prayer room in the airport and imagined it full of Moslem worshippers prostrating themselves on rugs facing Mecca.

When we finally boarded the plane to leave Liberia, a young, well-educated Nigerian man occupied the seat next to me. I told him that my visit to Nigeria was to do agricultural research. He was impressed and offered to assist me at the Lagos airport. During a visit to the United States he had developed a great liking for apples. In fact he was carrying apples with him and offered me some. In New York State apples are common and not considered a delicacy, but I appreciated his willingness to share with me his scarce item. Apples do not grow well in tropical Africa and are considered a luxury.

It was a relief to have my new friend help me through the airport in Lagos. I had heard disturbing stories of thieves who approached newcomers with offers of assistance and then later made off with their passports. I had determined not to surrender my passport under any circumstances. Fortunately nothing unforeseen arose as my young guide led me through the airport.

A van from IITA met me at the airport. When I saw the driver holding a banner that read "Dr. Mondy," I sighed with relief. I had expected trouble, but now I was safe and would be cared for by IITA.

Another passenger in the van, a young entomologist PhD from New Hampshire, had come from the Rockefeller Foundation to offer assistance in entomology at IITA. We immediately became friends for both of us were nervous as to what we might find in this region of the world. Fearing illness, we agreed to look after one another. Our fears were well founded for soon I had the opportunity to fulfill my part of the bargain. My new friend ate something that made him very ill. He lost weight, became weak, had difficulty eating, and looked terrible. He recovered when I provided him with packages of chicken soup that I had brought from the U.S. Because I always used caution with both food and drink, I never had a digestive upset during my entire stay in Africa. As supervisor of the biochemistry laboratory, I had a ready supply of distilled water available, and I always kept a bottle of water in my large purse.

The driver of the IITA van spoke English and was very helpful. Along the way to Ibadan, I saw a fruit stand with many Nigerian women, and I had a sudden urge to photograph them and their babies which were strapped to their backs. They looked so graceful and serene. My camera was positioned when I realized that something was wrong. The women were shouting at the driver of the van and waved their arms frantically, pointing at my camera. Soon I learned that Africans do not like to be photographed. When I realized their distress, I decided to photograph their fruit instead. Many spoke their tribal Yoruba language rather than English, and I could not understand them. English is a Lingua Franca for the Nigerians, a remnant of the years of British colonialism. However, there are competing languages and dialects in Nigeria corresponding to the nation's three main tribal groups: Ibo, Yoruba, and Hausa. Although English is the national language, many rural Nigerians speak it only as a second language. However, all major Nigerian newspapers are printed in English.

Although I could not understand why the women were shouting, I sensed that they were very upset about the camera, so I pointed first at the camera and then at the fruit and finally convinced them of my intentions to take a photo of the fruit. They agreed to let me take photos of the fruit. Thus my first photos in Nigeria were of bananas, mangos, and pineapples, not women and babies which I had desired.

As we started to go back to the van, I realized I was being impolite for I had alarmed them. The least I could do was to buy some of their fruit. Being very fond of bananas, I picked out a nice bunch and then suddenly realized that I had no Nigerian currency. There had not been time to exchange American money at the airport for Nigerian nira. Fortunately, the driver came to my rescue and paid for the bananas, and I reimbursed him the next day. The women seemed to like my idea of buying fruit and as I left, I smiled at them and waved goodbye and they smiled and waved to me.

After that experience, I always made sure I was accompanied on my excursions by someone who spoke Yoruba. My escort would explain to the local people that I was in Nigeria to help produce a better yam. Since yams were their favorite food, I was permitted to take photos.

Some Africans believe that taking their photo captures their soul. Others believe that tourists are taking their pictures back to the United States to make money. I do not know what came into the minds of those women at the fruit stand or other Nigerians whom I encountered. Most Nigerians avoid having their picture taken unless they know the photographer. Many innocent photographers who have not understood the African culture have had their cameras snatched by the natives.

The International Institute of Tropical Agriculture (IITA) is a beautiful place, including 1,000 hectares of farmland set beside two large lakes. The Institute area, allotted by the Nigerian government, had previously been jungle and swampland before being drained. A tremendous amount of work had gone into establishing the IITA complex, and it was designed by experts in agriculture from around the world. One was Dr. F.F. Hill, former vice president of Cornell who later worked for the Ford Foundation.

Founded in 1967 as an autonomous, nonprofit corporation, IITA received its initial funding from the Ford Foundation. Their start-up capital enabled IITA to construct this spacious compound. Current funding is provided by the Consultative Group on International Agricultural Research (CGIAR), a collective of nations, development banks, international agencies, and foundations. Other assistance is provided through support for specific research initiatives or training programs.

There were two major areas of focus at the Institute: farming systems and crop improvement in humid and sub-humid tropical zones. IITA studied crops that include cereals, such as maize and rice; grain legumes, including the cow pea and the soybean; and my specialty, roots and tubers—yams, sweet potatoes, and cassava.

The high surrounding fence and security guards give the IITA compound a military appearance. The guards expected to know why you were entering or leaving the compound before they would clear passage past the gate. Although I initially found this annoying, I learned to appreciate the protection it afforded those of us staying at IITA. The security also protected the researcher's experimental plots from raids by Nigerian natives.

During my stay at IITA I was furnished a white Ford which was a great convenience since the compound consisted of several acres. The car also provided relaxation at the end of a busy day as I drove slowly around the lakes observing the birds and beautiful flowers.

Gasoline stations were located on the compound so the first time I needed a refill, I drove up to the station and asked for gas. Immediately I was directed to go to another area where I found only heavy steel tanks. Confused, I drove back to the station with pumps. Another lady was waiting so I asked her what I had done wrong. She said I should have asked for "petro." I did and this time had no problem getting the tank filled with gasoline.

I was warned of the driving dangers in Nigeria. Nigerians are not noted for their driving skills or for their adherence to road rules. As a result, serious accidents are far too commonplace there. I was told that if I had an accident I was never to stop and help the other people involved because the natives tend to take things into their own hands. Some have been known to kill those trying to offer assistance. Sometimes the natives hurt in an accident feel obliged to kill the other driver as a means of retribution. This mind-set was completely foreign to me, so I avoided driving outside the compound. Instead I traveled with Nigerian friends or hired a driver who was accustomed to native drivers.

In addition to aggressive, reckless drivers, the roads are filled with potholes. Tires and axles subjected to brutal road conditions may be ruined or damaged without warning. There was always danger of becoming stranded in a remote area since replacement parts and tires were hard to come by and very expensive.

Nigeria is different from the western world in many ways, and I quickly experienced mild culture shock. I was surprised to see women walking bare-breasted in public. Many carried large baskets balanced precariously on their heads. The women managed to distribute the heavy weight of the produce-filled baskets evenly throughout their bodies by maintaining a straight spine. They had excellent posture.

I arrived in Ibadan exhausted and found the weather to be extremely hot. I was taken to the International House where I had been assigned a room. Fortunately the International House was air-conditioned most of the time. Occasionally the air-conditioner broke and I felt the full extent of the intense Nigerian heat. Following my long journey from the U.S., I was exhausted, and I fell into bed and slept for hours.

There was much activity at the International House the next day. It was Halloween, and the researchers' children were having a Halloween party. The children were from many different countries including Japan, Sweden, Canada, Germany, France, Switzerland, the United States, and many African countries. It was a pleasure to see them having so much fun together. I took several photographs of the children playing and soon came to think of the International House as "International Heaven"—a place where people from all nationalities got along together.

Thanksgiving was the next celebration. Americans, who were in the minority at the International House, were the only ones who celebrated Thanksgiving, so we agreed to quit work in the early afternoon on Thanksgiving Day to share a traditional Thanksgiving meal. This took much effort since turkeys, as well as other traditional American foods, are hard to find in Nigeria. We divided the responsibility for gathering the meal items and put together a rather nice menu: turkey, cranberry sauce, and ice cream. It was a pleasant relief from the unbearable Nigerian summer heat. The men even played football for us to watch—an additional USA touch.

Christmas in Nigeria was different from any Christmas I had ever known, for people were wearing shorts since the weather was so hot. Dressed in his traditional red suit, Santa Claus arrived at the Institute aboard a fire truck. He hurried into the Institute's air-conditioned auditorium where the children eagerly waited. Santa distributed candy, balloons, and gifts to each child. The international children, Japanese, Finnish, American, African, and Swedish, eagerly ripped open their packages which revealed a diversity of gifts, each suited to the individual culture of the child. (Santa, of course, was assisted by each of the parents in selecting and providing the special gifts.) Eyes widened with excitement as the children discovered toys they had wanted from their respective home countries.

Afterward everyone attended a dessert party and the children sat together at low tables, eating their desserts and enjoying each other's company and the excitement of the holiday. What a wonderful world it would be if adults from different countries got along as well as the children at IITA. It was a joy to observe the children in a variety of activities, including the Christmas pageant. Even the children from other religions joined in the celebration, making the time very enjoyable.

Normally there was little to do at the compound besides the children's activities and an occasional party at the International House. Movies were shown weekly, and although most were old French films, they were always well attended. While public entertainment was lacking, there was much social life. Most families lived in nice houses on the compound, and I was pleased to be invited to dinner in the homes of several friends. I felt fortunate to live in the International House. Everyone was friendly, and because we all resided on the compound we became very close.

When I arrived, I was offered the use of a nice large house of my own, complete with a cook and servants. Instead I chose to take a room at the International House because it seemed more sensible to stay where adequate, safe meals were provided rather than to direct a cook to go out, buy food, and prepare them for me. Besides it would have been difficult to keep everything running smoothly for just one person.

The meals at the International House were fairly good although quite different from the food commonly served in the United States. Even pizza and hamburgers were prepared quite differently; I often longed for good old American food. Our food was always prepared by trained cooks in clean kitchens with stainless steel equipment, so I never worried about getting sick from contamination.

Most disappointing, however, were the potatoes. The flavor and texture were very poor. For the first time in my life, I *avoided potatoes*. Much of Nigeria is tropical and not ideal for growing potatoes. It is just too hot to grow potatoes properly in most of tropical Nigeria so most were imported and poorly stored. And to make matters worse, local cooks knew little about their preparation. As a result, I secretly vowed not to eat potatoes until I returned to the United States—but I attempted to teach the natives the proper way to store potatoes. Most placed them in the hot sun.

In contrast to the virtually inedible potatoes, pineapples were delicious. The sweet taste of the perfectly ripened pineapples is indescribable. I also enjoyed the bananas which came in numerous varieties and shapes, colors, and sizes, all of them good.

My fondness for bananas became widely known among members of the compound. Frequently, when I returned to the International House from work, I would find the desk clerks smiling, telling me they had a package for me. Invariably the package contained bananas, mangos, oranges, pineapples, or an occasional papaya sent over by my friends. From these I made fruit salad in my room, a wonderful before-dinner treat.

While the fruits and most vegetables were good, I had some difficulty with the meats. In Nigeria meat is very scarce and expensive except goat meat which was served frequently. It was often tough.

In my luggage I had brought several packages of Jell-O gelatin. I prepared some for the young men at the laboratory. They tasted it warily and told me it was too sweet. After spreading the Jell-O on slices of bread as though it were jelly, they thought it was much better. The Americans quickly devoured every bite. Because of the hot climate, Jell-O is rare in Nigeria.

I also brought powdered milk with me from the United States, but because it was available at the compound, I rarely used my own. Instead I gave my packages of milk to mothers in the countryside where there is a tremendous need for milk for small children.

Each night at ten o'clock I listened to "Voice of America" news broadcasts on my short wave radio. While listening I ate my nightly portion of peanut butter—exactly one spoonful. The news, as well as the peanut butter, provided a special American touch. It is interesting how little things can be so important when one is so far away from home. I had brought two jars in my suitcase because I knew that I would not be able to find peanut butter in Nigeria. Although Nigeria is a major peanut producer, they did not seem to know how to transform peanuts into peanut butter. My final spoonful of peanut butter was consumed the last night I was in Nigeria.

Dr. Hahn, Director of the Root and Tuber Division, was a specialist in plant breeding. He had done extensive research on the cassava, a staple food in Nigeria and in recognition for his research, the natives bestowed on him the honor of "chief," a very high honor. Similar to the recent British tradition of bestowing knighthood upon high-ranking civil servants for exemplary service, the honor of being named chief is bestowed in Nigeria to recognize years of outstanding service. Dr. Hahn welcomed me and was very cooperative in providing excellent support for my research.

My research began almost immediately upon arrival. I was in charge of the biochemistry laboratory and quickly determined that it was in need of many things, including chemicals which are unusually scarce in Nigeria. The laboratory did, however, contain a still where we could prepare distilled water. Water supplied to the compound came from a local lake and was treated chemically so it was safe to drink but had an off flavor, so I consumed distilled water from my laboratory. I attributed my excellent health while in Nigeria to the enormous amount of distilled water I consumed and my caution in selecting foods.

When chemicals were available, I conducted experiments. Unfortunately, when we ran out of chemicals, we could expect a delay of weeks or even months before receiving more. My work with yams provided a way around the delay. When I was unable to get chemicals for the chemical analyses, I chose to become a food technologist and developed new food products using the native yams or cassava. I also carried out similar experiments on the yam that I had carried out on the potato at Cornell. I was pleased that my findings on the potato were duplicated with the yam. Yams resistant to the nematode had lower phenolic compounds than susceptible yams.

I was the first food technologist to work at the Institute. After I left, however, other food technologists were brought in to continue the work I had begun. IITA realized the value of having food technologists who could develop new products from the native foods of Africa.

Just as chemicals were hard to come by, certain pieces of laboratory equipment were also scarce. A cooker imported from Holland with which I could obtain different cooking conditions by controlling the temperature was used. Various yams were sliced and fried as chips. Chips were almost unknown in Nigeria at that time, but most of the roots and tubers could be made into chips which were delicious.

With the student's help, I prepared chips from the different yam clones to determine which ones worked best. To present my findings, I arranged for a photographer to take pictures of the various chips, but the next morning the chips were gone. I asked Patrick, one of the four young men who worked with me, what had happened. Sheepishly he suggested that the laboratory might have rats. I smiled at him and said, "Yes, two-legged rats." He got the point. After we made the chips over again, the boys were told that they could eat them only after the photos were taken.

When I arrived, I had been warned that the young workers never showed up on time, so at our first meeting, I said that I was giving my time to help their country, and if I could be at the laboratory at eight in the morning, perhaps they could join me as well. They did and they took great pride in their work and were very pleased with their accomplishments.

It was a pleasure working with these young men. Although they did not have the scientific training to which I was accustomed with my students at Cornell, they followed instructions well. At first I furnished them with written instructions outlining each experiment so they could review the details before starting to work. Our accents differed greatly although all spoke English. Despite our language difficulties, we got along well.

I began to share the yam chips at coffee hour when researchers from different countries gathered. Encouraged by their popularity, I checked several different clones to see which would make the best chips. The water yam, *D. alata*, made excellent chips, but the regular yam, *D. rotundata*, gave very bitter and unacceptable chips.

A favorite Nigerian food is pounded yam (somewhat similar to mashed potatoes but stiffer) made by pounding the boiled and peeled *D. rotundata*. It is rich in nutrients but very expensive because it is so difficult to grow. Only a certain section of this yam can be used as seed material to produce another plant. Growing *D. rotundata* is very labor intensive, requiring a trellis for growth which takes many months. Because it is nutritious and very popular with the Nigerian people, I chose to concentrate my work on this variety.

The chemicals and equipment were unavailable to adequately test my hypothesis that the bitterness was due to glycoalkaloids. A researcher who followed me was able to prove that my hypothesis was correct.

We peeled the yam, boiled it, placed it in a vessel, and pounded it with a pestle. When cooked in homes, this procedure required two people to pound the yam in a mortar with long pestles for approximately an hour. A huge white mortar was found in the biochemistry lab, and the young men proceeded to pound the different clones of *D. rotundata*—to just the right consistency.

Pounding yams was always a popular activity among my assistants, since they enjoyed eating the pounded yam after the experiment was completed. We took photographs to show the differences in degrees of discoloration of the different clones. Some turned black while others remained white. Most people prefer white yams in terms of color and flavor, and the dark color was found to be positively correlated with phenolic content.

In addition to my work with the water yam and the regular yam, I also studied sweet potatoes. This was difficult since it was not the best season for harvesting, and due to the scarcity of pesticides, many potatoes had been consumed by weevils. My assistants and I discovered that by placing a crushed cyanide-containing cassava leaf beside the sweet potatoes, we could destroy the weevils. Although we couldn't encourage the use of poisonous cyanide, it was good to know that the crushed cassava leaves could control the pesky weevils.

Cassava, also known as tapioca, is perhaps the cheapest food source in Nigeria because it grows at all times of the year under adverse conditions. It contains mostly empty calories with few minerals or nutrients, but it is a chief source of energy among Africans. The widespread reliance on the cassava is one of the main reasons many Africans are malnourished. Yam is very expensive but nutritious, and cassava is inexpensive but lacking in nutrients, so I attempted to develop products that contained blended flours from both the cassava and the yam in different proportions. We made these mixtures into products that were fried in various oils (i.e., mainly African palm oil and different vegetable oils).

I discovered that Nigerians send their palm oil out of Nigeria to be processed in order to remove its natural reddish color. This also removed its Vitamin A content and I considered this totally unnecessary. Thus we used a variety of vegetable oils commonly found in the American market. We also compared the effects of different fats and frying temperatures in order to determine the optimum conditions, and we came up with a formula. My young associates were very enthusiastic and impressed with our product. They even showed their wives how to prepare it and their wives were also pleased with the product and felt they could sell it in the market place. (Often African women make extra money by selling foods on the street.) This product was popular at once.

In the United States, potatoes are sometimes peeled at the industrial level by dipping them in a bath of concentrated alkali and then rinsing off the peel. Unfortunately, this method did not work for the cassava. I decided that it might be a mistake to develop a more efficient method for peeling the cassava anyway. Many Nigerian women earn their livelihood by peeling the vegetable at various processing plants, and I did not want to eliminate their source of income.

It pleased me when my assistants liked a new food product. Since I was unfamiliar with African foods, I used my assistants as a taste panel, a practice they enjoyed. After they tasted a new product, we discussed whether they liked it or didn't and so forth. I attempted to teach them about nutrition during these discussions.

It was a relief to know that my associates enjoyed working with me because I was aware that they had had difficulty working with the previous director. Their positive feelings toward me were confirmed during a party they threw for me before I left Africa. There were many big speeches. One assistant said, "Dr. Mondy, we have worked for a lot of different scientists here at the Institute, but you're so different, you're more like our mother." In Africa, where mothers are treated by their children with reverence and respect, that is the highest compliment I could have received.

International people at the Institute were conducting research on different commodities from rice to soybeans. The soybean was new to Africa, and native Nigerians were unaware of its properties. My colleagues at IITA were developing soybean varieties that would grow well in Nigeria.

Two of my former students from Cornell lived in Nigeria and were teaching at the University of Ife. Dipo, a native Nigerian, had studied Food Science at Cornell and Pat Ladipo, an undergraduate student of mine in Food Chemistry at Cornell, had worked in my research laboratory. A native of New York State, she married a Nigerian graduate student whom she met at Cornell while he was studying for his doctorate in Economics. He also was a teacher at the University of Ife and in addition was head of his family clan.

Pat and her husband lived on a farm outside Ife in a village called Iwo. When Pat learned I was in Nigeria, she drove to the Institute to invite me to her home for Thanksgiving. I gladly accepted. Pat had been in Nigeria for many years and had endeared herself to the native peoples. Dipo told me that Pat had virtually become a native Nigerian. He was pleased with her contributions to Nigeria.

I visited her farm, and Pat introduced me to Chief Rohm, an American woman who had gone to Nigeria as a missionary in 1953. She was held in such high esteem by the people of her adopted village that they elected to make her a chief. At the time the title was bestowed, the villagers held a big celebration and showered her with gifts. She always wore the bracelet designating her a chief and was greatly respected by the Nigerians.

Chief Rohm was a native Texan, and, after forty years in Nigeria, she remained staunch in her beliefs. She wanted to show me the Kersey Children's Home in Ogbomosho thinking that, as a nutritionist, I could advise the Home's personnel. I agreed to make the visit at Christmas. Pat and her husband drove me to their home on Christmas Eve, and on Christmas Day I, along with the Chief and her native driver, paid a visit to Ogbomosho. Plans for this trip had been made during my Thanksgiving visit because Nigeria's communication technology was poor since the telephones never worked properly, and we knew we would be unable to alter our plans later.

On Christmas Eve, Pat and her husband came for me as promised and drove me to their farm. Pat wanted to celebrate a traditional American Christmas and set a little tree (decorated with a few Christmas lights) in front of the house. Although Pat is a Christian, her husband and some of their children are Moslems, so we had a mixed celebration. The next morning, Pat took me to meet Chief Rohm. After attending the Christmas service at her church we traveled to Ogbomosho.

At the Children's Home, I met many foreign missionaries, some of whom taught at the local Southern Baptist Seminary. Together they ran a huge hospital, considered the best in the area. They were attempting to train Nigerians to fill their positions in case they were required by the government to leave the country. Deportation was a constant concern of the missionaries, especially during the time of my visit just a few months before a major coup.

The Kersey Children's Home was part of the larger complex, caring for children who were malnourished (often due to a lack of protein) but were not otherwise ill. The Home was well known and women came from all over Nigeria with their sick children. Waiting lines for admission were always very long.

The nurses who ran the Home were highly trained, some of whom had a master's degree in nursing. They had studied medicine to enable them to meet the particular needs of the people they served. They were doing an excellent job.

Ruth Romack, the head of the Children's Home, was assisted by Sharon Hawk, both very capable nurses. Ruth accepted me right away and gave me a guided tour of the Home. During my tour, Ruth introduced me to the two abandoned children she had chosen to take care of—a boy and a girl. They had recovered physically from their deficiency disease and were ready to be released, but there was nowhere for them to go. Moved, I told Ruth that I would support them until they were adopted by a good Nigerian family. I did so for several years following my return to the United States.

In the Home, I was able to meet the children, talk with their mothers, and take a few pictures. The nurses told me what protein foods and nutritional supplements were used for treatment. They explained what I had already suspected—the main cause of malnutrition among children at the Home was a diet consisting largely of cassava, the food staple of the Nigerian poor.

Ruth told me that her main concern was providing the children with adequate sources of protein. Because she had only a few eggs to spare, she used blood cheese until she could acquire some laying hens. She used soymilk with the smaller children. Unfortunately soymilk was foreign to Nigeria, and Ruth had to fly to Togo to pick up shipments of the milk imported from Holland. As a food technologist, I knew how to produce soymilk, and this practice seemed an inordinate burden. If they could acquire soybeans, I thought, they could make their own soymilk.

After visiting the Home for a day, Chief Rohm took me to the leper colony in nearby Ogbomosho. The Chief, who spoke fluent Yoruba, told me she would serve as my interpreter at the colony since most of the residents spoke little English.

The leper colony occupied a stretch of farmland surrounded by a fence. Over the entrance gate hung a sign that read, ironically, "The Promised Land." Because leprosy was considered so contagious, most of the lepers had been abandoned by their families and forced to live alone, separated from the people of their village. This colony was an attempt by Baptist missionaries to provide the lepers a sense of community and belonging. For many of its residents perhaps it was indeed a sort of promised land after what they had been forced to endure.

The residents lived in sheltered rooms. The Chief explained that because of the warm climate, houses were not necessary, only a roof to shield them from the rain.

Many of the lepers I saw there were badly deformed, with no fingers, toes, or in some cases, even hands. But they were a determined group. Despite their handicaps, many worked in the fields to grow enough food for themselves and for the older lepers who could no longer work.

Others made inexpensive goods such as fly swatters and hand-held fans. These goods were quite attractive and were sold to bring money into the compound. Impressed that they could produce such workmanship with missing fingers, I bought most of what they had. The Chief later told me that, although poverty stricken themselves and malnourished due to their reliance on the cassava, the members of this colony managed to send a portion of the money they raised to another colony. They had also built a chapel.

I was moved by the lepers. One man had lost so much of his legs that he was unable to walk. Instead he got around by way of a battery-run cart. The battery was dead, however, and residents pushed his cart manually. He was most grateful when I supplied him with a fresh battery as a Christmas present.

After Christmas, the Americans made preparations for a New Year's Eve celebration at the International House. Unfortunately, our celebration was abruptly spoiled by worrisome news. On New Year's Day it was announced that the Nigerian government had been overthrown by a military coup. A curfew was imposed, ruining any hopes for a party, if anyone still had the desire for one.

I was frightened. In all my travels, I had never been present during a period of internal conflict. My colleagues and I worried about what would become of us as foreigners visiting at the behest of the outgoing government. We were told not to panic but to stay in the compound until instructions came from the army whose generals had seized power. Instead of celebrating on New Year's Day, we sat nervously around a television listening to the words of a stern Nigerian army officer. To our great relief, he indicated that foreigners in Nigeria would not be harmed.

One disturbing consequence of the coup was that the nation's borders were sealed. Nothing could go in or out. I had thought about spending a few days in Togo for a brief vacation from the Institute but had decided to stay since my laboratory work was not as complete as I wanted it to be. Had

I gone on that vacation, I would have been stuck in Togo, unable to return to the Institute for weeks. I do not know how I would have managed.

Although we seemed to be in no physical danger, the situation at the center was not easy. Children who had come to visit their parents at IITA for the holidays were now stranded. The children of the ambassador and his wife had come all the way from the United States where they were enrolled in college. They were unable to return to classes at the beginning of the second semester.

When I considered the ban on international travel and trade, I thought of the Children's Home and Ruth's trips to Togo for imported soymilk. How would the closing of Nigeria's borders affect the already "protein deficient" children who depended on the milk?

I remembered Dr. Les Root whose work at IITA involved soybeans. With soybeans, instructions, and the proper equipment, I thought, Ruth could produce her own soymilk. She would need only a grinder and a place to heat and strain the milk. Immediately I began typing up instructions. When I told Dr. Root of the situation at the Children's Home in Ogbomosho, I was surprised to learn that he did not even know of the Home. When I asked to buy some of the soybeans he had harvested, he told me he would think about it. Later he informed me that he would be delighted to supply the soybeans free of charge.

As it happened, he had been looking for a place in Nigeria to illustrate how soybeans could be used in Africa, and this looked like a good opportunity. Transporting the beans to Ogbomosho was our next problem. I had a car but did not feel at all comfortable on the highways. On the road between the compound and Ibadan, about ten miles away, I had seen bloated human bodies lying in the ditches. I was told the bodies were probably accident victims or people who unwisely had offered assistance to the injured and had been repaid with a bullet or a knife. The bodies had been left to decompose because in Nigeria anyone who touches a body may be accused of being responsible for it.

Because of what I had seen and heard, I was simply not prepared to drive outside the compound. However, the delivery was important, and I began to consider hiring a seasoned, native driver. When Dr. Hahn, my supervisor at the Root and Tuber Division of IITA, heard about the project, he told me that I must take the soybeans in the department's van and suggested I use IITA's best driver. I was impressed by this expression of support and cooperation.

Because of the non-functioning phone system, I could not let Ruth know that I was coming, so the delivery would be a surprise. Loaded up with bags of soybeans and my typed instructions on converting them into soymilk, the driver and I set out for Ogbomosho. It was a long trip. Although a trip of a few hundred miles can take hours in the United States, the roads in Nigeria are so filled with cracks and craters and the traffic is so dense that such a trip can seem endless.

When we finally arrived at the Children's Home, the nurses met us. I told them why I had returned and handed them the instructions I had prepared. They read the procedures and said they believed they could complete the process. With tears in their eyes, they said, "Little did we know when we saw you a week ago that God would send you back on his mission."

As the driver unloaded the sacks of soybeans, I spent time making my instructions clear to the nurses. I told Ruth that I wanted her to meet Dr. Root and the other scientists at IITA who were growing the soybeans. This was arranged a few days later. After she visited the Institute and met with Dr. Root and the others, regular shipments of soybeans began to flow from the Institute to the Children's Home.

The project was immediately successful and since 1983 has grown dramatically. Nurses at the home train mothers to grow soybeans and to process them into soymilk. Recently I heard that some of these women have traveled as far as neighboring Ghana to teach other women how to process the beans into soymilk. They believe their efforts are making a difference in the fight against malnutrition there. Reportedly even residents of the leper colony have gotten word and are now able to use some of the soybeans. Because soybeans are much richer in nutrients than cassava, their use seems to have had a positive effect on leprosy patients.

I still have letters both from scientists at IITA and the nurses at the Home telling me how grateful they are that I was able to get them together. Sharon Hawk, one of the main nurses at the Home (along with Ruth) wrote to me after I had returned to the United States:

> The Lord sent you our way, and your visit has completely changed our treatment program and Kersey's Children's Home. I want you to know how grateful we are. We are using a ton of soybeans a month and have started a program of teaching the mothers to grow their own soybeans in addition to teaching them to prepare them. You may already know all this but I just want to thank you again. May God bless you as he has used you to bless us.

I also heard from Dr. Root: "We maintain our contact with Kersey Children's Home. It is the best example of what we hope to accomplish by promoting soybeans in Africa." He mentioned as well that they were initiating a collaboration with UNICEF.

As proud as I am of my involvement in this meaningful project, I take little credit for its success. I simply feel that God placed me, with my skills and knowledge, in that situation at that time for an important reason, and I am pleased that I was given the opportunity to contribute.

Despite the important work I did with soybeans, my main job at the Institute remained my work on yams. My most valuable contribution in this area was perhaps to show Dr. Hahn how his team could develop yams that were more resistant to the nematode which is present in the soil and can destroy the yam. I also showed him how to make the yam richer in nutrients.

I enjoyed living in the International House, but during my free time, I found myself venturing out to get a better sense of what the Nigerian people were like. I frequently visited people with the help of my former students, Pat and Dipo.

Both were so pleased that I had come to Nigeria that they invited me to visit their university, the University of Ife, and lecture on my research concerning the yam and the cassava. I was delighted to accept their invitation and had a wonderful time meeting the faculty. The campus was beautiful—spacious and well laid out. The buildings were tastefully done in African style, and I was impressed with the aesthetics of the university. However when I toured the library I was shocked at the scarcity of books. I sent books back to the university when I returned to the United States.

The audience for my lecture was large, and they seemed to appreciate the fact that I wore an African dress to the event. It was a long, flowing cotton pullover with delicate embroidery around the neckline and sleeves. Everyone was gracious and the lecture went very well. Afterward I retired to my guesthouse to prepare for my trip back to IITA where Dipo was to take me the following morning.

I awoke early the next morning and studied the beautiful African art that decorated the guesthouse. As I was looking around, my foot slipped and I fell to the floor, skinning my knees. I had fallen on a step. In Nigeria steps are typically very small and unmarked, and consequently easily overlooked.

I immediately rinsed the wounds with distilled water which I always carried in my purse and I applied Merthiolate which I also had in my purse. When Dipo arrived and observed my knees, he told me he did not think the Merthiolate would be enough. He was afraid I might become infected, so he took me to the university's health clinic. We spent a lot of time waiting at the clinic, but I was treated well there, and I appreciated Dipo's concern.

While in Nigeria I was able to work with Dipo on his research manuscripts and later to help him get his manuscript published in American journals. When he was considered for full professorship, I was honored that the University of Ife requested me to serve on his review panel. The review process was time consuming but very interesting. I was instructed to analyze each of Dipo's publications minutely, to make special comments, and to analyze the value of his research to the scientific world.

In addition to bringing me to his university, Dipo also wanted me to visit his home and meet his family. I was pleased to go and meet his lovely wife and children, all of whom were very cordial to me. I have always found it interesting to see how children behave in the presence of a senior guest. These children were very respectful, perhaps to a fault. I spent one night in the house, and the next morning the children greeted me by curtsying on the floor, as though bowing at the feet of a saint. It was simply their way of being polite.

Dipo's wife was very pretty, and the day I met her she was wearing a lovely dress that was perfect for her. I commented to her that I thought she looked very pretty. Almost before I had gotten the words out, she accompanied me out of the house to meet some woman she knew. I had no idea what this was about but played along because she seemed excited. A week later, I learned that she had hired this woman to make me a dress just like the one I had complimented. Well, as beautiful as it looked on her, the dress simply did not match my coloring. I still cherish the dress, however, because of her thoughtfulness and generosity in having it made for me. I have now given it to the costume collection at Cornell University.

During the course of my stay in Nigeria, I was given other dresses as well. Being given a dress is a compliment, often the best gift one can bestow. Nigerian dresses were hand-made with quality materials. One of my favorite dresses was a gift from a young woman named Sidi who worked in the biochemistry laboratory. She had received her master's degree in food science from Ohio State. I helped her with some of her research, including attempts to prepare soy flour to use in bread and cookies in order to enrich the diets of her people.

She presented me with a beautiful lavender eyelet and lace dress. I felt honored to receive these dresses and wore them whenever possible. The Nigerians at IITA appreciated this, and the night I wore the lavender dress to dinner at the International House, people at the tables applauded me as I entered the room.

Several Nigerians told me that I had just the right figure for wearing African clothes. I knew that being plump with wide hips was admired in Nigerian women. The wife of the United States Ambassador who stayed at the International House for a time was very slender with a nice figure. However, some Nigerians thought she looked sick and did not understand why she chose to be thin.

In Nigeria extra pounds are considered a sign of prosperity. If the wife is fat, it means the husband is well to do. For this reason, Nigerian women like to be plump. It is customary for a bride-to-be to attend a special school for last minute fattening prior to the wedding. This appreciation for plumpness was new to me but enjoyable nevertheless. I felt appreciated in Nigeria for another reason—my age. Nigerians have great respect for their elders, particularly older women, perhaps because most were raised by their mothers and grandmothers. Younger family members curtsy to older women.

One time I was out with a group of people from the Institute on a very hot day in the marketplace and a young man noticed that I was uncomfortable. He brought his chair over to me and placed it in the shade of his tent. Because of my age, people often treated me with courtesy and respect.

Each Sunday a van appeared outside the International House to transport residents to whatever place of worship they desired. As a Baptist, I chose to attend the local Protestant church. The Nigerian parishioners, dressed up in native finery, were very friendly. The children were very well behaved, and sometimes the sermon was delivered by a child who stood on a table in order to be seen over the pulpit. My main regret was that I did not have a tape recorder with which to record the wonderful sermons of the children and the church music as well. Children often participated in the music. In Nigerian churches it is common for churchgoers to dance as they sing and this was no exception. In this church, balloons were released, lending the service a festive and exuberant atmosphere.

The Institute had very few women visitors. A friend of mine from Iowa State visited one weekend. Dr. Quak, a tissue culture researcher from the Netherlands, came for a few weeks to teach a course in tissue culture. One time a women's group came for a day's conference at IITA. Among the group was an extension worker from Ogbomosho. We talked for some length about her work and afterward I gave her a copy of the food book that I had published, knowing that books were scarce in Nigeria. She did not need to reciprocate, but she insisted on giving me something as well. She handed me a book that she had used in her extension teaching. It contained recipes and instructions on personal hygiene in the kitchen.

When I left Ithaca, I worried about the length of my stay. Three months seemed such a long time in an unfamiliar location and I worried about getting ill. I experienced periods of anxiety. Not only was the coup a trying experience, but I was also concerned about my responsibilities at Cornell in Ithaca. At the time, I was the national president of Graduate Women in Science (GWIS) and had many obligations to fill, including a speech at the national conference. I had established committees of hard-working, dedicated women, but my nerves were working overtime because I was unable to call the United States to check on their progress. One night in Nigeria I had a nightmare about the meeting. I dreamed that I arrived unexpectedly in a huge auditorium filled with people and nervously asked, "What's on the program?" only to be told there was no program. "Well," I asked, "Who's the speaker?" "You are," I was told. I was terrified and then I awoke, to find it only a dream. Ultimately I had nothing to worry about. GWIS holds its annual meeting in conjunction with the American Association for the Advancement of Science (AAAS), typically in January or February. Fortunately in 1994, AAAS had postponed its meeting until May, giving me plenty of time to prepare for the meeting after returning to Ithaca in February.

As my time in Nigeria grew short, I began to realize that I enjoyed my work so much that I did not want to leave, but I had eager students at Cornell waiting to start the spring semester. The young men who worked with me in the biochemistry laboratory in IITA felt sad to see me leave, and I certainly felt sad to leave them as well as the friends and acquaintances I had come to know. I would miss Pat and Dipo, Chief Rohm, Ruth Romack and the dedicated nurses at the Children's Home, and, of course, my colleagues at the Institute.

Early in my visit to Nigeria, while facing a number of hardships, I thought I would be anxious to return home at the end of my three months. I realized, however, that it's easier to endure the hardships if you have the love of the people and feel you are making a difference in their lives.

African yams in storage. International Institute of Tropical Agriculture Ibadan, Nigeria, 1983

Yam Market — Ibadan, Nigeria
Nigeria, 1983

Kersey Children's Home
Ogbomosho, Nigeria, 1983

SHARING SCIENCE WITH AFRICA
IVORY COAST: 1984

In 1984, I represented Graduate Women in Science at a conference held by the American Association for the Advancement of Science (AAAS) in Grand Bassam, Ivory Coast. The conference was titled, "The Role of Scientific and Engineering Societies in Development," and was attended by the presidents of several major scientific organizations, as well as by a host of African researchers. It was designed to bring together the best minds from a variety of countries and scientific disciplines to address national development problems in Africa.

The invitation to participate in this event was quite an honor, and despite my busy schedule at Cornell, I accepted. I had read the literature about the conference and was particularly pleased with its intention to bring together individuals from very different backgrounds to address concerns that affect all.

I was excited about visiting the Ivory Coast in December. However, when I accepted the invitation, I was unaware of the hardships I would face.

In February of 1983, after returning from my three-month visit to Nigeria, the winter weather in Ithaca seemed particularly harsh to me since I had been thrust from tropical weather to sub-zero temperatures. My responsibilities at Cornell teaching classes and catching up on research were enormous. However, when the opportunity arose to participate in the AAAS sponsored conference in the Ivory Coast, I felt compelled to go. During my stay in Nigeria, I had learned about Africa's scientific and technological needs and felt that I could contribute to the conference.

A friend in Graduate Women in Science, Sr. Helen Haller wrote to AAAS headquarters informing the administration of my experiences and activities in Nigeria. This information may have played a role in my selection for the Ivory Coast. From the large number of scientific organizations represented in AAAS, only a few individuals were selected to participate in these meetings. I was honored to be among the chosen few.

Participants were asked to prepare a paper recommending to African scientists and policy makers ways to elevate their people's living conditions. The assignment was daunting and represented new territory for me. However I had already developed firm opinions on this subject because of my stay in Nigeria, and voicing them to a responsive audience was a challenge I was eager to accept.

A frightening event occurred prior to my departure. Before I had heard about the conference I learned that I had a cataract in my left eye. My optomologist assured me that this condition was common and could readily be corrected. He scheduled an operation to remove the cataract in October. When I learned of my selection for the conference by AAAS, I immediately contacted the doctor and inquired if the operation would interfere with my attendance of the Ivory Coast meeting in December. He assured me that he anticipated no complications and that the surgery should in no way impede my plans.

However complications arose following my surgery. Neither I nor the doctor knew what had happened, but it soon became evident that rather than being restored, my eyesight was rapidly deteriorating. Within days I was blind in my left eye. Matters grew worse because whatever had afflicted my left eye soon spread to my right eye and I faced almost total blindness. I could barely make out the difference between light and dark, and could recognize only large objects. I could not read—not even street signs or the numbers on a telephone dial. A friend of mine who had been blind for years, Dick Flight, was wonderfully supportive, helping me adjust to my new situation. His wife brought a huge magnifying glass for reading, but it did not help much.

I tried to maintain my usual optimism but with only partial success. Facing blindness was torture for me. I could not imagine anything worse. Often healthy individuals think that they understand the handicapped: how they live and what they are forced to go through in their daily lives. We empathize with them and often even feel moved to help, but my experience with blindness taught me that one could never fully understand a situation without having experienced it.

When my other eye became blind, I was horrified. My vision was getting progressively worse, and I still did not know the cause. I called the office, but my doctor was out of town. Fortunately his colleague, Dr. Philip Lempert, answered. Recognizing the distress in my voice, he offered to meet me that night at his office. I was relieved.

When I arrived, Dr. Lempert attempted to comfort me, although he knew that concerning my sight, anything could happen. The problem still had not been solved, but his concern lifted my spirits. When I returned, I was determined to have my speech ready for the conference even though

I could not see. However, as I set this goal for myself, I realized that I would need help assimilating the material.

Friends offered to read to me the material I needed for the preparation of my speech. Professor Gene Delwiche, a retired teacher of microbiology, graciously agreed to help me, as did Marion Howe, who had recently retired from Cornell United Religious Work. Thanks to their efforts, I was able to get a sense of what was expected of me for my own speech. Soon I began dictating my speech to my secretary, Mrs. Mary Wheaton, who helped proofread the completed manuscript. I was required to have the speech translated into French since the conference would be divided between speakers of English and French. For this I contacted a French instructor in the language department at Cornell who translated my speech into French.

My surgeon, Dr. Levitt, was impressed that I had composed my speech under such adverse circumstances. He consulted with other area doctors who together decided I would be able to attend the conference. However, there was a problem. My new lens did not filter out ultraviolet light, leaving the eyes unprotected from Africa's dangerous ultraviolet sunrays. To help remedy this situation, Dr. Levitt provided a lens insert for my glasses that would screen out the UV radiation. The doctors admonished me to be very careful in my trip abroad. Although my eyesight improved somewhat during the weeks leading up to my scheduled flight, I still could not see very well and knew that even a minor trip or fall could result in serious damage. (Fortunately, my sight gradually did return after I returned home.)

The AAAS had sent a list of the participants who would be attending the conference. Most were presidents of various organizations, such as the American Physical Society and the American Chemistry Society. Among the participants was Dr. Rodney Briggs of the American Society of Agronomy. He was scheduled on the same route I was taking, and since we would be traveling on the same flights, I asked for his assistance because I was particularly insecure about getting through the airport in Paris. Dr. Briggs graciously agreed to help. He met me in NYC and accompanied me to Grand Bassam.

The trip to the Ivory Coast was challenging, especially since my vision was impaired. We arrived there at night and were met by the conference committee assigned to greet us. They took our passports and cleared us through customs which took an enormous amount of time. Despite the lateness of the hour, I found the airport quite hot due to lack of air conditioning. It was an interesting experience after leaving from snow covered Ithaca hours before.

We were taken by bus to the dormitory where we would be housed during our stay. The dorm was not air-conditioned, and the rooms were sweltering hot. Never have I been hotter in my life than that first night in the dorm.

As uncomfortable as I was, however, the other participants had a worse experience. They had underestimated the importance of bringing drinking water with them, perhaps assuming that they could simply purchase safe drinking water when they arrived. However our arrival was quite late and there was no place to find water that was safe to drink. I shared what little water I could spare, but that wasn't much because I had brought only enough water for basic tasks such as brushing my teeth and warding off dehydration.

Jointly sponsored by the AAAS and the Science Association of the Ivory Coast (ASCI), the conference was held in Grand Bassam, December 10-13, 1984. Scientific and engineering society representatives from sub-Saharan African nations, the United States, and Western Europe attended. The total number of participants was nearly 100, and all had been selected by the organizing committee from a pool of 350 nominees. The participants represented a large number of societies, including non-governmental disciplinary, multidisciplinary, and federative. We had been selected because of our commitment to scientific advancement, shown by various scholarly activities such as holding a position of leadership within one's own society and being involved in a scientific activity. As one of the few women delegates, I represented the United States and Graduate Woman in Science.

On the first day of the conference, we heard two speeches, one from the Minister of Education in the Ivory Coast and one from the United States Ambassador to the Ivory Coast. We gathered in a large, nicely appointed auditorium. Fortunately, the auditorium was air-conditioned because we waited over an hour for the Minister of Education to arrive. We were told later that it was customary in the Ivory Coast for important individuals to always make the audience wait. Making an extremely late entrance was considered stylish rather than rude. Americans and Europeans thought otherwise.

Television cameras had been set up on stage, and as soon as the minister arrived, they began rolling tape. Because of the bright lights cast by the video cameras I was able to take some excellent photos. At one point, I became so engrossed with snapping photos that I was unaware that the television cameras had temporarily focused on *me* in the audience wearing my colorful Nigerian dress. The local people seemed to appreciate my knowledge of and affection for Africa, particularly when I wore my Nigerian dresses. I was pleased to wear them since these long, flowing cotton dresses were more comfortable than my American dresses. That night when coverage of the conference appeared on national television, I was featured, and my colleagues later referred to me as the TV star of the Ivory Coast.

Spending time with other delegates at the conference who represented so many different cultures was enjoyable. Our purpose was to examine the role of African scientific and engineering societies in national development both on their own and in cooperation with the industrialized nations.

The written objectives of the conference included:

1. Examine the current status of sub-Saharan scientific and engineering societies.
2. Identify ways in which existing societies can be strengthened and new ones established.
3. Consider ways in which the scientific and engineering societies can address developmental problems of Africa.
4. Develop plans for scientific and engineering society pilot projects and other activities.

To meet these goals, participants were divided into workgroups, each responsible for addressing a different issue. These included:

A. Scientific and technological communication.
B. Education, training, and popularization of science and technology.
C. Role of scientific and engineering societies in linking universities, industry, and government.
D. Strengthening and initiating scientific and engineering societies in Africa.

The first day each workgroup began by summarizing relevant background papers and then proceeded to a discussion among themselves. Based on their discussions, the members prepared conclusions, recommendations, and proposals for action. These were presented in preliminary form at an evening plenary session on the second day. The session became a forum for groups to exchange and integrate the ideas that each group had developed. I was pleased to have been selected to work in group D which had been charged with strengthening scientific and engineering societies in Africa. Through this group I presented my speech, the abstract of which follows:

> Science is one of the most important factors in the improvement of life in any country, and societies play an important role in development. Societies play a major role in making science meaningful to the public at large, and these serve as a catalyst for promoting innovative experiments and useful programs both on the national and international scale. In the development of a nation, a strong science base is essential, and citizens must become aware of the advances in science and technology. Societies provide an important interface between industry, universities, and government. The basic sciences, e.g., mathematics, physics, chemistry, biology, and sociology, form the base from which science can be utilized in agriculture, public health, nutrition, etc.
>
> Food production and distribution are important factors in the improvement of life in any country. Special consideration should be given to appropriate agricultural technology, nutrition, and health.

African women should play a prominent role in development, and participation of women in the modern world of science and technology should be encouraged. Training should be in keeping with overall manpower needs, and women should receive training suitable to their aptitude.

In 1921, Sigma Delta Epsilon (SDE), Graduate Women in Science (GWIS) was established in the United States. Its purpose was to advance the participation and recognition of women in science and to foster research in science through grants, awards, and fellowships. Representatives from this organization helped establish the Federation of Organizations for Professional Women with over 100 affiliated organizations in all fields. Professional societies in developed countries should assist societies in developing countries. Establishment of societies similar to SDE/GWIS should prove useful for the advancement of science in Africa.

After I delivered my speech, I was approached by African women scientists who were interested in starting a similar organization in their home country. I encouraged them to do so and provided them with materials about our organization. In 1990, the Third World Organization for Women in Science was created and is progressing nicely today. I take pride in thinking of my role in its establishment. It is good to know that I was able to help women in another part of the world.

FOOD AROUND THE WORLD

SPAIN, SOVIET UNION, FINLAND, TAIWAN, THAILAND, SINGAPORE, CHINA, PHILIPPINE ISLANDS: 1987

Nineteen eighty-seven was a year filled with professional international travel. In March I attended international meetings in Spain, and I visited Russia and Finland in August. September found me in Taiwan, Thailand, Singapore, and Hong Kong, while in October I participated with a group of food scientists on a lecture tour of Mainland China. Following the tour, I visited the Philippines, where I lectured at the University of the Philippines in Manila and toured the International Rice Institute at Los Alamos.

Participating in the Second World Congress of Food Technology in Barcelona, Spain was different from many of the food congresses I had attended. It focused largely on the food industries rather than on European research institutes.

Of special interest to me were the sessions on food irradiation. At that time controversy persisted in the United States regarding the safety of irradiated food. My particular research concerned the effects different levels of irradiation had on the chemical composition of potato tubers. European countries seemed less concerned about the safety of irradiated foods than the U.S. and irradiation was used to a much greater extent than in the United States.

Other points of interest at the congress included a large exhibit hall featuring many commercial products, including numerous varieties of candies. Huge equipment for commercial production was on display and was very impressive. Also included were miniatures of processing plants which exhibited all the stages of processing. These photos were useful in my graduate courses in food science at Cornell.

Although I enjoyed the food congress, my experience in Barcelona was not entirely pleasant. Air pollution in Barcelona was especially bad which made breathing difficult for me. I am allergic to smoke, and the cigarette and automobile exhaust fumes often caused me to experience spasms of coughing. Smoking was permitted in all meeting rooms at the congress, as well as on the airplanes, and the methods used to divide smokers from nonsmokers were completely ineffective. On planes smokers were permitted to sit on the right side of the aisle while non-smokers sat on the left. Smoke passed freely from one side to the other and filled the entire cabin with fumes.

In spite of the smoking problems, I enjoyed seeing beautiful Barcelona. Following the meetings, the participants were invited to tour the little island of Mallorca where we saw many windmills and several different types of agriculture. As we flew over the island, the view of the windmills in action was spectacular. I was also impressed with the numerous olive groves and the pearl factories.

At the conclusion of the congress, a banquet was held at the base of the fascinating Columbus Monument. International Congresses provide a wonderful opportunity to make friends in the scientific community of the world. While in Spain I met many interesting people, mostly food scientists from different European countries.

During the summer of 1987, I traveled to the Soviet Union (the appropriate name at that time, for the Union had not yet broken up). Moscow Technological Institute of Food had invited me to visit, conveniently at the same time a study group from the Cornell Adult University had planned to visit Moscow.

While in the USSR, I left the Cornell group for a day to visit the Moscow Technological Institute of Food where I was the special guest of Dr. Krasnikov, Rector of the Institute. Some years later, in 1993, Dr. Krasnikov visited Cornell University and signed an Agreement of Understanding for his Institute to cooperate with the University. I was pleased to have played a role in bringing about the cooperation of these two institutions.

In Moscow, the Institute's representative, who served as my interpreter, called to tell me that she would escort me to the Institute. When she arrived with a beautiful bouquet of red roses, I immediately felt welcome because of her friendly gesture.

At the Institute, a welcoming reception had been set up in the room adjacent to the chairman's office. In addition to the faculty of the Institute, some special nutritional faculty guests were there to greet me. An American flag stood proudly along side the Soviet flag on the huge table.

Following a discussion of our special teaching and research interests, I was taken on a tour of the Institute. I was surprised to find that their equipment was extremely outdated and the laboratories in need of repair. Yet despite the bleak decor, the laboratory workers were cordial and gave me a very warm welcome.

For lunch I joined the faculty at the faculty club. I had never sampled Russian cooking before, and because the food was so different, I found that I could eat very little. The Rector apologized for the meal, but I attempted to downplay the issue, saying that my appetite was small when I traveled.

During the tour of the laboratories, I enjoyed speaking with the faculty about their research interests and had a memorable conversation with a female professor who was in charge of the baking and bread department. We talked about her department and also discussed potatoes, which are a major crop in Russia. The institute had several varieties of potatoes on exhibit.

Following the tour, the faculty showered me with presents. Because I had heard that Soviets welcome books from other countries, I presented them with a copy of my book, *Experimental Food Chemistry*. They presented me with books on the chemical composition of the Russian foods as well as books on Russian history and art.

Although they were written in Russian, I appreciated receiving them and have shown them to my students. Presently I have Russian students who can translate them for me.

Knowing that the political situation between the United States and the Soviet Union was still tense, it was even more of a pleasure to be treated so well by these people. At the start of the trip, I was unsure of what was in store for me, but my discomforts were eased by the friendly attitudes of all the Soviets I encountered.

I later joined the Cornellians for a boat trip on the Volga River. A Soviet reporter for *Pravda*, the government-run Soviet newspaper, approached our group and attempted to be friendly. Wondering if he might be some sort of spy attempting to get information from us, we were at first hesitant to converse with him, but it soon became evident that he was sincere in attempting to break down barriers. Our guards were lowered, and we then had a pleasant time comparing cultures and traditions.

My visit to the USSR gave me better understanding of the Soviet people. A highlight of the trip occurred at Getowa where the Cornellians were guests of a group of university students. Most of the students spoke English, and each Cornellian was assigned to sit at a table of students to ensure maximum interaction between our hosts and us.

The students at my table were intelligent and interesting, and I enjoyed their company. They were anxious to learn about America, and much discussion followed concerning our home countries. I had brought along some Cornell souvenirs, and seeing their curiosity about Cornell, I suggested that they accompany me to the boat to look at slides of Cornell. They seemed thrilled, and accepted and this interchange was most helpful to both countries.

Before leaving Russia, we were instructed to pack our bags early so they could be inspected before our departure for Finland. Upon our arrival in Finland, I was shocked to learn that some items had been removed from my luggage, including Russian coins and trinkets. This was regrettable, but I chose to remember the good times rather than the bad. I went on my way remembering the many friends I had made in the Soviet Union.

On our return to the United States, we stopped briefly in Finland. There I visited with two good friends, Dr. Eini Laakkonen, a specialist in food science, and Dr. Hilkka Halkilahti, a nutrition specialist. Both had been students at Cornell, and we had continued to correspond since their graduation.

They came to my hotel, presented me with delicious Finnish chocolates and escorted me to places in Helsinki that I had not seen in my previous visits to Finland. My time in Finland was so limited that there was no time to visit their homes.

I returned to Ithaca in late August, only three weeks before I was scheduled to attend the Seventh World Food Congress for Food Science and Technology in Singapore. I had accepted an invitation to speak at the congress after which I would join a group of select food scientists from the United States and Canada to lecture at several universities in Mainland China.

During the short time in Ithaca, I was in a terrible accident. While driving on campus, I was knocked unconscious by a speeding Cornell student who slammed into my car, demolishing it. I suffered a concussion, but to my relief recovered quickly. However, this incident left me with no means of transportation. Since I had only a few weeks to complete my lectures for Singapore and China, I did not have the time to purchase a new car. My friends loaned me a model that was similar to my demolished one. However, the shock resulting from the accident made driving difficult.

Arrangements had to be made for my graduate students and the research they would do while I was away, and I had to polish my speeches for Singapore and China. Amazingly I completed all the tasks before my departure date on September 20. During that time when I felt particularly distraught, I remembered my motto: *You Never Fail Until You Stop Trying*.

Visits to Taiwan and Thailand had been scheduled prior to the meetings in Singapore and fortunately, I was able to continue with these plans despite the accident. During my visit to Taiwan I visited Dr. and Mrs. Paul Ma before proceeding to Thailand and the World Congress in Singapore.

In 1983, I had met Dr. Ma, the director of the Taiwan Food Research Institute, and his wife in Ireland while attending the sixth World Food Congress. At that time they invited me to visit them in Taiwan, and now seemed the opportune time. Dr. Ma graduated from the College of Agriculture at Cornell in the 1920s and had many fond memories of his time in Ithaca.

My reception in Taiwan was very cordial, for Dr. Ma was a wonderful host. He had planned all the arrangements for my visit in minute detail. He presented me with my itinerary upon my arrival at his office, and after a short visit he and I were photographed standing alongside the flags of our respective countries. This was followed by a guided tour of his Institute.

The next day I lectured and had tea with a group of young scientists, all of whom spoke fluent English. Some were conducting research on irradiated potato tubers, my specific research interest. I was very impressed with the Institute, especially with the high quality personnel, the modern equipment, and the excellent research. During my visit, Dr. Ma also played host to Dr. L. Den Drijuver, a female physics professor from South Africa. She and I discovered that we were both lecturing at the Commercial Food Irradiation Session of the World Food Congress in Singapore. We enjoyed discussing our common interest: irradiated food. Dr. Ma arranged for us to take a joint tour of the irradiation facilities of the Taiwan Chemical Laboratory and Center for Measurement Standards.

Dr. Ma also arranged for me to tour the gem and sculpture markets as well as the wonderful fruit markets. I bought many tropical fruits, some of which I had never seen before. Other tours arranged by Dr. Ma included various types of restaurants where I sampled Chinese cuisine. Before my departure for Thailand, Dr. and Mrs. Ma hosted a dinner in my honor at their home, a most enjoyable occasion.

When I mentioned to Dr. Ma that I planned to visit Thailand before going to Singapore, he informed me that a delegation of food scientists from the Taiwan Institute of Food Technology (IFT) was also planning to tour Thailand before the Singapore meetings and arranged for me to meet the group. They invited me to join them and as the only American touring with the highly educated Chinese scientists, I found myself in the minority, but the tour was very enjoyable. Being able to tour with this IFT group was a marvelous opportunity because my companions knew all the best hotels, restaurants, and points of interest. The high quality accommodations made the trip especially memorable. We were served special Chinese foods, which included roast suckling pig. In Bangkok our group visited a Chinese medicine store, and in addition to purchasing Chinese medicines, I met young students who asked many questions about the United States. They gathered around me in large numbers for a photograph. They had no difficulty with English and were very curious about the United States.

In addition to visiting many historic places in Thailand, including the palace, I also rode among the "boat people" of Thailand and was able to photograph the "boat market."

The Seventh World Congress of Food Science and Technology was held in Singapore in the fall of 1987. While in Singapore I stayed at the Westin-Stanford Hotel and my room, near the top of the very tall building, had a spectacular view of the beautiful city from my balcony. Singapore was a joy to visit.

The lecture I presented to the congress, "Effect of Gamma Irradiation on Potato Quality," was well received. It was interesting to learn about food irradiation around the world for many other countries did not appear as hesitant to use this new tool as the United States was.

At the congress, special recognition was given to Dr. John Hawthorne, founder of the World Food Congress at the 1960 meetings in Glasgow, Scotland. He gave the Founders Memorial Lecture, entitled "The End of the Beginning International Union of Food Scientist, 1962—1987." Dr. Joe Hulse of Canada, who also participated in the original meetings in Scotland at which the World Food Congress was launched, gave the plenary lecture, "Human Resources and Technological Developments."

The food exhibits were especially informative; they depicted the latest foods and food processing methods in Singapore and neighboring Asian countries. The young women in charge of the exhibits were well informed and especially friendly to me; they offered to show me their lovely city and took me on a tour of the famous lion fountain and some government buildings.

Official tours included spectacular orchid gardens and special stores with beautiful gems and sculptures. The Congress banquet was elegant, with beautiful food service and outstanding entertainment by professional singers and dancers.

Following the Congress in Singapore, I joined a group of food technologists on a seventeen day tour of the People's Republic of China. Sponsored by the Institute of Food Technologists, the tour began after the Seventh World Congress of Food Science and Technology and was led by Dr. John R. Whitaker, Professor of Food Science at the University of California at Davis. The twenty-eight member Food Science and Technology Delegation gathered in Hong Kong on October 2. Many of us had already become acquainted in Singapore and were pleased to have the opportunity to explore China together. Hong Kong is a city of great diversity—skyscrapers and lush hills meet the sea, and high-density high rises have magnificent harbor views as backdrops. After spending the night there, we departed for the People's Republic of China.

The tour included visits to Chinese universities, research institutes, and food processing facilities in several major cities. These professional visits allowed us to have personal contact with students and food researchers, resulting in effective exchange of information between scientists from the east and west. When the busy schedule permitted, we saw some of the magnificent tourist attractions of China, including the Great Wall, the Forbidden City, and the Ming Tombs. Our first destination was Xi'an, which served as capital for eleven dynasties, spanning more than eleven hundred years. Xi'an's main attraction is its magnificent collection of terra cotta warriors sculpted in the second century to guard the tomb of Emperor Qin Shihuang. The 7,000 life-sized warriors were accompanied by 600 clay horses and 100 chariots. We also visited the seven-story Big Goose Pagoda and the Hua Qing Hot Springs, once a favorite resort for Xi'an's emperors.

As memorable as Xi'an's archaeological treasures were, the people made the city special for me. I clearly remember the children in their brightly colored clothing, as well as the many cyclists and friendly street vendors.

On October 5, the delegation arrived in Beijing, the capital of People's Republic of China, where we visited Beijing Agricultural University. Members of the newly established food science department told us of their strong interest in the processing and storage of fruits and vegetables.

China's various research institutes specialize in different areas. Whereas one institute concentrates on the analysis of pesticide residues on agricultural products, another focuses on the application of irradiation to fruit and vegetable processing.

The campus of Beijing Agricultural University was especially attractive at the time of our visit, filled with flowers in honor of the October Revolution. Bouquets surrounded the university's imposing statue of Chairman Mao Zedong.

Our third full day in Beijing was devoted to two technical visits. As members of the delegation, we were guided to the Food and Fermentation Industry's Scientific Research Institute. Again presentations by members of the delegation followed. During the two-day period afterwards, we visited the Beijing Institute of Microbiology, the Forbidden City, the Ming Tombs, and the Great Wall. The Forbidden City, where twenty-four emporers resided and ruled China for five centuries, was breathtaking. Also built on an enormous scale was the 100-acre square in the center of Beijing, the site of Chairman Mao Zedong Memorial Hall. This houses Mao's crystal coffin, the Great Hall of the People, and numerous museums and monuments. On the way to the Great Wall we stopped at the Ming Tombs on the outskirts of Beijing.

Seeing the Great Wall was a high point of our trip. The restored section north of Beijing is a small part of the 4,000 mile-long structure which was begun in the 5th century B.C. and completed in 221 B.C. Climbing the wall was as memorable as catching my first glimpse of it winding along the mountain tops in the distance. The Great Wall and the unsurpassed vistas of autumn forests from the Wall's towers were not only places to observe and enjoy but also places which inspired reflection.

Nanjing, which served as China's capital several times in the past, lies on the Yangtze River. Arriving on October 9, we saw the famous Chang Jiang Bridge which spans this wide river. The next morning we were off to Nanjing Agricultural University. Following an informative video that provided essential facts about the university, we were given a tour of the campus. The university's impressive library contains 600,100 volumes, including 1,000 Chinese and 263 foreign journals. The food department, most of which was established in 1985, has divisions of meat, poultry, milk, and seafood technology. The primary concern of the food chemistry laboratory is fruit and vegetable storage.

On the morning of October 11, we departed for Wuxi. Our pleasant three-hour train ride through the countryside from Nanjing was followed by a cruise on beautiful Lake Taihu. The next morning we visited the Wuxi Institute of Light Industry, a growing, modern campus situated on the hillsides of the city. The two sessions that followed included presentations by the delegates. Simultaneous interpretations for the 250-plus audience were handled by able interpreters.

After lunch we visited the Fresh Water Fisheries Research Center of the Chinese Academy of Fishing Sciences. While sipping hot green tea, we learned that this international center has three functions: research, training, and the distribution of information. Upon our return to the Wuxi Institute of Light Industry, Professor Wang treated the group to a guided tour of the campus. The tour included visits to the three largest departments: food science and food engineering, cereal chemistry, and fermentation.

One laboratory used high-performance liquid chromatography to study polyphenols in wine and chlorogenic acid, a metabolite common in plants which I had studied extensively in potatoes. Another laboratory used spectrophotometric equipment to investigate flavonone antioxidants found in Chinese green tea.

We later joined our hosts at a lavish banquet hosted by Professor Ding at the Gong De Lin Restaurant. The extensive menu included local fish, scallops, shrimp, crab, eel, Wuxi spareribs, assorted vegetables, dumplings, straw mushrooms, duck, chicken, pineapple, apples, and soup. Professor Ding proposed a toast to friendship and health. In response Dr. Whitaker thanked the hosts for their hospitality. Dr. Richard L. Hall, President of IUFoST, joined him in thanking the institute on behalf of the delegation.

On October 13, after another comfortable train ride through rural and industrial regions, we reached Shanghai, a city of eleven million at the mouth of the Yellow River. Breakfast in the ballroom of the Shanghai Sheraton Hotel started the day of technical visits. At the Shanghai Research Institute of Industrial Microbiology, we were warmly received by Dr. Liu Jie-fu, council chairman of the Shanghai Society of Food Science. Two simultaneous sessions followed. One session consisted of my lecture along with lectures by Dr. Freda M. Rubin, Dr. Ramunas Bigelis, Dr. Othmar O. Silberstein, Dr. Edward Mendez, and Dr. John Whitaker.

After lunch, we were escorted to the Children's Food Factory in Shanghai. The tour included a close-up look at the packaging of baby cereal foods. The manufacturing operation, equipped with Swiss machinery, was donated to China by UNICEF. Our next stop was the Shanghai Gourmet Powder Factory which has 1,000 workers and manufactures lysine, alanine, asparagine, flavor nucleotides, soya sauce, and condensed soups.

On our final morning in Shanghai, we began a day of tours with a drive along the Bund—the main thoroughfare along the Yellow River—and a visit to the Jade Temple, a Buddhist shrine with an awe-inspiring white jade seated Buddha. While there we witnessed a funeral ceremony in progress;

the temple was filled with incense and the sounds of the monk's drumbeats. Afterward the delegation toured the old city and its square. As always I especially enjoyed seeing the throngs of schoolchildren in their colorful uniforms. We spent the evening enjoying a Shanghai acrobatic troupe performance.

From Shanghai we traveled to Guangzhou, also known as Canton, a major city on the Pearl River. Guangzhou reminded us of Hong Kong with its fast pace, heavy traffic, noise, and urban sprawl. Since our technical program there was cancelled due to unforeseen circumstances, the delegation spent its time touring the busy metropolis.

October 17 began with a visit to a huge goat monument overlooking Guangzhou, "The City of Goats," a tour of a lovely orchid garden, and a stop at the palatial White Swan Hotel on the Pearl River. Our ten-course evening meal was sumptuous—a fitting finale to our China tour. The most memorable dishes were the roast suckling pig, the delicious soup served in the hollowed half of a watermelon, and the cake and sweet agar dessert.

An air-conditioned train awaited us at the station the next day. After passing through passport control, we took our seats and watched the fertile countryside roll by. We saw vast fields, water buffalo, fish ponds, and field workers, and were able to discern many of the major crops of South China: rice, cassava, papaya, taro, lotus, sugar cane, tangerines, bananas, hemp, ginger, and loofah. Finally we reentered Hong Kong.

On October 19, the food technology group left for the Chinese University of Hong Kong, where the Department of Biology had arranged a Symposium of Food Science and Technology. Professor Chang welcomed the delegation and described the four-year university and its 6,000 students.

The symposium consisted of four lectures by members of the delegation and two by university faculty members. After the symposium, we had lunch at the Royal Hong Kong Jockey Club hosted by Mr. Eddy Lee, president of the Lee Kum Lee Food Company. The gourmet meal consisted of fifteen courses.

Our tour concluded that night with a festive thirteen-course banquet at the Royal Garden Hotel. The food and service were impeccable. All the members of the delegations were deeply grateful for Dr. Whitaker's leadership and appreciated the friendships made during the adventure. The historic tour was something each of us would long remember.

Although I had traveled extensively in 1987, I wasn't ready to relax. An invitation to the Philippines helped me decide that a visit to these famous islands would be a fine conclusion to the year's travels.

Although I was excited about the opportunity to take this final trip, the timing made my friends from the U.S. delegation concerned about my safety. At the time there was much unrest in the Philippines. Tanks were rolling through the city of Manila, and the national scene was particularly violent. I weighed the pros and cons of the trip extensively.

Throughout my travels, I had found myself in many dangerous situations. In this instance, I had to make a decision whether or not to willingly put myself in danger. I had already purchased my ticket and arrangements had been made for my arrival, so I decided to make the trip. I remembered my motto! *You never fail until you stop trying.*

My friend, Mrs. Paredes, greeted me at the airport. Although there was military activity in close proximity to us, I never felt personally threatened or frightened. She took me to the university campus at Quezon City because I had been invited by Professor Sonia DeLeon, Director Food Development Systems, to lecture on food irradiation. Following my lecture, the faculty invited me to dinner.

The next day, Mrs. Paredes and I visited the International Rice Institute in Los Banos and she introduced me to Dr. Corazon Barbo, a professor of food and nutrition at the University at Los Banos. I had heard many good things about this particular campus and received an excellent tour. This confirmed my opinion that the institute was a top-quality research facility.

Much of what I was able to accomplish in the Philippines was due to the gracious hospitality of my hostess, Mrs. Paredes, who lived in Quezon City and provided needed transportation.

One of Mrs. Paredes' daughters was a special reporter for Mrs. Corazon Aquino, who, at the time, was president of the Philippines. Another of her daughters, Dulci, had been a student at Cornell University and had frequently visited in my home.

Everywhere I went, people showed warm friendship toward Americans and Cornellians. Many were familiar with Cornell's role in their agriculture program, for several Cornell faculty had spent time in the Philippines helping with projects in food science and agriculture in Los Banos. I met many Cornell alumni during this trip. When I met the dean of the Human Ecology Institute at the University of the Philippines at Los Banos, I learned that she was planning a visit to Cornell. It was gratifying to see Cornell held in high regard in the Philippines.

One thing that was particularly characteristic of the Philippines was the oppressive heat. Most of the hotel rooms and automobiles were air conditioned, or I might not have survived the trip. I did contract a viral infection that lasted for weeks after my return to the United States

My tight schedule limited my free time during the trip, but I did manage to get in some shopping. The local fruits and foods held my attention; I was escorted to different fruit markets by Professor DeLeon as well as to nice restaurants where I tried the wonderful island foods. I was able to purchase dolls, angels, and wooden birds that often remind me of the wonderful time I spent in the Philippines. The country is renowned for its lovely embroidery and elaborate handicrafts, and I bought several beautiful blouses.

I shall never forget the warm hospitality of the Filipino people and the gorgeous sunsets I witnessed on the island. When I returned to the United

States, the vice president of the Philippines was on my same flight, and we exchanged ideas concerning the political role of the United States in the Philippines.

I returned to Cornell in late October, exhausted but happy that I had been privileged to visit so many interesting places during 1987. International travel can be exhausting but stimulating. I felt much better educated after visiting so many interesting people in such a variety of countries.

TEACHING RESEARCHERS IN INDONESIA
GADJAH MADA UNIVERSITY: 1989

In 1989, I was invited to Gadjah Mada University in Yogyakarta, Indonesia, to assist in an effort to develop an area of study in food science. Since the potato is not a common food in Indonesia, I considered my role to be that of a general food scientist. I made recommendations to the Indonesian scholars that would strengthen their academic efforts in research.

Indonesia is the largest archipelago in the world. It consists of five main islands and thirty smaller archipelagoes, totaling 13,667 islands. It forms a crossroad between the Pacific and Indian oceans and a bridge between two continents, Asia and Australia. Indonesia's land area is continuously replenished by volcanic eruptions like those on the island of Java. There are between one hundred and fifty and two hundred and fifty languages and dialects spoken and written in Indonesia. The national language, however, is called Bahasa Indonesia. Its structure is mainly based on the Malay language but is enriched by Indonesia's lexicon of multi-local languages.

For my month-long stay in Indonesia I was selected to serve as a visiting professor at Gadjah Mada University in Yogyakarta. I felt honored to have been chosen for Gadjah Mada, for it is among the oldest and most prestigious universities in the country. Most Indonesian universities are new, having been organized following the country's independence on August 17, 1945 in the days following Japan's surrender at the end of World War II. Although universities are relatively new to Indonesia, education is taken very seriously, and efforts are being made to strengthen the nation's academic standing.

I arrived in Indonesia in time for their Independence Day celebration which began August 17. Red and white Indonesian flags were displayed throughout the countryside, and the celebration continued for a week, during which time there were many exhibits of machinery and food. It was a pleasure to witness the people's pride in their country.

The food in Indonesia was quite good, and I was able to photograph several particularly interesting dishes. Also I made a point of conversing with individuals at the local food stands. Indonesians were very open and friendly, quite different from the people of Nigeria who were suspicious and cold unless I was accompanied by a Nigerian escort. Indonesian children often followed me during my visits to the markets. They especially liked to pose for my photographs.

When I arrived at Gadjah Mada, I found a relatively new food science building which was beginning to be furnished with modern chemistry equipment. Dr. V. Wahyuni welcomed me to the university, and Dr. Slamet Sudarmadji, director of the Inter University Center (IUC) and the Food and Nutrition Development and Research Center (FANDARC), discussed the activities I was to carry out while at IUC. Their determination to achieve academic recognition was impressive.

One of my assignments at Gadjah Mada was to give direction to the university's food science research program. I assisted them in their research efforts and encouraged them to publish their results. In addition I helped to oversee plans for the new laboratories, making certain that they obtained the necessary modern equipment. I assisted faculty in developing and improving their research techniques.

Another assignment was to deliver a special lecture in September during Seminar Week which was a special annual event at Gadjah Mada University. Students and faculty from other Indonesian universities participated, and a variety of topics were selected. For my special lecture, I chose the title, "Food, Chemistry, and You," which can easily be adapted to a wide range of audiences. My lecture was delivered in the large, air-conditioned lecture hall on campus. I showed how chemistry is used in food science and how important it is to teaching and research in the area. All went well, and I enjoyed answering questions following the lecture. The lecture room was decorated with beautiful orchids, flowers that are native to the island.

I also taught two-week courses in food chemistry which were offered to students who had made the trip to Gadjah Mada from their homes on other islands. September was a time when students from all parts of Indonesia congregated at Gadjah Mada to acquire new information. Teaching these students was pleasant; for they were bright, friendly, and eager to learn. English was difficult for most Indonesians, and it sometimes was difficult for me to understand them. Fortunately, I had the assistance of an interpreter in case a problem arose. Despite the language barrier, both the students and faculty often visited my office. My numerous international experiences had helped me understand even the most broken English. I enjoyed especially the visits from fellow professors with whom I had stimulating conversations concerning their research. We also discussed the importance of higher education to their nation's future. All were friendly and took a keen interest in what I had to contribute.

I was well cared for—even pampered—throughout my stay in Indonesia. A government representative had met me on August 15 upon my arrival at the Jakarta airport and drove me to Hotel Kemang Jakarta where I spent the night before continuing my journey to Yogyakarta the next day. While in Jakarta, I was given a thorough orientation program regarding my role as visiting scholar. Dr. Chester Tsai, Sue Dechow, and Dr. Avanella Kirksey informed me of the arrangements that had been made for my visit and related the historical background and needs of the project. Following the orientation, I flew via Garuda Airlines to Yogyakarta, the home of Gadjah Mada University.

I was assigned a lovely, air-conditioned guesthouse and provided with a modern van and two drivers to escort me wherever I needed to go. The first driver would appear at the guesthouse at 7:00 A.M. and remain at my command until 2:00 P.M. The second driver arrived at 2:00 P.M. and remained until 9:00 P.M. At first the arrangement seemed strange, but it proved very useful for my busy schedule. Without this ready source of transportation, I could not have accomplished my goals. Frequently I transported books between the guesthouse and my office at the university.

Both drivers were very polite and insisted on carrying my briefcase and opening all doors for me. With so much attention, I felt like royalty. One of the drivers had worked for the Rockefeller Foundation in previous years and was fluent in English. He was so knowledgeable concerning his country that I began to rely on him as an information resource. However, the other driver was shy and did not speak nor understand English very well. As a result, confusion sometimes arose. On one occasion, I asked him to drive me to the house to pick up a book that I needed. I asked him to wait for me while I went in to get the book. When I returned, he and the van had disappeared. He did not understand and assumed that I had dismissed him for the day. Following this incident, I was especially cautious with him, providing careful instructions and making sure he understood what I wanted. Sometimes it was necessary to enlist the help of the first driver to relay messages to the second driver.

Since I was being transported so well, I felt that I was not getting the proper exercise, and one afternoon I decided to walk from the guesthouse to the campus store. I knew the campus store was a short distance away, and I thought that I could make it easily. This decision proved to be overly optimistic. The streets in that particular area fan out in complicated patterns. I reached the campus store without any problem, but on the return trip to the guesthouse I got lost.

I knew that I was relatively close to the guesthouse, but none of the landmarks were familiar. Nightfall was only a short time off, and I became worried for my safety. Also the temperature was quite high, and I never tolerated hot weather very well.

As I wandered around trying to find the streets that would lead to the guesthouse darkness settled in, and two young men on a motor scooter approached me and offered their assistance. Aware that I might suspect them of having ill intentions, they produced their professional cards which led me to believe I could trust them. They were kind, helpful young men and after a few minutes of discussion, we agreed that the best way for me to return to the guest house was for one of them to dismount the motor scooter and allow me to get on the back seat. That was the first time in my life I had ridden on the back of a motorcycle. Thanks to the two young men the day turned out well. Afterward I became more cautious about doing things on my own.

Although both the van and the guesthouse were air-conditioned, my office at the university was not. Fortunately the building was built in such a way that it picked up the breezes. With the windows open, the office was bearable. The classrooms, however, were not air-conditioned and were often very hot. Having come prepared for the heat based on my previous journeys to Africa, I survived. I had prepared for high temperatures and had brought cotton clothing. Because I had a driver at my disposal, I could make brief trips from the university to the guesthouse for a shower and a change into fresh clothes. Since the drivers were always on call, such trips were entirely appropriate.

The faculty at Gadjah Mada was very proud of their new facilities and was attempting to conduct meaningful research. I was impressed with the facilities and equipment available at the Food and Nutrition Research Center as well as in the physics and chemistry departments. However, when I visited the library, I experienced a shock. The library was new and quite large, but it was lacking in journals and books. It was particularly deficient in science journals. I found a few very old issues of *Science*. To my surprise I found that among the few books it had acquired, the library contained two copies of my own book, *Experimental Food Chemistry*. The discovery was quite pleasant, for apparently their familiarity with my book was one reason they had invited me to come to Gadjah Mada.

I often spoke with Mary Astuti, a faculty member in food and nutrition with whom I became a close friend. She had been especially impressed with the experiments I had described in my book. We had many interesting discussions about food science. Many other faculty members approached me as well, asking questions about my research publications.

When I returned to the States, I thought that the greatest contribution I could make to the faculty who had made my stay at Gadjah Mada so enjoyable would be to send them recent copies of *Science* and other journals for their library. Shipping the journals was expensive, but I felt it was worthwhile, and the faculty expressed their appreciation to me for this effort.

Little emphasis had been placed on the publication of research at Gadjah Mada. When I inquired of different professors as to what was considered appropriate for advancement in rank, I was told that advancement came almost solely as a result of seniority, not publications. If one stayed in the same position long enough, he or she would be promoted. A problem with this system was that it failed to reward achievement and discouraged professors from engaging in ambitious research projects. In fact a scholar who has earned a doctoral degree in the United States might actually be lower in rank and salary than someone who had remained at home and had not pursued further study.

During my stay in Indonesia, I presented faculty seminars in addition to presenting the main lecture during Seminar Week. I also visited cottage industries where I saw the preparation of tempeh, tofu, and soy sauce—all soy bean products. The natives refer to soy sauce as ketchup. I worked long hours, staying at my office until five or six in the afternoon, then retiring to my room where I worked some more. The office was equipped with a computer, but I found it difficult to use and instead chose to use the typewriter provided for the reports and recommendations I generated for the university and its food science program. I also worked on Saturdays, often in the morning. Sundays were free, and I spent time exploring notable locations throughout the country.

The arrangement with the university allowed me access to the van and one of the two drivers. I compensated him for his time and paid for the fuel. With my driver, and the company of friends from the university, I visited a number of interesting sites, including a beautiful palace, and attended one of Indonesia's famous puppet shows. The puppet show was delightful and the musicians played exotic instruments.

Dr. Slamet Sudarmadji, the chair of the food science department, was aware that I was interested in learning more about Indonesian history and culture and recommended a number of interesting places to see. One Sunday he and his family accompanied me to a number of their favorite historic locations.

Perhaps my favorite weekend excursions were the ones to the great stone temples of the Indonesian island of Java. The mountains and plains of central and eastern Java abound with the remains of temples dating roughly from the eighth to fifteenth centuries. Together they tell the story of the rise and decline of Java's Hindu and Buddhist civilizations. Generally, the central Javanese monuments, most of which were built between 750 and 950 A.D., predate those in the eastern part of the islands. The temples of central Java were the work of master builders who drew their inspiration from Indian architectural models. The principles upon which they are built are reportedly older than either Hinduism or Buddhism and are connected to the belief that humans are influenced by subtle astrological forces.

The Javanese temples were earthly replicas of the spiritual mansions where gods and spirits would be inclined to congregate and hopefully mingle with humans. Temples also sometimes functioned as shrines for departed leaders. Two famous monuments near Yogyakarta are Prambanan and Borobudur. Scholars are uncertain as to who built the Temple of Prambanan.

According to legend, however, it was constructed by the warrior, Prince Brandring, in exchange for the hand in marriage of Loro, a beautiful young woman.

Prambanan consists of a series of peaks, which represent mountains in miniature. Its inner courtyard is dominated by giant temples. A unique event in Yogyakarta is the performance of the Ramayana Ballet at the Prambanan Theatre, using the temple as a backdrop. The ballet, which involves more than one hundred dancers, is staged on four consecutive nights around the full moon during the dry season between May and October.

The principal Buddhist monument in Java is Borobudur which many consider one of the great architectural wonders of the world. It measures 369 feet on each side and stands 126 feet high. Built around an artificial hill, the temple takes the form of a square stepped pyramid consisting of fine walled terraces and crowned by a large bell-shaped stupa. It contains 504 statues of the Buddha and more than 2,500 carved relief panels.

Borobudur can be seen as a representation of the Buddhist journey to enlightenment. Pilgrims to the temple re-enact the Buddha's spiritual path by circling the terraces, gradually ascending to higher levels until they reach the central stupa which symbolizes Nirvana, or the ultimate truth. Whether or not one is a Buddhist, after emerging from the enclosed terraces a feeling of liberation is quite noticeable. I discovered this during my own journey to the top of the steps. It was a difficult climb for me, and my fair skin became sunburned as I ascended. However, the magnificent mountain scenery more than made up for my temporary discomfort, for I could see the mountain peaks of Sumbing, Sindoro, and Merbabu to the north, and the smoking summit of Merapi on the eastern horizon.

Before leaving for Indonesia, I bought a book detailing Indonesian customs in order to prepare to live there for a month. I have always considered it important when traveling to observe the norms of indigenous cultures and to appreciate their customs. The native people seemed pleased with my efforts to understand them because so many international travelers do not make the effort.

One of the Indonesian customs I learned was that it was impolite to eat with one's left hand. This presented me with a problem, since I am left-handed. When the chair of food science at Gadjah Mada invited me to a wedding reception—itself quite an honor—I was very careful not to eat with my left hand for fear of offending the other guests. Eating with my right hand was awkward and I ended up not eating very much. Concerned, the chair asked if I was ill.

At that point, I had only recently arrived in Indonesia and did not feel comfortable telling him of my predicament. Later when I told him why I had eaten so little that night, he was amused and told me that the custom I had read about was in fact quite old and no longer strictly observed. No one would have been offended had I eaten with my left hand.

Because the island of Java is predominantly Moslem, despite its Hindu and Buddhist history, the rules of social conduct may have seemed restrictive to many Westerners. I was not bothered by them. Being a teetotaler, the stricture against alcohol consumption suited me well. I came to appreciate the order of the Moslem community in Java, and I never worried for my safety or the safety of my belongings even at night when I did most of my shopping. Of course, on these occasions, I had the added protection of a male driver who always watched my movements when I was away from the van.

I enjoyed my trips to the various shops and became familiar with a couple of the stores and the merchants who owned them. I was most intrigued by the clothing stores in which clothes were made on the spot for the customers. One simply purchased material and indicated what sort of garment one wanted made. A week later, the dress or blouse would be ready at a typically low cost. Compared to dressmaking in the United States, it was very reasonable.

I found the dresses to be attractive and well made and liked the materials used by the tailors, especially the lovely batik prints. It is generally agreed that the batik process originated in Indonesia, and I was pleased to have the chance to visit a factory where batik was being produced. I bought several pieces, and it was fascinating to observe the different methods the workers used. Some prints were completely hand-done, including the pattern, which was hand-crafted by an artist. Less expensive prints were done by stamping the fabric, a process similar to screen-printing.

I was sorry for the people who produced the batik because they worked in cramped, stuffy rooms filled with harmful fumes. The working conditions seemed very unhealthy. I do not believe Indonesia has any equivalent of our Environmental Protection Agency or OSHA to rectify such abuses.

While I was teaching in Yogyakarta, a young medical doctor, Dr. Gde Pinatih from Bali, took my course and seemed very interested in nutrition and food. His English was not perfect, but he often stopped by my office to chat. He inquired if I would be visiting Bali while I was in Indonesia. I said no, for I was very busy and only had Sundays free.

He invited me to come to Bali, where he lived with his family, to visit them for a long weekend. I decided to accept his invitation and had a wonderful time. Both he and his wife went all out to show me a good time. Bali, in contrast to Java, is largely Hindu, and I was fortunate to be there on one of their special holidays and witnessed some of their customs.

An interesting interaction occurred during my weekend with them. It concerned their young daughter, a darling child who had not seen many Caucasian women. The first time she saw me she cried and pulled away because she was afraid of me.

Soon, however, I learned that the little girl was very fond of chocolate, a rare and expensive treat in Indonesia, probably due to the hot climate. Since I had brought some chocolates with me, I decided to share some with her. I would sit at one end of the room and hold out a piece of chocolate, and the child would warily make her way over to me, grab the chocolate, and scurry back to her mother on the other side of the room. Soon she became more friendly. We became very good friends through chocolates.

At the conclusion of my stay in Indonesia, I traveled by plane to Jakarta where I again visited top officials and was entertained overnight before continuing my journey back to the States. I had hoped to visit the Agricultural University at Bogor, located near Jakarta, because many of my colleagues in food science had spent time there. Unfortunately I was unable to see the campus because on the day I was to visit, a riot erupted in Jakarta, and I was informed that it would not be safe for me to be out on the streets in that area. Not being able to visit Bogor was perhaps the single greatest disappointment in what was a very enjoyable stay in Indonesia. My visit to Indonesia was delightful, but my work at Cornell called me back to Ithaca. It was difficult to adjust from my life of freedom from "household chores" back to a lifestyle where I did everything for myself. I often think fondly of those days in Indonesia where I had efficient help, beautiful surroundings and very interesting friends.

Dr. Nell Mondy — Visiting Scholar, International University Center, Food Science and Technology, Gadijah Mada University, Yogyakarta, Indonesia, 1989. Dr. Mondy was the featured speaker at the seminar.

ADVENTURE ON PARADISE ISLAND: MAURITIUS
AFRICAN POTATO ASSOCIATION: 1990

In 1990 I received a fax from the Potato Association of Africa inviting me to speak at its Second Triennial International Meeting in Reduit, Mauritius. The meeting was also sponsored by the International Potato Institute in Lima, Peru.

At that time, I knew little about Mauritius, but I was intrigued by the request for two reasons. For quite some time I had been interested in the potato's development in tropical and subtropical regions, an interest that had been strengthened during my three-month assignment at the International Institute for Tropical Agriculture in Ibadan, Nigeria. Progressing through my career, I have become convinced that the potato is a food for the world, including the tropical countries where it had previously been difficult to grow crops due to the greater prevalence of disease.

A second reason that the Association's request captured my interest was that it had specified an appropriate topic for me to address concerning research which I had done a few years previously. The topic they had selected for me was "Nutritive Value in Relation to Potato Disorders." As it happened, I had recently published several papers on this topic and I was impressed that they were aware of my research interests and had tailored their offer to me accordingly. I returned a fax agreeing to go.

The president of the African Potato Association was a Mauritius citizen. For many years he had worked in the area of sugar cane research, but in recent years much of his research interests had been directed toward the potato; by this time the potato had caught on nicely in this island nation—particularly a variety called *spoonta*, a potato that looks and tastes very much like U.S. grown potatoes. The International Potato Institute developed this variety, among others, for farmers in tropical climates.

Many Mauritian farmers grow potatoes between the rows of sugar cane,

Mauritius' largest cash crop. Rather than let the cane grow to its full height, a process that typically takes years, farmers wait only until the stalks overshadow the potatoes before harvesting potatoes.

Because of the potato's success in Mauritius, many there hope that through increased efforts they will be able to produce a surplus that could be exported to neighboring countries. My visit to this tiny country in the middle of the Indian Ocean became a visit to paradise.

As pleased as I was about the research aspects of my visit, I had no idea that I had been invited to paradise. My first clue came when I was still in Ithaca. Two of my graduate students from India informed me of the island's natural beauty, and they were so enthusiastic in their description that I became a bit suspicious. Nothing can be that wonderful, I thought. But before the plane even landed, I saw that my students had not exaggerated.

A volcanic island with white, red, blue, and blue-black soil, Mauritius consists of approximately 1865 square kilometers, with 160 kilometers of coastline almost entirely surrounded by coral reefs and impressive mountains. As the Mauritius Airlines jet descended toward the airport at one end of the island, I was taken aback by the sight below. The island looked like a rich green carpet with its lush fields of sugar cane surrounded by a rim of white beaches and the wide blue expanse of the Indian Ocean.

Bounded by Africa, India, and Australia, Mauritius lies near Madagascar, halfway between Nairobi, Kenya, and Johannesburg, South Africa. Known to the Arabs in antiquity, the island was visited by the Portuguese and colonized by the Dutch, the French, and finally the British before winning its independence in 1968. With no well-defined rainy or dry seasons, Mauritius maintains a green cover of vegetation throughout the year with mid-day temperatures averaging a comfortable 67 degrees Fahrenheit.

My flight into Mauritius carried several other scholars as well, most of them from England and the Netherlands. Our hosts for the conference met us at the airport, took our passports, and quickly cleared us through customs—our first indication of the lengths to which the African Potato Association would go to make our stay enjoyable. After our long twelve-hour flight from London, stopping only briefly in Geneva, Switzerland, we were exhausted and it was a relief to be taken care of by our hosts.

After quickly finishing our business at the airport, we boarded a special van that had been provided by the Association and were driven to Villa Caroline, a little village on the other side of the island. Although I was tired, I found the trip exciting as we sped past the vast fields of sugar cane and wound our way through the tiny island's villages.

One thing I noticed in particular was the field equipment used for irrigation. The potatoes were typically grown side-by-side with the sugar cane, and I was somewhat surprised to see the local farmers irrigating these fields in a Western manner with sophisticated equipment.

As we drove along, I became more interested in this small island about-which I knew little. My curiosity was satisfied through many first-hand experiences there. I learned that Mauritius contains slightly over one million residents, most of them Endo-mauritians, Creoles (people of mixed European and African origin), and Sino-mauritians. Since its independence in March 1968, Mauritius has been a sovereign state within the British Commonwealth governed by a prime minister and cabinet.

The island features virgin beaches embraced by coral reefs, translucent sea lagoons, wonderful landscapes, sophisticated cuisine, charming cosmopolitan people, and civilized politics. Within its 720 square miles are more than 1000 miles of good roads lined with bougainvillea and palm trees. During my visit there, I saw violet moonscaped mountains; deep craters; wild gorges; thick forests; tumbling streams; twisting rivers; waterfalls; rainbows; and villages hidden in the lush, coastal vegetation. Flowers and trees grew out of the red earth in a variety of colors amid the golden mantle of sugar cane. No wonder Mark Twain was moved to exclaim that "God modeled heaven on Mauritius."

Our accommodations at the Villa Caroline were lovely. I was housed on the second floor of a two-story cabin on a gorgeous sandy beach. My balcony commanded a full view of the ocean, and because it faced the west, I was treated every night to a spectacular sunset. It was lovely riding back to the Villa from the conference hall in the late afternoon with the sun descending over the ocean.

I quickly made a point of interacting with the Mauritian people who were unique in their diversity. With their soft features, infectious smiles, and disarming personalities, they made Mauritius more than just another exotic island in the sun; it is a nation shaped by the richness of Asia, Europe, and Africa, yet free and fully independent. While preserving their original cultures they live, work, and play together, achieving a unity in diversity which offers the rest of us an inspiring vision of tomorrow's world.

In keeping with the nation's multicultural flavor, the shop signs are typically listed in French, English, and Chinese. Television and radio programs are broadcast in a dozen languages, and there are more than thirty newspapers and magazines for a population with one of the highest literacy rates in the world. They celebrate almost every festival under the sun, from Christmas to the Hindu Diwali to the Chinese New Year. The spectrum of colors, customs, creeds, and languages stimulate the senses and the soul.

Heirs to the culinary secrets of three continents, the Mauritians can turn out a feast of international foods calculated to revive the most jaded palates—Indian and Creole curry, French peppered steaks, English roast beef, and a host of Chinese and Moslem delicacies. Excellent seafood is commonplace, including lobsters, freshly harvested oysters, shrimp, and crayfish. Venison, hare, and wild boar are also available, along with vegetables such as boiled watercress. The island also contains an abundance of sweet pineapples, papayas, mangos, peaches, guavas, jack fruits, watermelon, avocados, custard apples, and bananas. Indeed one can survive happily on the luscious fruits of the fertile volcanic soil.

Our meetings were held at the Mauritius Sugar Industry Research Institute located in Reduit, not far from the university. The conference itself was quite an event and was attended by the island's prime minister, among other local dignitaries. Delegates from twenty-six nations attended the meetings, and I was pleased to be one of the two Americans invited to speak. Of all the conference participants, I was most interested in the African delegates who had only recently begun growing potatoes. All excitedly reported on how well the crop was doing in their respective countries. The Kenyan delegates seemed particularly eager to share the success story of potatoes in their country.

I was also impressed with the meals that we were served, all in an outdoor setting among the lush Mauritian countryside. Breakfast consisted of coconut yogurt, tropical fruit, and "bacon and eggs"—a combination that did not at all resemble an American's idea of bacon but was delicious nevertheless. Special potato cakes and other delicious dishes were also prepared from locally grown potatoes.

Before I had gone to Mauritius, I had heard of the country's reputation for rare and beautiful stamps. I wanted to collect a few, but unfortunately I was unable to locate a post office. Luckily one of our hosts heard of my interest and offered his help. I was driven to a quaint post office, where I was permitted to sample from an extensive catalog of lovely stamps featuring native flowers, butterflies, and wildlife. A few depicted the sugar cane fields, and I wondered if someday they might also feature the potato as is already done in Peru.

I had brought with me several pictures of Cornell. The people were particularly impressed with the photographs of Ithaca's snowfall. Several students expressed their interest in Cornell University and I was pleased to discuss it with them, hoping Cornell might soon welcome a few Mauritian students.

By the time the conference ended, I wanted to stay in this paradise island. In fact the Mauritian government had extended the invitation for another week in order to fully take advantage of what the island had to offer. I would like to have accepted but knew that it was impossible. In the height of the tourist season I couldn't change my airline reservations. Consequently I declined, a decision I have since regretted.

The only negative aspect of my Mauritius experience was the departure. The flight was delayed, then delayed again, and shortly after take-off, we were informed that the plane had developed engine trouble and would be forced to return to Mauritius. Due to these delays, I missed my connections and the long hours and spending long hours at Heathrow Airport was very discouraging. I was informed that my luggage had been lost and rescheduling a connecting flight would take awhile. I was stranded. Finally I departed for New York without my luggage which was finally sent to me several days later. Upon arrival I was taken to a hotel to await my rescheduled flight to Ithaca. However, despite the problems with my return flight, I will never forget my wonderful experience in paradise.

Dr. Mondy in Potato Research Lab with students and faculty.
Dr. Mondy was one of two from U.S. invited to lecture at the Triennial African Potato Association Congress. Redait, Mauritius, 1990

POTATOES DOWN UNDER

AUSTRALIA, NEW ZEALAND: 1991

I embarked on my long overdue fourth sabbatic in February of 1991. For years I had postponed my leave because my various commitments at Cornell placed enormous demands on my time. At last I found the time to go, and I made plans to visit universities and fellow potato researchers in both Australia and New Zealand.

When I arrived in Melbourne, Australia, I was greeted by my friends, Mr. and Mrs. Bryan Burrell, and their young son, William. I first met the Burrells at the Treetops lodge in Kenya, and the three of us formed an immediate friendship; we even traveled together on a safari to Samburu, Kenya. The Burrells were younger than I but they were great companions. Before we returned to our separate parts of the world, we agreed to visit one another in the future.

I was doubly pleased to see the Burrells again because this was my first trip to Australia and on my travels abroad one of the greatest pleasures is visits with friends. Upon my arrival, I was too exhausted from the travel to talk, but they understood this. They showed me to a guest bedroom, where I changed my clothing, put on my satin cap to maintain my hairdo, and fell asleep immediately.

Knowing that I was likely to sleep for some time, the Burrells left to fulfill another engagement. In the meantime, Bryan's brother and his family came to visit, not realizing that I was asleep in bed. Their young son tiptoed into my bedroom, then quickly went out again, stating that someone in bed "looks like a nanny wearing a bonnet." Thus my Australian nickname became "the nanny with a bonnet."

I stayed in Melbourne for a few days, visiting its beautiful botanical gardens, the food research laboratories, and food departments at the

University of Melbourne and the Royal Melbourne Institute of Technology. Next I took a scenic bus trip to the city of Adelaide where I met my friend, Margaret Ewing. Margaret was a wonderful hostess who threw parties for me and toured me all around Adelaide. She took me to Mount Lofty, which rises 711 meters above sea level, and to the Cleland Conservation Park. There I hand-fed kangaroos and parrots, hugged a koala, saw ostriches and wallabies, and photographed joeys nestled in their kangaroo mothers' pouches.

I had learned that Australia is famous for its high quality opals, and since the opal is my birthstone, I asked Margaret to help me shop for one. We spent many hours searching through various elegant stores before I finally purchased a lovely blue opal which I cherish.

Margaret notified local potato researchers and growers that I would be coming, and they arranged a trip for me to the Lenswood Horticulture Center where I discussed the growing practices and problems regarding the mineral composition of soils which are high in boron. Next we went to a large potato farm where we observed the mechanical harvesting of potatoes. I found it similar to the procedures used on the large potato farms in the United States. I was also pleased to meet some individual potato growers on small farms. One that I remember in particular was Mrs. Jane Bourne. I looked over her potato crop and had an illuminating conversation about her cultivation practices. She even invited us to have lunch on her farm.

From Adelaide I moved on to Canberra, the capital of Australia. I decided to travel via bus and on the way met an elderly shepherd who had emigrated from England many years before. He had become very successful in raising sheep and later diversified into fruit farming. Like most of the Australians I met, he was very friendly and regarded Americans as friends.

In Canberra I visited the capitol building and was invited to take a seat in the observation section where I witnessed the legislature in a raucous session. A stern-looking man wearing a George Washington-style white wig, the chairman, attempted to keep order by stopping legislators from shouting at each other. At every outburst, he would pound his gavel and say, "Order, *please*! Order, *please*!" Despite the session's theatrical aspect, I understood much of what was being said. I enjoyed seeing this special different form of government.

My next stop was Sydney, the beautiful port city in New South Wales with its famous opera house and elegant shopping district. Over the course of several days, I toured the opera house, visited the Old Town, sailed on boat trips, shopped, and did the usual sightseeing activities. In the Queen Victoria Building, a stately structure with inlaid marble floors, I took pictures of a lovely fashion show held on the first floor. From my vantage point on a third-floor balcony I could observe very well. I also attended a few seminars at a woman's conference that was being held in Sydney at the time.

Following my stay in Sydney, I flew to Auckland, New Zealand. I had been invited to New Zealand by Dr. Peter Meredith, ("Mr. Potato"), a famous potato researcher. I had been invited to lecture to the New Zealand Institute of Food Technologists at the University of Canterbury in Christ Church. Peter had alerted the potato researchers in Auckland about my visit and they met my flight.

My plane landed in Auckland in the late afternoon. Because Dr. Meredith lived in Christchurch, which is some distance from Auckland, he and his wife could not meet me at the airport. I had resigned myself to finding transportation on my own. However, Dr. Meredith was a step ahead of me. He had alerted a group of potato processors from ETA, a large potato processing company, of my arrival time, and they were at the airport to welcome me. It was a pleasant surprise, and the gentlemen took me to my hotel in the heart of the city located near the University of Auckland. I had received an invitation to consult for ETA's main processing plant in Palmerston North. The Auckland processors supplied me with enough potato chips (or crisps) produced by their company to last for most of my stay in New Zealand. The crisps were thicker than American chips and were delicious.

The researchers suggested various points of interest in Auckland for me to visit. These included Kelly Tarlton's Underwater World which featured a glass tunnel extending along a stretch of the ocean floor with a magical view of many types of fish overhead. While in Auckland, I took a Harbor Cruise, toured the Auckland War Memorial Museum, saw Waitomo Cave with its Glowworm Grotto, and visited a preserve for the indigenous kiwi bird. The kiwi is a wingless fowl roughly the size of a chicken and lives in hollow tree trunks or holes in the ground. Some New Zealanders refer to themselves as Kiwis.

From Auckland I took a day trip to Rotorura, a city in the middle of a thermal region. There I encountered the Maori people, descendants of New Zealand's first settlers. I viewed cemeteries filled with aboveground tombs; the thermal activity prevents underground burial. They reminded me of the cemeteries in New Orleans, Louisiana, where tombs are above ground. Many Cornellians know about Rotorura because one of Cornell's former presidents, Dr. Frank Rhodes, a geologist, frequently leads tours of the city's geysers and thermal sites. The geysers were interesting: The Prince of Wales Feathers Geyser had twenty-foot bursts of water, and the Pohutu Geyser had eruptions rising sixty feet.

I also toured a kiwi fruit plantation. Flying over the plantation earlier, I had been puzzled by its appearance from the air. It looked like a green carpet with symmetrical rectangular designs. Upon landing I realized that the rectangular patterns were rows of trellises that held the kiwi plant. Like the African yam, the kiwi grows on vines, and the pickers walk under the trellises to harvest the fruit. The kiwi fruit has a tart taste and is rich in ascorbic acid; I prefer to let the fruit ripen until it's sweet. To this day, whenever I see kiwi fruit in a supermarket, I am reminded of beautiful New Zealand and its kiwi plantations.

From Auckland I flew to Palmerston North, the home of ETA, a large potato processing plant where I consulted with the researchers. I was fortunate to be there at harvest time and observe the mechanical harvesting as well as the processing. Representatives of the company took me on a tour of the plant and later the potato fields. The soil was excellent for potato cultivation and growers had few problems with stones which can bruise the potatoes during harvest. Bruising often happens during potato harvest in New York State. I was a luncheon guest of the researchers and I thoroughly enjoyed talking "potato-shop."

In Palmerston North, I also visited the family of Dr. Martha Stipanuk, a colleague from the Division of Nutritional Sciences at Cornell, who was at that time on sabbatic leave from Cornell, working in the Department of Biochemistry at Massey University. The Stipanuks were wonderful hosts and helped me plan a visit to the Department of Food Science at Massey University and take a side trip to Wellington, the capital of New Zealand. Wellington is a beautiful city built on hills overlooking a magnificent harbor. The views reminded me of Ithaca, N.Y. with the houses spilling down the distant hillsides; however, the houses were at much higher elevations than those in Ithaca.

Next, I embarked to the city of Christchurch to visit Dr. and Mrs. Peter Meredith. I spent several enjoyable days with them, staying near their home located near the campus of Canterbury University. Dr. Meredith's car license plate read POTATO and in his office he displayed a small figure of a man holding a fishing rod; on the hook dangled a large potato. I had been invited to lecture before members of the New Zealand Institute of Food Technologists. Peter introduced me to several of Canterbury's biochemistry faculty and to the university research sections where we had enlightening discussions concerning their research projects. Some of these projects included the irradiation of potatoes. Peter also drove me to Lincoln University, an attractive institution with a young and alert faculty, where I met several more potato researchers. Studying potatoes is such a pleasant and worthwhile profession, and I'm thankful that so many people all over the world share my particular research interest. It is a pleasure to visit other researchers.

In between my professional activities in Christchurch, I managed to find time for sightseeing. The Merediths showed me Christchurch's scenic beauty—hillsides covered with flocks of grazing sheep, a stately lighthouse perched like a sentinel at the edge of the harbor, and the lovely banks of the Avon River in the heart of the city, perfect for an afternoon stroll. In addition to their work on the potato, Peter and his wife also raised sheep on their farm just outside the city. They served me some of the best lamb chops I have ever tasted.

My next professional stop was the University of Otago, located in Duneden, New Zealand. It was a pleasure to compare the beautiful English city of Christchurch with the Scottish city of Duneden. I chose to travel to Duneden via bus rather than by air, for I wanted to see the New Zealand countryside. This turned out to be a wise decision. The lovely views from the bus windows were spectacular and revealed the beauty of this island nation. I was especially fortunate to be traveling just after the first winter snowfall on the mountains. As usual I got to know some of my fellow bus passengers; among them was a Japanese family whose son spoke fluent English and several friendly New Zealand women who enjoyed talking about their nation's history. The women gave me some of their native recipes; one being "pavlova", a very special dessert sometimes served with kiwi fruit and considered a New Zealand specialty.

Late in the afternoon, the bus stopped for the night in the Resort City of Queenstown. On the way I had watched a group of fearless young people bungee-jump from a bridge, but I opted for the much less dangerous activity of riding a lift high above the city for a magnificent look at the picturesque mountains and bay. I arrived in Duneden the following day. The city was founded by Scottish immigrants and closely resembled the cities I visited in Scotland. It was quite different from the English-settled City of Christchurch with its ornate Old English architecture.

After the long day's bus ride from Queenstown, I was a bit weary, but when I saw the faculty members from the food science department at Otago University eagerly awaiting my arrival, my energy level was restored. The next day I was escorted to a tour of the food laboratories at Otago University and was given directions to some very special places of interest, including the Albatross Center, a sanctuary for enormous, awe-inspiring birds. Less awe-inspiring but perhaps more charming was watching the arrival of a family of penguins as they waddled up the shore from the sea, returning to their nesting grounds on a high hill. Later I visited a farm where penguins were kept as pets, and I was allowed to feed them.

I decided to fly from Duneden to Auckland since I had already had an opportunity to see the islands from the bus. A friend had invited me to visit her on the Fiji Islands following my tour of Australia and New Zealand, but time ran out and I returned home via Hawaii. I have since regretted not visiting the Fiji Islands, but perhaps in the future I may be able to go there. My trip home was broken only by a few hours stop in Hawaii—a respite not nearly long enough to recover my energy. Never in all my travels have I been more physically exhausted than from my trip "down under." The month following my trip was spent recuperating. However, when I remember the kiwis, kangaroos, potato people in both Australia and New Zealand, and the beautiful scenery, the exhaustion seems worthwhile.

Research:

Microbes, Rats, and Potatoes

In the 1950s and '60s, many Cornell professors held nine-month appointments. There were few, if any, full-time research professors. The summer months were off salary; they were supposed to be used for professional growth and vacation. Since I had a full-time teaching load, I chose to use all three months to advance my research. During the academic year throughout my first eighteen years at Cornell, I taught a ten-credit undergraduate course in food chemistry, two graduate-level courses, was in charge of the graduate seminar and served on numerous college and department committees. Little time was available for my own research.

I had conducted research during my graduate training at Texas and Cornell and knew that I enjoyed the intellectual stimulation it provided. I firmly believe that the most accomplished scholars are those who are committed to both teaching and research. Therefore, I sought out opportunities to carry out both in my professional life.

In the three months of summer vacation, freed from teaching responsibilities, I pushed forward with my own research projects: designing, conducting, and publishing original studies. My mother, seeing how hard I was working, urged me to curtail the research. Knowing that teaching was my first love, she reasoned that since I had already been successful at it in many places—Ouachita, Texas, Sampson, and Cornell—it would be easier for me to concentrate on teaching.

Mother's advice was reasonable, but because of the pleasure I received from my previous research, I was determined to challenge myself as a scholar and produce meaningful research even if the research had to be done on my own time. In fact I have actively pursued my own research over the course of my career. Although in more recent years my work has focused largely on potatoes, my research has actually been conducted in three distinct phases: first dealing with microbes at the University of Texas, secondly with rats during my Ph.D. study, and more recently with potatoes at Cornell and around the world.

Microbes

My first research was conducted at the University of Texas during the years 1943 to 1945 where I worked with Dr. R. J. Williams and Dr. Esmond E. Snell on the B vitamins. Methods used in the analysis of these vitamins involved the use of microorganisms such as various bacteria. Shortly after I arrived at Texas, Dr. Snell discovered two forms of vitamin B6, pyridoxal and pyridoxamine. He invited me to help in the development of methods for the analysis of these vitamins. These methods were included in my masters thesis. In addition, I also performed animal studies, examining the ways in which these vitamins are metabolized by rats. Later I conducted the first human study on the metabolism of these compounds. Besides the B6 Vitamins, I also studied the B vitamin folic acid and the compound para aminobenzoic acid, which was later found to be a component part of another B vitamin. Some of these studies were published in the *Journal of Biochemistry*. In addition to the research for my thesis, I held the responsible position of maintaining the stock cultures for the entire Biochemical Institute.

Rats

In 1951 I entered the Ph.D. program in biochemistry at Cornell. The Biochemistry Department was widely known for its specialization in the study of enzymes. For my Ph.D. research, I selected to study enzymes. Under the direction of Dr. Louise Daniel and Dr. J. B. Sumner, I studied the properties of two specific enzymes in rat liver: chlorine dehydrogenase and betaine aldehyde dehydrogenase.

The Department of Biochemistry at Cornell was an exciting place in the early 1950's. Dr. J.B. Sumner had recently been awarded the Nobel Prize for his work in crystallizing the enzyme urease. Enzyme research was at an interesting stage, due in part to Dr. Sumner's efforts. New types of equipment had arrived and greatly expanded the range of research that was possible. An example of this new technology was the "ultracentrifuge." Although it is a common instrument today, at that time it was considered on the cutting edge of technology. Suddenly, we were able to fractionate cells and study their different fractions.

My research with rats was not always pleasant, especially the sacrificing of the rats. I injected rats with chemicals such as aminopterin (a folic acid inhibitor) and then analyzed the liver enzymes. In order to accomplish this it was necessary to secure the rat liver immediately following the death of the rat. As a scientist, I realized that in order to gain valuable knowledge, it is sometimes necessary to perform unpleasant tasks. Since I believed that my research would generate useful information to help mankind, I accepted the unpleasant job of sacrificing rats.

The use of anesthetic in sacrificing the rats had to be avoided because the enzymes I was using might respond to it. The rats were sacrificed by decapitation; a swift blow to the head followed by immediate decapitation was the usual procedure. The liver tissue was then immediately removed for analysis.

Cornell was up-to-date on the latest developments in biochemistry, and I was fortunate enough to take the most advanced biochemistry laboratory courses offered. As the only woman in these classes, I was pleased to have earned the highest grade in class.

Publishing my research was an additional challenge. Each laboratory experiment was lengthy and time consuming, and the written summary of each experiment resembled a thesis. A young biochemistry professor at the University of Wisconsin, Dr. J.N. Williams, was conducting studies similar to mine and friendly competition developed between us. I was challenged to publish my results first in the *Archives of Biochemistry and Biophysics, Journal of Biological Chemistry,* or *Proceedings of the Society for Experimental Biology and Medicine.* This competition motivated me to work harder. I completed my Ph.D. dissertation in two years, in 1953, by which time I already had several publications to my credit. This record pace was possible because of my strong background in chemistry both at Ouachita Baptist University and at the University of Texas. Also I was fortunate to receive the Cornell Sigma Xi fellowship which permitted me to devote full time to research.

Potatoes

As a new Ph.D. who had just been installed in my almost full time teaching position at Cornell, I was faced with a dilemma: In what area would I choose to conduct research as an independent scholar? I had little enthusiasm for continuing work on rats, despite having several publications in this area. To pursue independent research in the same area as my Ph.D. work might also infringe on the domain of Dr. Louise Daniel, chair of my graduate committee, whom I greatly admired.

It was at this point that I discovered an exciting enzyme problem with the potato. In reading the scientific literature I became very interested in enzymatic darkening in potatoes. The more I read, the more fascinated I became. My background in enzymology lead me to consider studying this darkening effect using the enzyme techniques which I had applied to rat livers.

It was not the practice at Cornell for a scientist to suddenly begin conducting research in an area in which another professor was working. Instead it was appropriate to approach the foremost expert in that area on campus and clear the project with him or her. This useful procedure often served to head off intra-campus rivalries and ill will.

Several individuals affiliated with Cornell were working on the potato and two had interests similar to mine: Dr. Richard Sawyer, a professor who served as director of the Cornell Research Farms on Long Island, and Dr. Ora Smith of the Department of Vegetable Crops, who was known as "Mr. Potato" around campus. Dr. Sawyer had been a former student of Dr. Smith and many years later he went on to become director of the International Potato Institute in Lima, Peru, and a world-famous potato researcher in his own right.

Because of Dr. Smith's proximity, I approached him first with a proposal to study a troublesome physiological disorder in potatoes called "blackspot." I scheduled an appointment with him and briefly described my ideas. I told him I planned to address the problem using enzyme techniques from recent biochemistry studies.

Cordial and enthusiastic, Dr. Smith told me that he would be delighted to have me join the community of potato researchers at Cornell. He went so far as to offer to grow potatoes for me, an offer repeated by Dr. Richard Sawyer in Long Island when I contacted him. I was fortunate to have acquired two new friends who accepted me and welcomed my research. It was gratifying to find that both Dr. Smith and Dr. Sawyer welcomed my biochemical approach and thought my ideas sound. Our work was complementary instead of competitive, with each of us providing a separate perspective on the potato.

To expand my knowledge of the potato and plants in general, I audited several courses in plant physiology, an area not totally unfamiliar to me since I had minored in physiology as a master's student at Texas. I also delved into the voluminous literature on plant physiology and invited graduate students studying vegetable crops and plant breeding to join me and my graduate students in research discussions or seminars. Over coffee and cookies on Saturday mornings, my students, all of them female at that time, discussed potatoes with the male students from the other agricultural departments. I put forward my ideas and discussed the different experiments I was carrying out in my laboratories. All seemed interested and before long students attended from other departments such as Plant Pathology as well. At one point, Dr. Robert Plaisted, the chair of the Department of Plant Breeding, asked if he could join the discussion group, and he made significant contributions to the discussions.

These seminars were rewarding and enlightening. Many interesting experiments resulted from the discussions as our thoughts were combined and analyzed. It was enjoyable to be among a group that was so intelligent and interested in this area of research. As these seminars continued and I continued my research on the potato, I came to realize that I had joined the community of outstanding potato researchers. Originally I had not planned to remain long in this one area; rather I had hoped to solve the problem of enzymatic darkening known as "blackspot" and then move on. However, I became fascinated with research on potatoes and decided to continue for many years. I have never regretted this decision for I have thoroughly enjoyed my work on this highly nutritious food. The potato has many benefits for the world and particularly for populations in developing countries. It has been a pleasure to add significant information regarding the potato's growth, chemical composition, and its retention of nutrients during storage and processing. My studies have been challenging, especially since they blend the fields of chemistry, nutrition, food science (1967), and toxicology. Over the years I helped to organize the Institute of Food Science and the Institute of Toxicology (1981) at Cornell.

As my research on the potato progressed, I was invited to join the Potato Association of America (PAA), an international organization covering both North and South America. Later I was invited to join the European Association for Potato Research (EAPR) and participated in its meetings for many years. In 1983, the PAA bestowed upon me Honorary Life Membership, the organization's highest honor. It is good to be a member of this unusual family of potato lovers.

Although my scholarly research on potatoes did not develop until after I had received the Ph.D., my initiation into potato mysteries began at an early age. In my "Baby" book mother had listed my favorite foods. The first on the list was "mashed potatoes." My mother, who was an expert gardener, frequently won prizes for her flowers and vegetables, and I was appointed her chief assistant in the garden. Gardening was time-consuming and often physically draining, but now I look back on these experiences with appreciation since they prepared me for the work I would do later.

Mother grew Irish Cobbler potatoes in her garden and in Arkansas they were typically ready for harvest by Independence Day. She always chose this holiday to harvest potatoes because she could depend on having the day off from her work at the newspaper office. So on July 4, instead of lighting fireworks, Mother went to the potato patch to dig the tubers from the ground. She was an expert at freeing the potatoes from the soil without cutting or bruising them, using a digger with multiple long prongs for this operation. My job was to carry the potatoes to the cellar and carefully store them for the winter.

Grandfather had built the cellar as a shelter against tornadoes which were frequently known to ravage parts of northern Arkansas. The cellar was partially underground and furnished with tables upon which I stored the potatoes. After a nice peel formed on the freshly harvested tubers, I sprinkled them with lime. We rarely had problems with rot, and our supply lasted for months. Later, when I became familiar with the potato research literature, I understood the importance of the steps Mother had taught me.

As a researcher, I have had wonderful relations with scholars from various departments at Cornell, beginning with my induction into Cornell's family of potato researchers in vegetable crops and continuing throughout my career. Many times I developed a research experiment that required the special knowledge of a scholar in a related field. I approached him with an informal proposal, and if the researcher thought the idea sound, he would offer his cooperation.

Collaboration is a vital aspect of research. By blending my knowledge of chemistry with the specialized knowledge of scholars in other areas, I was able to broaden the range of my research.

Shortly after my decision to pursue research on the potato I began to suspect that the solution to the problem of potato darkening lay in the area of plant breeding. As a chemist with little first-hand knowledge in this area, I approached Dr. Robert Plaisted, chair of the Department of Plant Breeding, who was developing new varieties of potatoes. I suggested that by conducting some controlled chemical experiments we might be able to ascertain why the enzymatic blackening was occurring and possibly address the flavor question as well. Dr. Plaisted was interested and offered his cooperation.

I took some of his potato clones and sifted through them for polyphenols, the compounds I suspected were causing the problem. After analyzing fifty clones for phenolic content, the ten that were highest and the ten lowest in phenols were selected for the study. A highly significant positive correlation between enzymatic darkening and phenolic content was found. Those clones highest in phenols also exhibited a bitter and astringent flavor.

Dr. Plaisted was pleased with our results, and he invited me to speak at a major potato conference, the Potato Utilization Conference. Our work was later published in the proceedings of the Nineteenth National Potato Utilization Conference and in proceedings of Fourth Triennial of European Association for Potato Research.

I discovered that vegetables, like animals, could become infected by many different types of viruses. One of the viruses to which potatoes are susceptible is Virus X, which affects the plant's ability to grow and produce new tubers. For this study on the effects of viral infection on tuber nutrients, I consulted with Dr. Ed Jones in the Department of Plant Pathology who immediately expressed an interest in exploring this problem. An experiment using four varieties of potatoes was designed in which tubers free of virus X infection were compared with the same four varieties known to be infected by the virus. By comparing the virus-free with the virus-infected tubers, we discovered that nutrients such as ascorbic acid and lipids, as well as nitrogen compounds, are affected by the virus. I prepared the original project statement and the manuscripts, but Dr. Jones was cooperative at every stage of the experiment. The results were published in the *American Potato Journal, Journal of Food Science, and Experientia*.

Another focus of my research was to study factors that affect the texture or firmness of the tuber. Dr. Malcom Bourne, an expert on texture and

Professor of Cornell Food Science, Experiment Station Geneva, New York, agreed to cooperate and through his work using the Instron we were able to determine factors affecting potato quality as related to texture. Dr. Leonard Mattick, Professor of Food Science at Geneva, was also very helpful as I developed methods for determining the lipid composition of potatoes.

I also worked with Dr. Louis Naylor, Department of Agricultural Engineering, on studying the effect of growing potatoes in sludge-amended soil. We discovered that potatoes do pick up cadmium and other toxic chemicals from the sludge when it is applied to the land.

Another focus of my research has been the study of factors involved in the synthesis of naturally-occurring toxicants (glycoalkaloids) that accumulate largely in potato skins and give potatoes a bitter and undesirable flavor. Consumption of potatoes with high levels of glycoalkaloids can lead to cholinesterase inhibition. This enzyme affects the nervous system and glycoalkaloids can cause acute intestinal tract irritation as well. If consumed at a high level, glycoalkaloids have been shown to result in death in both humans and animals. Glycoalkaloid levels above 20 mg per 100 grams of fresh potatoes are considered toxic. Some varieties have been shown to exceed these levels. Unfortunately I, along with several other researchers, was made very ill by the Lenape variety which contains high levels of glycoalkaloids. This variety later had to be removed from the marketplace because of its glycoalkaloid content.

Numerous factors determine glycoalkaloid levels in potatoes. These include varietal differences, tuber maturity and size, soil type and fertilization practices, climate and altitude of growing regions, light exposure, and mechanical- and chemical-induced stresses. I have studied these factors to find ways of controlling the synthesis of glycoalkaloids. These studies have helped growers and processors to produce potatoes and potato products with reduced levels of these toxic compounds.

Since the toxic compounds are more concentrated in the peel, I recommended caution in the consumption of peels. Since peeling potentially involves increased costs for the potato processor, my recommendation was not universally well received, especially by those who value profits more than health concerns. At the time of my retirement, Dr. Glenn Vogt, Manager of Agricultural Services, J. R. Simplot Company, wrote:

> ... You are also a person who conducts and reports research with an unusually high level of professionalism, courage and integrity. I will never forget how you maintained those admirable qualities even when you were being publicly and unjustly vilified by certain fellow 'professionals.' [Your] contributions to the body of potato research literature in the areas of nutrition and quality improvements, particularly in relation to glycoalkaloids and blackspot bruise, will be of lasting value and significance to the potato industry and to consumers of potatoes everywhere.

His comments were greatly appreciated.

Northeast Regional Research Team

At the suggestion of Dr. Nyle Brady, Director of the Cornell Agricultural Experiment Station, I joined the Northeast Regional Research Team, an organization of researchers from Connecticut, Georgia, Maine, Maryland, Massachusetts, Michigan, and Rhode Island. The overall project was given the title "Quality Maintenance and Control in the Marketing and Storage of Vegetables." Many productive years were spent working with this team, and I was honored to become the first woman to chair this group.

In 1978, I made an around-the-world tour in thirty days. The tour had been shortened to thirty days in order that I could return in time to chair the Northeast Regional Research Team's annual meeting in Washington, D. C. My concern was that all should go well, since, after many years, I was the first woman selected to chair such a group. I felt a special responsibility to perform well for the sake of the women who were to follow. Since that time, other women have been asked to chair the group and I am pleased to have opened the door for them.

Referring to my work with the regional team, Dr. W. F. Shipe, Professor of Food Science, Cornell University wrote:

> Dr. Mondy is recognized both nationally and internationally for her expertise pertaining to the biochemical changes in potatoes. . . . I have heard her give a number of seminars and reports on her research. She presents her material very well, and the contents reflect a high level of scientific competence. . . . Dr. Mondy was elected to be Chair of the Northeast Cooperative Regional Research Project on the Quality of Vegetables. This is a reflection of the high esteem with which scientists regard her research performance.

Another team member, Professor F. M. Clydesdale, Chair of the Food Science Department at the University of Massachusetts, wrote:

> I have had the honor of serving on a regional Hatch research project with Dr. Mondy for the past ten years. In that capacity I feel I have had a unique opportunity to not only judge the quantity and quality of research she is involved with, but as well to observe her ability to present ideas and interrelate with her peers. In all these areas she has proved to be outstanding. Her list of publications, international work, honorary societies and background speak for themselves. However, what cannot be listed is her great ability to articulate her fine research and present arguments in a clear, concise and convincing fashion. She is always pleasant and helpful yet firm

in her ideas and commitment, a truly rare combination of talents. Her research is characterized by excellent science applied to basic agricultural problems. . . . Nell is a joy to have at a meeting, and she always adds to it by her personality and contributes with her research.

Prof. Elmer Ewing, Chair, Dept. of Fruit and Vegetable Science, Cornell University, also wrote, commenting on my collaborative work.

The Potato Association of America has recognized Dr. Mondy's contribution by bestowing its highest honor, making her an Honorary Life Member. This was done not only for her loyal service to the organization, but also for her many publications on the potato. The record of her research is well represented in the *American Potato Journal*, which is where scientists interested in the American potato industry look first for manuscripts that deal with the potato. Of course she has also published extensively in other scientific journals when the subject matter or audience made this more appropriate; but her loyalty to the *American Potato Journal* has been much appreciated. Dr. Mondy has not limited her focus to the United States. The potato is grown in more countries than any other crop except corn. Thus it is appropriate that Dr. Mondy has taken a worldwide perspective on potatoes. She has traveled extensively in potato producing countries, speaking at conferences and visiting with research colleagues. As a result, she has made friends and gained recognition from around the world for her dedication to the potato. A final point to be mentioned in surveying Dr. Mondy's career is her continuing effort to link human nutrition and agriculture. Too often there is a gap between what is done in colleges of agriculture and departments of nutrition. It is to Dr. Mondy's credit that she has worked to bridge this gap. No doubt it has been tedious at times for a food scientist and biochemist to sit through meetings dominated by agriculturists (usually men, needless to say), but Dr. Mondy has shown admirable perseverance in enduring our lopsided presentations. With patient good humor she has reminded us by her presence that the reason for producing potatoes is so that people will eat them, and that therefore their nutritional quality is important.

Letters from Industry and Fellow Researchers

Over the course of my career, I have had the pleasure of working with a number of research professionals and representatives of the potato industry. Many of these people have written to me expressing their thoughts about my research and our work together. Below are some excerpts from these letters.

Prof. Richard Sawyer, former Executive Director, International Potato Center, Lima, Peru, presently President, International Fund for Agricultural Research

When I received the letter about your retirement, my mind went back to the many years ago and the harvesting of potatoes at the Long Island Vegetable Research Station. As a young research professor taking over some of the collaboration that others had started the importance of saving the samples which Nell Mondy wanted from research plots was underscored. This collaboration went on for a number of years and I don't believe any sample was forgotten. Many changes have taken place in our lives and the collaboration, which started with you, has gone on to include most of the developing world. It was indeed a great pleasure to meet you again after a number of years at the Triennial Meeting of the African Potato Association at Reduit, Mauritius as you represented the Potato Association of America. I wish you the best as you move to new challenges and opportunities.

Professor Milton Workman, Colorado State University

"The publications of Dr. Mondy are exceptionally well written. The experimental approaches and methodology appear to be carefully planned and executed. . . . Her presentation of papers at scientific meetings also reflects the care and accuracy with which she directs and performs the experiments. The presentation and analysis of the data are always clear and concise."

Professor Elizabeth Murphy, University of Maine

I have known Professor Mondy for several years. I have recognized her as an able biochemist in an area of research in which I was actively engaged, viz. the chemistry of foods as associated with sensory quality, especially that of the potato. She has done outstanding research work and has made many valuable contributions in her field of endeavor.

Professor S. Chang, Chair, Dept. of Food Chemistry, Rutgers University

Dr. Mondy has uniquely demonstrated herself to be an expert in potato research. Her accomplishments in the chemical composition of potato, particularly, the effect of processing, fertilization, sprouting, and diseases upon the composition of potato, has been regarded by her peers as the foremost. She contributed greatly, not only in the generation of new, basic knowledge concerning the chemistry of potato, but also contributed a great impact to the utilization of potato.

Professor R. Dennison, Chair, Food Science Dept., University of Florida

Dr. Mondy has made a number of extremely valuable contributions to our knowledge of the chemistry of potatoes. As a result of her work, it has been possible for various segments of the potato industry to make some important improvements in storage and handling practices. Her research studies have always been well designed and the interpretations of the data appear sound.

Professor I. Howard Ellison, Rutgers University

Dr. Mondy is one of the leading potato research scientists in foods, nutrition, and physiological disorders in the country, and indeed enjoys an international reputation. Her research concerns serious problems of the potato and food industry, and her papers reflect distinction upon herself, her Department, and Cornell University. Her work on potato blackspot, potato discoloration, off-flavor, and other quality factors of tubers is outstanding.

Professor Robert Kunkel, Washington State University

I noticed in the program that you presented a paper as you've done each year for so many years. You are the only one left who is doing anything of importance on the biochemistry of the potato.... I hope that you will be able to continue in your biochemical work because it is not only important to know what happens, but to explain why it happens, when possible.

Raymon Webb, Chief, Vegetable Lab., Federal Research Northeast Region

Dr. Mondy is highly respected by her peers in several disciplines (breeding, genetics, horticulture, plant physiology, food technology, etc.), for her research on nutritive values and flavor in the potato and, equally important, as a person. Her counsel is sought on a myriad of subjects, including pest management practices as insect dynamics relates to nutritional composition of genetically diverse potato parental materials. In fact, Dr. Mondy is the leading adviser to the potato scientific community in the U.S. on various aspects of composition and flavor of the potato.

Glenn E. Vogt, Manager, Agricultural Services, J. R. Simplot Company

Dr. Mondy's contributions to the body of potato research literature in the areas of nutrition and quality improvements, particularly in relation to glycoalkaloids and blackspot bruise, will be of lasting value and significance to the potato industry and to consumers of potatoes everywhere.

Alvin Mosley, Past President of the Potato Association of America

I have never properly thanked you for your assistance in preparing the original nine proposals which led to [the] formation of the

ARS/NPC National Potato Research Program. I understand that approximately $3 million in new monies is available to U.S. potato researchers each year due in part to your leadership in focusing attention on needed research related to utilization and quality.

Mike Groskoff, University of Wisconsin, American Potato Co,
In all the years I was involved in potato research at the university of Wisconsin and American Potato Company, you helped me in so many ways in your field of expertise. I thank you for your willingness to share your knowledge involving the many effects of micronutrients on potato quality.

Richard Chase, Extension Specialist, Michigan State University
Dr. Mondy has enjoyed a productive career and has contributed in many ways to the increasing knowledge of the potato. A good example has been related to the problems of blackspot.... Her research has certainly contributed to a better understanding of this problem.

Letters from International Colleagues

One of the joys of research is sharing knowledge with colleagues both at home and abroad. My research has taken me to forty-seven countries and one of my colleagues, Magdalena Krondl, Professor Emerita, Faculty of Medicine, University of Toronto, at the time of my retirement wrote:

It was in 1966 at the World Congress of Food Science and Technology held in Warsaw, Poland that first time I met Nell. She had with her an astounding number of friends and acquaintances. I was happy that since then she has included me in the category of her friends. After the conference Nell came to Prague, met my family and took a liking to our then 5 year old son Michael. It was characteristic of her that on her return to Ithaca she sent him a lovely white shirt, an article in short supply at that time in Eastern Europe. Two years later, when our family had succeeded to escape from behind the Iron Curtain, Nell was the one who helped me to settle in an academic position in Canada. The many scientific meetings that I have attended since had the attraction of providing an opportunity to meet Nell and to catch up on her incredibly eventful life. Nell has one specific peculiarity. She likes angels. Whenever I come across an angel in art, folklore, literature, or scripture, I think of Nell. In fact, in my mind she represents an angel. Ability to create such an image is a big achievement in a person's life.

Professor Patricia Ladipo, University of Ife, Nigeria, 1997
Thank you for your generous advice and recommendations

which have helped me at many points over the years. Every once in a while I remember when I was your student. Twenty years later I really saw the nonprofessional side of you. You were working in Nigeria at the International Institute of Tropical Agriculture (IITA) in Ibadan and traveled to give a seminar at the University of Ife where my husband and I were teaching. After your talk, we drove you back to Ibadan. Unfortunately, before we could reach IITA we got caught in a traffic jam and found ourselves completely locked in by petrol tankers. You were as calm and pleasant as ever in that highly flammable situation. After several hours, my husband was able to inch us out backwards. By then it was too late to go back to Ife so we brought you to our cottage in Iwo where you shared the kids' room with them, slept in one of their bunk beds and woke up looking perfectly cheerful. That visit was actually the beginning of your relationship with my family and it is one of my fondest memories.

Acknowledgements

My research over the years could not have been accomplished without the help of others. I want to thank Cornell faculty at the Cornell Agricultural Experiment Station, Riverhead, Long Island, Drs. R. L. Sawyer, D. I. Cotter, Stewart Dallyn, P. A. Schippers, G. W. Selleck, and J. E. Sieczka, who were very helpful in growing, harvesting and transporting experimental potatoes to Ithaca.

In the Ithaca area, I thank Drs. Ora Smith, Robert Kunkel, Paul Muneta, George Collins, Robert Plaisted, Ken Paddock, L. C. Peterson, Ed Jones, Larry Hymes and Don Halseth who were also very helpful in the growing and harvesting of experimental potatoes.

For the potato studies at Florida State University my gratitude goes to Drs. Ray Dennison, Dale Hensel, and Pete Weingartner.

Conclusion

Someone once said that success in research is achieved by one percent inspiration and 99 percent perspiration. I have found this to be true, for throughout my career as a teacher and researcher, my recognition of the value of hard work and commitment has been vital to the contributions I have made. However, I believe that one must not underestimate the power of that one percent inspiration, for without the fundamental desire and pleasure in exploring the unknown, the work becomes drudgery. Successful researchers must have the ability to combine inspiration and serious commitment with hard work.

Mondy—Potato Queen Celebration
Dr. Mondy with her graduate students in her laboratory 218 MVR Hall,
Cornell University, 1981
Students named her Potato Queen.
Cake states "Congratulations to the Potato Queen"

Dr. Mondy receiving "Honorary Life Membership" award from the American Potato Association (both North and South America) East Lansing Michigan, 1983

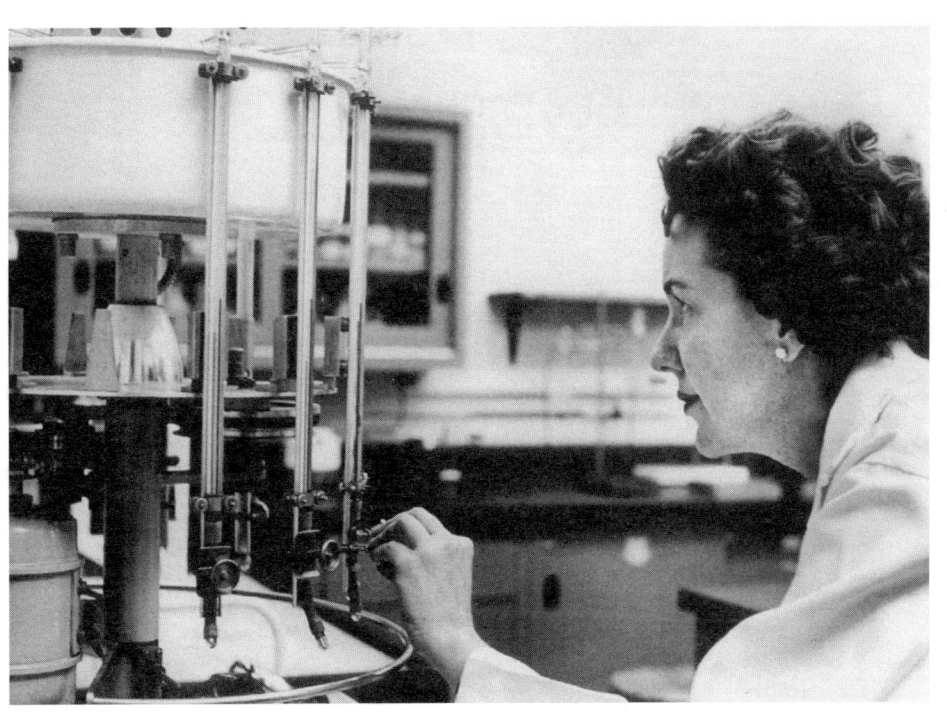

Dr. Nell Mondy in her research laboratory, Cornell University.
Using the Warburg respirometer to test the oxidative
enzyme activity of potato tissue.

PHILOSOPHY OF TEACHING

Teaching is both an art and a science. Through the experience of trial and error, a teacher may become more adept at his or her craft, mastering the fundamentals of public speaking, proper preparation, and the use of illustrative materials. However, the best teachers go beyond craft, establishing a relationship with their students through their care and commitment which is mutually enlightening. This sort of relationship, based on sensitivity to the different ways that students learn, reflects the art of teaching.

I was blessed to have worked with and studied under excellent teachers throughout my educational career. From each I learned about the profession of teaching and added their insights to my store of knowledge. I also learned from the few poor teachers I encountered. Often it is as important to know what does not work as it is to know what does.

To me teaching means much more than simply performing in a classroom. Rather it is a commitment to sharing knowledge, whether in the classroom or outside. A good teacher must be informed about the subject matter and must present it in such a way that students can comprehend it. It is always important to understand that even the most elegantly prepared lecture is of no worth if it fails to convey its message to an audience effectively. Therefore, a good teacher should be alert to signals that his or her message is or is not getting through.

Tutoring

My work as a teacher began when I was quite young. In grade school in Pocahontas, Arkansas I was often asked to teach all or part of a class when the teacher was called away for some reason. I believe I was asked to do this both because of my academic standing as valedictorian in sixth, ninth, and twelfth grades and because I was often perceived as mature for my age. People who did not know me often thought me much older than I was, and even when they were informed of my true age they seemed to bestow upon me acceptance and authority. I never felt nervous about leading my classmates for they gave me their respect and attention, and I never had problems with discipline, even with my peers.

I gained a bit of teaching experience in Latin class in high school. The teacher was not very good or committed to her work. It seemed as though she did not want to be there, and she displayed no enthusiasm for her subject. In fact her knowledge of Latin was shallow, and we students found that if we studied from our textbooks, we would know more than she did. Often students in the class corrected her, not in a mean way, but simply because something she had said was inaccurate. Finally, she began producing excuses to be out of class and would assign a student to lead the group. This assignment often fell to me and served as a wonderful opportunity for me to develop my teaching skills at an early stage.

One of the things I learned from this Latin teacher, as well as from the many good teachers I had, was that in order to be effective in the classroom, preparation is crucial. I have always believed that by the time a teacher steps into the classroom, he or she should have fully digested the material and not have to rely upon reading stale lecture notes. Few students enjoy being read to, and many will simply tune out a professor whose nose is always buried in notes.

I also gained valuable teaching experience and a feel for understanding individual learning styles by tutoring. I began tutoring as early as grade school, in order to help my best friend Barbara. She was talented in many ways but found mathematics and science to be difficult. At the end of the academic year, students who had excelled in these subjects were allowed to exempt the final exam. Since I had maintained the highest marks in class, I was included among these. Since I did not have to study for the final exams, I tutored Barbara in order to help her raise her mark. I learned from our tutoring sessions, since in preparing materials to show to her, I added to my own knowledge.

I tutored at Ouachita as well, accepting a fee of ten cents an hour from each of the young women who came to my class. I enjoyed doing this and began to seriously consider the possibility of teaching at the high school level, should the state of our family finances prevent me from immediately going on to graduate study or medical school. Accordingly, I minored in education and became certified to teach both chemistry and home economics in high school.

By the time I finished the bachelor's degree at Ouachita, I had received several assistantship offers and made plans to enter the Department of Biochemistry at the University of Texas. At Texas I was unable to tutor in the Department of Biochemistry, for that would have represented a conflict of interest. However, members of the Department of Organic Chemistry were aware of my strong background in organic chemistry and invited me to serve as a tutor in that department. There were many struggling students, so I accepted their offer. I soon found that the rate of pay for tutoring was higher than that for my assistant's salary. There were many more applicants than I had time to tutor.

More knowledge about teaching was gained with each individual I tutored. I tailored the materials to fit the needs and abilities of each student. At Cornell I also continued to tutor in organic chemistry but on a somewhat more limited basis. I was able to apply much of what I learned in tutoring to my teaching at the university level.

I. University Teaching

A good teacher should be able to illustrate his or her material visually. In chemistry I achieved this by using demonstrations during my lectures. My food chemistry course took place in a large auditorium covering two floors. I was aware that the students on the second level were quite far away. In order to make the demonstrations effective for everyone in the class, I secured help in designing a demonstration platform with lights underneath. With this device, I could carry out titrations and other reactions over the illuminated desk and even the students in the back of the room could see the color changes in the illuminated flasks.

Often I received comments from students who had taken the course that the demonstrations coupled with the lectures were more effective in teaching the principles of chemistry than lectures alone. Such comments confirmed what I had already suspected—that visualization is a powerful teaching tool. It engages students' eyes and minds better than the written or spoken word alone.

I believe laboratory work can be extremely effective in training students in the fundamentals of chemistry. As a young chemistry student at Ouachita, I could read all about copper sulfate ($CuSO_4$) in a textbook, but when I actually worked with the beautiful blue crystals, mixing them in various solutions, I was able to grasp what I had read much more quickly. Instead of merely memorizing formulas, I always tried to get a mental image of the chemical so that I could better understand its properties. I have often recommended this technique to my students.

I am saddened to learn that the number of laboratory hours for food chemistry have been reduced. I hope that eventually the pendulum will swing back and that laboratory work will again become a priority. I remain convinced that when students are able to observe and work with a substance, they grasp the subject more readily.

I have always tried to involve my students in hands-on activities in the classroom, particularly through the use of problem sets and questions designed to challenge students to think independently and put the information into practice. Sometimes these sets were graded, while other times they were given solely for the benefit of the students in order to help them review material they had already learned. Preparing these problem sets required diligent preparation on my part, but I was pleased to do it, for I considered it an important learning tool.

The appreciation of former students is always gratifying. In 1986, Carol Menzel Viertel an undergraduate in the mid-1960s, wrote: "To this day, I remember your sincere straight-forwardness, your warmth, enjoyment of teaching and your concern for us students. Your dedication to your career and your belief in the value of the scientific method has stayed with me, and continues to inspire me."

I always wanted to make certain that the information was correct and comprehensible to my audience. Accordingly my lectures were typed well in advance of the date on which they were presented. At my lectures these served only as an outline. I refused to read my notes to the class, and often gave the students the opportunity to ask relevant questions. Because I allowed these questions, my lectures did not always run the exact length I had planned, but I nevertheless found it a worthwhile practice. Often, when a student requests clarification, the answer benefits other students who also might have been confused but lacked the courage to ask.

Regardless of these interruptions, I usually managed to cover the material intended for each lecture. Over the years I developed a good sense of the time required to cover a certain amount of material. This skill is similar to that of an experienced cook who can predict the time required to prepare each of the dishes for a meal.

Young teachers have a tendency to pack too much material into a lecture. In their desire to convey as much knowledge as possible, they sometimes overwhelm students with dense information that may be difficult to assimilate. It is important to remember one's audience and their needs, and abilities, and, most importantly, the pace at which they are capable of understanding new material.

Teaching Undergraduates

During my first eighteen years at Cornell, I carried a heavy teaching load, due primarily to my work on the ten-credit food chemistry course, FN 214–215. Six credits of the course were assigned to chemistry and four credits to foods. The course was very demanding for me as well as the students.

The chemistry component of the course involved both general and organic chemistry and was intended to prepare students to go directly into biochemistry. I felt the need to present as much general and organic chemistry in six credit hours as other students in the chemistry department were receiving in the eight credit general chemistry plus the four credit organic chemistry courses. These courses also served as a prerequisite to biochemistry and were taught in the chemistry department. My course was a challenge, both for me and for the students, but I believe it succeeded, for many of my students made top marks in biochemistry. In 1967 Dr. Louise Daniel wrote:

> Miss Mondy's courses FN 214-215 served as a prerequisite for Biochemistry. There is an excellent correlation between student attainment in Miss Mondy's courses and how well they do in Biochemistry. To understand the full meaning of this, one must be aware of the fact that 200-250 students take my biochemistry course. This past year there were 177 undergraduates most of whom had taken Organic Chemistry in the College of Arts and Sciences. Thus, the competition is great. However, the top student had taken Miss Mondy's courses in preparation for Biochemistry. Students with whom I have talked have been most enthusiastic about her teaching. Throughout the years I have found the students from home economics well able to compete with their counterparts from other colleges.

Because of the large amount of material that had to be covered, I was forced to push students to work harder than perhaps they had been made to work in other courses. I assigned worksheets and often held extra discussion classes. Some students thought my course was difficult, a charge I didn't mind so long as they also thought they had been treated fairly. My goal was to challenge them and to prepare them to the best of my ability.

The food chemistry course has always been dear to my heart. Previous to Cornell I had taught at the college level, both at Ouachita and at Sampson. It was a pleasure to assist Dr. Pfund in developing materials for the course, and she always highly regarded my input. Later when I directed the courses, I developed many experiments for the laboratory. I reviewed both chemistry and food journals, adapting the newest innovations to food chemistry.

I look back fondly on my days of teaching undergraduates. One of the great joys of having taught is the feeling that perhaps I had influenced a young person's life for the better, either by fostering a love for a particular field, or by instilling a sense of discipline. Sometimes a teacher doesn't realize the impact he or she has made until years later when a grateful student comes forward to acknowledge the teacher's contribution.

Susan Brown Matson

In September I entered the nursing program at Ulster County Community College in hopes of becoming a registered nurse. In the battle to transfer my chemistry credits I had occasion to review my FN 214-215 notes. What a joy it was to recall those classes. Just today, I've read your article on Sulfur Dioxide and Safety Standards in the summer issue of *Forum*. Again, I was reminded of you and your classes. I've not retained a great deal of chemistry knowledge, nor am I a food expert, but I'm still greatly influenced by the necessity for hard work and self-discipline you taught. We all worked hard and, I'm afraid, heaped verbal abuse upon you! But when we were finished, how grateful we were! Oh, that I could once again have the privilege of being your student!

One of the most memorable letters on my desk at the end of the academic year, 1959, was from Mabel Fisher, an undergraduate who had struggled with chemistry and considered dropping the course. I spent much time with her, calling to her attention the motto on my office wall: *You Never Fail Until You Stop Trying.* Mabel wrote:

> I want to thank you for all the helpful advice you gave me this year. F.N. was more than an ordinary learning experience for me, for I have learned a lot about self-control and attitudes towards a course and how they can help a person. You have really been wonderful to me, and having your understanding helped me a lot. I am so glad I decided not to petition for withdrawal because even though my mark ended up to be just passing, withdrawal would have meant acknowledgement of failure. Again, thank you so much for everything. I shall never forget this year and your advice. It has carried through to my other courses, and I don't think I shall ever let anything get the best of me again. Incidentally, I managed to get through my other courses OK too!) I really appreciate the time you and your staff have given to me.

Nineteen years after this letter was written, I contacted Mabel to see how she had fared in her life since leaving Cornell. Responding to my call she wrote:

> Almost nineteen years have passed, so what a surprise it was to hear from you yesterday. Also to experience you once again, as the interested and sympathetic and human person which makes you the great teacher you are. Like you, I too have saved those notes that come occasionally from students. They do serve as reminders that the effort we put into teaching is really worthwhile. I've traveled in many directions since graduating from Cornell. I started out teaching in Westchester. . . . [Later], I took a job at Rye High School. . . . In the meantime, I married a math teacher and we built a home. . . . I completed my masters degree at New York University and started to teach graduate courses in the area of consumer education. . . . I have continued as a consultant developing materials for a variety of clients, including publishers such as Guidance Associates, materials for corporations such as J.C. Penney, Proctor and Gamble, and Johnson and Johnson. Professionally, I have kept

active over the years in various home economics organizations. Reflecting on my experience in FN 214-215, I must say again that it was a major life lesson. Being twenty years older now, I understand the meaning of the lesson better, though I guess I was on track even then.... As I've continued to mature, I've come to understand that life is far too short to spend it in ways that are not personally satisfying. I am very fortunate that I have been gifted with certain talents, and I have had rich opportunities for self-development. I regard my Cornell education as one of those important experiences that has helped me to become and will continue to help me to become.

Nikki Goldbeck (Schulman)

It is unlikely that you will remember me, having influenced so many students over the years, but as a former student (Class of '68) and now engaged in writing about food and teaching nutrition workshops, I have greatly appreciated the excellent education and personal attention you gave to me when I was in your class. I have been following your work with potatoes and am presently engaged in writing a consumer guidebook that is aimed at helping people make safe and nutritious food purchases. It will be called *The Super Market Handbook* and is actually an all new version of a book my husband and I co-authored about ten years ago. In the section on produce we talk about some of your findings regarding the glycoalkaloids in potatoes and particularly how this relates to fried potato skins. In preparing the snack food section it came to my attention that many "natural" potato chips are prepared from unpeeled potatoes. I am wondering now if this is ill advised, or if perhaps a low-solanin variety of potato is used by the snack food industry. If you could give me any information on this subject it would be very helpful in making the book complete and accurate. Unfortunately, we are now facing a deadline for the manuscript, and although I am sure you have a good deal of your own work to tend to, if you could spare a few minutes to answer this question it would be very valuable to us.

Betty Lou van Splunder

As I look back on my four years at Cornell, I feel that the course I had from you, FN 214-215, was one of the best ones I have had. FN 214-215 was an excellent introduction to chemistry, both inorganic and organic, and to food science. The course tied the chemistry background to actual examples in foods, both in lecture and in the laboratory. I personally feel that having the chemistry integrated with the foods makes both much more meaningful and relevant. I would never have continued with the major had it not been for the significance of this course.

Self-Help Classes

In order to assist the students in food chemistry, I adopted the practice, which I had innovated at Sampson College of setting up "self-help" classes so that any student having problems could come and ask questions in an informal setting. The class was conducive to student involvement and many students attended. I was there to answer their questions and guide them through various types of problems. Some had a mental block based on the erroneous notion that women were not intellectually suited to mathematics or science. First, I took them step by step through a problem. This was followed by a similar problem, which they solved in my presence. Their self-confidence grew.

The self-help classes were taught after regular hours, usually 5:00 to 7:00 P.M. I was never paid for the extra time, but I saw the positive effect these classes had on the students. In 1967 Virginia Ahrens, some years following her graduation, wrote, using a quote from Saturday Review (March 18, 1967):

> We must have scholars in the classrooms, people who love and understand that they do well. The effective teacher is always engaged in learning and by that continuing act makes all-teaching an adventure in mutual discovery. Such a teacher is rarely found, but always treasured by his students and colleagues, whether his forum is a kindergarten or a graduate seminar.

> I was thinking of you throughout the article, but I think the above paragraph summarizes my thoughts succinctly. . . . Your seminars or 'self-help sessions' were (to me) an 'adventure in mutual discovery.' Your knack for patiently following diverse trains of thought, I feel, laid the groundwork for a truly free spirit of inquiry. Somehow you made me want to 'gobble up' all the available information so that I could get on to the unknown. This is in sharp contrast to the method of spoon-feeding 'canned' information, which assumes rigid and homogeneous thought processes. I suppose I should be sorry that I stubbed my toe on calculus and didn't feel able to continue in chemistry, but I'm happy to find that this 'awareness' you sparked is readily transferable to other fields. Keep up the good work, and please don't lose your enthusiasm.

The Laboratory As Classroom

I took great delight in discovering talented students who were interested in food chemistry, and I was among the first at Cornell to hire capable undergraduates to work in my research laboratory. In recent years, this practice has become fashionable, and now faculty is encouraged to do this, but it was not customary in my day. I welcome this change in attitude and practice, however belated, for after hiring undergraduates for fifty years, I am aware of the benefits.

I involved the students in all aspects of the research for I did not want them to be merely dishwashers, or to assume only janitorial duties. Students were instructed to carry out an experiment that I had designed. I met with the student, explained the experimental design and coached them in the procedures. I demonstrated for them the equipment they would be using. Throughout this process, I treated them as professionals and expected them to respond professionally. These undergraduate students carefully collected and recorded data, summarized it, and drafted a report.

Some undergraduates advanced to such a degree through their work in the laboratory that they were ready to present papers at national conferences. In fact, several honors students did so. I encouraged gifted students to understand the basics of research. I receive letters from students thanking me for giving them the opportunity to work in my laboratory and gain practical experience at such an early point in their lives.

Mary Rose Kornreich, who worked in my laboratory as an undergraduate in the early 1960s, wrote:

> When Dr. Mondy recognized students with the potential to become good scientists, she offered us positions in her laboratory where she could train us to become researchers. She held regular conferences with us to discuss the progress of the research. She also worked closely with us in the laboratory, carefully supervising our analytical techniques. In her role as teacher, mentor, and role model, she enriched my learning experience at Cornell and was an inspiration. In her food chemistry courses, she presented inorganic and organic chemistry with clarity and depth. These rigorous courses gave me a strong foundation for Dr. Daniel's biochemistry course in the Graduate School of Nutrition at Cornell and for the advanced chemistry courses I took in my doctoral program at M.I.T. . . . I was extremely fortunate that she singled me out and gave me the opportunity to participate in her research projects. Her accomplishments in scientific research and her gratifying work off campus, often in exotic locales, were inspiring to me. Certainly her success in research and in applying her expertise in the 'real world" motivated me to enter a doctoral program.

Carla Rawcliffe Lafayette, an undergraduate in the late 1970s, wrote:

> I'm extremely thankful that you chose me to work in your laboratory and that I was able to take your course. My laboratory experience and knowledge I gained from the course were probably

two of the most important factors in my being hired. And I know that next August at the American section I.S.E.S. meeting I'll be thanking my lucky stars that I had experience in presenting papers because I'll be presenting one.

In 1991, Joseph Grondahl, wrote:

> I am writing to thank you for the opportunity I had of participating in your recent research project. . . . I know that lessons I learned over those months will serve me well in the future, both in and out of medical school. I enjoyed the continued practice of evaluating current research, learning to be reasonably skeptical while understanding scientific methodology. Also of value was the familiarity I gained with the informal presentation of scientific literature. I know that this in particular will be valuable to me as an intern and resident, as I learn the practice of medicine and present cases daily to my instructors. Finally, I believe that the experience of working in the lab kept me focused on the practical side of academics that is often neglected in the classrooms at Cornell. I enjoyed having the chance to apply principles in a practical way. Thank you again.

Gary Kaplan, undergraduate in the 1970s and presently the Director of Clinical Neurophysiology at North Shore University Hospital and Associate Professor of Clinical Neurology at New York University, wrote:

> I was searching Cornell's web page and found your address. I wanted to let you know what became of me. I received my Ph.D. in neural science, Washington U., St. Louis, and M.D. at University of Miami. I remember my time in your lab fondly.
> I arrived at the lab in 1974 after noticing a part-time job announcement posted in Day Hall. . . . I remember the looks of astonishment from my family when I announced that I had a job in a 'potato lab.' Soon, they embraced the idea, and it became a topic of conversation with their friends. They would ask me to recount what I had heard about Dr. Mondy's exploits, including her calls from potato chip manufacturers for emergency consults, to remedy blackening chips and the like. In the lab, I became adept at vitamin C assays on raw, washed potatoes, and separating the outer cortex from the inner flesh. Every so often, I was called upon to sort potatoes in cold storage. I remember the large tabletop adding machine we used for calculating our assay results. When I think of my career since then, having developed some expertise in the relatively narrow field of clinical neurophysiology, I often think back to the stories Dr. Mondy told us about her participation over the years in scientific

meetings—how in the 1940s, anyone doing chemical research (inorganic, organic, biochemical) could attend the meetings of the American Chemical Society, and be part of a group of a few hundred. The breadth and depth of our knowledge at present is based on the pioneering work of researchers 30, 40, and 50 years ago. Professor Mondy is one of those pioneers, and has watched the field of nutritional research grow up. She can take great pride in being instrumental in that growth, as I take pride in being one of her students.

Teaching Outside the Classroom

A good teacher teaches not only in the classroom or laboratory, but outside of these traditional locations as well—either by answering questions or by helping students apply what they had learned. Often at my own expense, I took food chemistry students to a food company to let them observe how what they learned in class was being applied in the corporate world. Such experiences changed the way students looked at the subject. In 1967 Barbara Ludder, an undergraduate, wrote:

> I want to thank you for including me in your trip to Rochester on Friday. I have wanted to visit the R. T. French Company after hearing Miss Ruth Dubois speak at Cornell last fall and greatly appreciated this opportunity. It is members of the faculty like you who take an interest in the student beyond the classroom that make me realize the value of my Cornell education.

Graduate Teaching

When, after eighteen years of teaching undergraduates, I became more involved in graduate training, I was sorry to lose the contact I had had with the younger students. I missed their energy, but at the same time I realized that if I were to advance in my profession, I would need to find more time to conduct research. Over the years, I have received many letters from former graduate students who have remembered me as a teacher. Their words, in many cases, express better than any I could invent, the experience of teaching and learning.

Emily Owens Mobly, graduate student
I want to express my high regard for Dr. Nell Mondy, who was my graduate school chairman at Cornell. I was a research assistant under Miss Mondy from 1959 to 1961 while working on my master's degree in foods. My two years spent with Miss Mondy were extremely rewarding and provided me with an excellent background with

which to enter a research career. I was offered several jobs upon completion of my graduate work and spent three years as a food chemist with the Department of Agriculture at Beltsville, Maryland. After my marriage and move to Seattle, Washington, I found my training adaptable to work at the University of Washington Medical School. In addition to developing professional skills, Miss Mondy maintains a genuine personal interest in each student. She did much to make my time at Cornell pleasant, and we have kept up our friendship throughout the years.

Penelope Byrne Rieley, graduate student
Recently I have had an experience I would like to share. I was approached by a professor from the University of Vermont's Department of Human Nutrition and Foods and offered a position as lecturer. . . . I felt that this incident is a compliment to Cornell, in general, and to Professor Nell Mondy, in particular. Professor Mondy was chairman of my Master's committee, and I believe that her guidance and rigorous training is responsible for my success in my chosen field of Food Chemistry. . . . I strongly feel that it was the thorough training given to me by Professor Mondy, the high standards she expected and obtained by her students, that enabled me to resume my career so easily.

Subhash Chandra, graduate student
I have known Dr. Mondy as my chairperson of special committee for M.S. and Ph.D. program in Food Science Department of Cornell University. Dr. Mondy is not only very well recognized in food research but also possesses excellent teaching qualities. She has always encouraged new ideas and our research discussions are very constructive. I am proud to say that because of her invaluable guidance, I have been able to publish ten research articles during my graduate program. She also falls in the category of one of the most excellent teachers I have ever had during my academic career. Her class presentations are very clear and very encouraging to the students who are interested in the area of food and nutrition research. As a person she is very truthful and a great friend to have. She has always been very helpful in difficult times.

Lisa Klein, graduate student
I have known Dr. Mondy for the past three years beginning at the time when I was an undergraduate senior majoring in Nutrition and working in her laboratory. Since then, Dr. Mondy has served as chairperson of my special committee during my masters studies, and presently heads my Ph.D. committee. I have always found Dr. Mondy to be a very sincere and devoted professor. She is very interested in

her research and has become quite an authority in her field. Her numerous publications and personal involvement with agricultural and food science associations make her a valuable asset to our University. Dr. Mondy also takes personal interest in her students. She tries very hard to motivate them and to encourage their involvement in research, and is always available for help and guidance. She also teaches a course that is unique since it gives individual students the opportunity to acquire comprehensive knowledge in an area that is of particular interest to them, yet students also share what they have learned with each other. Dr. Mondy is a dedicated and useful member of the Cornell community.

Rathy Ponnampalam, graduate student
   I indicated in my last letter that I applied to Technical University of Nova Scotia for a Food Chemistry position. . . . Today I was typing my publications, and I was surprised to see how many I had written when I was at Cornell (12 papers). I do appreciate the way you improved my communication skills. Now my papers come back with good reviewer's comments. I think it is time to say 'BIG THANK YOU.'

Barbara P. Klein, graduate student
   Dr. Mondy was my thesis advisor when I completed my master's degree at Cornell in 1959. She was a hard taskmaster, but ultimately I found that this was excellent training. Dr. Mondy has high standards and encourages her students to do the same. As a master's student under her direction, I developed what I believed is a very sound approach to research. Dr. Mondy taught me the importance of careful planning of experiments, development of good laboratory techniques, precision and accuracy. Under her direction, I prepared two journal articles and presented a paper at the Institute of Food Technologists' annual meeting. I have since that time completed my Ph.D. at the University of Illinois, and am now a faculty member. The lessons that I learned from Dr. Mondy have helped me immensely. From a professional standpoint, Dr. Mondy is one of the leading researchers in the area of potato biochemistry. She has long been recognized as one of the experts in that field, and has served on national and international committees. As a teacher, Dr. Mondy was one of the best that I have ever had, either at Cornell or Illinois, in foods and nutrition. Her material was extremely well organized and clear, as well as accurate. I still use my classroom notes from her courses occasionally. There is no question that she is a demanding professor, but I think her standards are clear and students know what to expect from her courses and exams. On a personal level, Dr. Mondy is a frank and straightforward person. She will tell you the

truth and is fair, and expects others to be the same. . . . These attributes do not always make someone popular, but they are a good example of the kind of integrity one expects from university scholars.

Elisabeth P. Sonoff graduate student
The work under Dr. Mondy was rewarding, particularly because of her ability to instill an appreciation for thoroughness, diligence, and follow through in conducting and in reporting on all research undertaken. The experience gained from work performed under Dr. Mondy has proved to be of substantial benefit to me in my subsequent research activities.

I received many more letters from former graduate students at the time of my retirement in 1992.

Tom Mueller, graduate student
Within this month you will be honored by your colleagues and friends for the many contributions you have made on both a personal and academic level. It is appropriate at this time to thank you for the role that you played in my life. I will never forget the conversation we had in December 1974, just days before Spring Semester. You described the opportunities in the field of food science, the opportunities to utilize my scientific background and the numerous job options available to food science graduates. You generously offered me a laboratory assistant position to conduct potato research as a means of supporting a master's program. Within one week I was totally immersed in a course of study that changed my life and that unfolded into a rewarding professional career. You counseled me on how to best cover the broad area of food science and nutrition as I completed and audited numerous food and nutrition courses. You assisted me in designing and completing research projects for my master's thesis, which eventually were published in three scientific articles. You worked with me through multiple drafts of my thesis to produce a final product of which I was proud. Your support from that first conversation to my final oral review allowed me to explore and embark on a career in food science.

Barbara H. Ingham, graduate student
What a pleasure it is to be able to write to you on the occasion of your retirement. It was an honor to have the opportunity to work with you. Your guidance and support were invaluable to me as I completed work on my Ph.D. and launched a career in Food Science. You have set a positive example for me and other young women looking for evidence of successful women with science careers.

Shirley Porter Reagan, graduate student, Florida State University

In 1969—over 20 years ago—I was your first graduate student at Florida State University. . . . Dr. Mondy, you were the teacher who finally made chemistry live for me. Prior to your instruction, I saw the importance of biochemistry, but was slow to recognize the significance of inorganic chemistry to food science instruction. Because of your modeling, my instruction in food science reinforces principles of chemistry and makes those principles live for students. Of course, I never see a potato that I don't think about you. I read research published on potatoes in the Journal of Food Science and always read your work with remembrances of determining the phenolic content of potatoes. Currently, I serve as Associate Dean of the College of Human Ecology at Louisiana Tech University in Ruston, Louisiana. . . . My family and I send you our best wishes on your retirement from Cornell.

Emily Mobley, graduate student

You have been one of the most influential people in my life, as a professor, mentor, and friend. When I came to Cornell as a graduate student and research assistant in 1959, I was extremely fortunate to have you as my advisor and major professor. There were times when I felt that you were too demanding and too much a perfectionist, but I have always been grateful that you expected the best effort from your students and would not settle for less. The self-discipline and work skills I developed as a graduate student have been extremely valuable in my personal and professional life.

Robert L. Koch, graduate student

Dr. Mondy helped me to achieve more than I ever thought possible. I never felt confident at public speaking, much less giving a presentation to a group of critical colleagues. Her tireless coaching and encouragement enabled me to present two papers—one at an international conference in Canada and another at IFT in Philadelphia. Add to this the research articles that I published from my master's thesis and you have a good idea of her skill, taking "wet behind the ears" seniors and transforming them into highly motivated, achievement-oriented graduate students! I consider it an honor to have studied under her and would not trade my experience for any other.

Cecil Sievwright, graduate student

Dr. Mondy's influence on us goes beyond academic pursuit and far beyond a student/professor relationship. We have benefited from her warmth, sensitivity and the friendship she extended to us, a foreign student family studying at Cornell University. The visits to her home are memorable. As her student, I am grateful for the guidance and encouragement she gave, but more so, the support and freedom to research special projects even when it might have been divergent to her own research interests. Yes, indeed, Food and Nutrition research for the Third World needs a different approach and special focus. She provided this.

Colleagues and Professors

A final category of much appreciated letters have come from my colleagues, other professors and working scientists as well as people in the food industry.

Louise J. Daniel, Professor Biochemist 1977
I have known Nell Mondy for many years. She was one of my Ph.D. students in the Field of Chemistry. Her research was original and meticulously performed, and her research publications of high quality. After Dr. Mondy became a faculty member of the Department of Food and Nutrition, I served on the committees of several of her graduate students who minored in Biochemistry. I found these students to be well trained and their theses the result of well planned experimental work indicating the standards to which they are held. These candidates worked hard and were rewarded by the satisfaction that comes with a job well done. All of them seemed to appreciate her assistance and interest in their work.

At the time of my retirement in 1992 Dr. Daniel wrote:

> On the happy and memorable occasion of your retirement from Cornell and the Division of Nutritional Sciences, I am pleased to be asked to reminisce about our association during the past many years. . . . You were one of my early graduate students. You were in a fine group of able and eager scientists who received doctorates in 1952 and 1953, having done research on various aspects of choline oxidation in rats. . . . Nell, you were very particular about not only the quality of your work, but also the exposition of the results as they appeared in scientific papers. Most of my students found me a taskmaster when it came to writing papers, but you were seldom satisfied as soon as I was. I am certain your students benefited from your suggestions. When it came to teaching Food Chemistry, you gave your students a splendid background for biochemistry, which I taught to undergraduate majors in food and nutrition for a number of years. Their preparation and understanding made my task much easier. I wish you good health and happiness in your next endeavor.

Marion C. Pfund, Professor Food and Nutrition 1951

Nell Mondy worked closely with me during the academic years 1948—1950 and independently during 1950—1951 while I was on sabbatic leave. Miss Mondy gave up an assistant professorship in Chemistry at Sampson to accept an instructorship at the College of Home Economics at Cornell because she wished to learn to apply the science of chemistry to food preparation. . . . During the three years she was with us, Miss Mondy was in charge of the general chemistry laboratory. She also helped graduate students who act as assistants in the course to understand the subject matter that was being taught and their responsibility efficiently and well. She worked cooperatively and well with younger staff members and also gained the respect and admiration of the senior staff members by carrying a share of responsibility for seminars at a high scholarly level. During the first two years she was with us, Miss Mondy carried her work so well that during the third year when I was on sabbatic leave, she was able to assume complete charge and entire responsibility for the work that we had been doing together. Her performance, again, was of excellent quality. At the end of the third year, Miss Mondy resigned so she could continue her graduate work though she would have been recommended for an advancement in rank had she continued to teach. Miss Mondy is unusually able, loyal, responsible, cooperative, and forthright. Her standards are unusually high. She carries her work with enthusiasm and derives great pleasure from it. If she has a fault, it is that she drives herself too hard to attain a quality of performance higher than many would strive to reach.

J. R. Christensen, Prof. of Microbiology, University of Rochester Medical Center, 1978

I have known Dr. Mondy for more than 25 years, since we were fellow graduate students in the Biochemistry Department at Cornell in the early 1950s. I know Dr. Mondy to be hard working, conscientious, and responsible. Both personally and professionally, she maintains very high standards for herself, and she expects others to do likewise. At times, this latter characteristic may have created some tension between her and others whose standards may have been less firm. My own opinion is that this is to her credit, rather than otherwise. The academic world has been subject to many extraneous forces over the past several years, and there has sometimes been a tendency toward too much compromise for the sake of this or that short-term goal. It is good that there are stalwarts like Dr. Mondy to remind us that, in the long run, academic institutions will have to stand or fall on the basis of their academic standards.

John W. Sherbon, Professor of Food Science, 1978
It has become apparent to me through contact with students that Dr. Mondy has the highest possible standards in her research, the work of students under her direction, and for the classes she teaches. It is generally recognized that it is not easy to earn a graduate degree under Dr. Mondy. Those that do, however, are very well trained and are among the best Cornell produces. The extra work demanded has occasionally lead to problems with less capable or less willing students. Dr. Mondy never waivers in her own adherence to her standards, nor in her expectation of her students.

II. Educating the Public

In addition to my formal teaching in the classroom and my instruction of graduate students in the laboratory, I am pleased to have presented information from my research to the public. Frequently I have been asked to speak to extension groups or have been called for advice by extension agents to relate some of my research findings to them. I find this enjoyable, because it helps me to place my research in a different perspective from that which I would adopt for a peer-reviewed journal. Although providing information to the public often requires the elimination of complex terms and concepts, it is personally rewarding to know that my research is being heard and understood by those most affected by its findings.

Other sorts of public "teaching" have included frequent questions I have answered for various newspaper reporters, private individuals, and food companies. Although I realize that I could charge a healthy consulting fee for much of the information I distribute freely, I choose not to do so. I have on occasion served as a paid consultant for national food companies, an experience I have enjoyed, for that is another form of teaching. On other occasions I have helped students who were not enrolled in any of my courses. For example, Scott Paseltiner, an undergraduate who came to me for help with a speech, wrote:

> I'd like to thank you for all of the help you've given me since I first approached you. It's great at such a large university to have an opportunity to get to know professors on an interpersonal basis. Your kindness and willingness to help me write my speech turned a difficult subject into an enjoyable one. As for the success of this speech, it has done extremely well. In my public speaking class it received an A. After that my class nominated me to represent our section and give this speech in the Woodford Stage Speech Competition. This speech ended up in 1st place. I even took this speech over to a speech tournament at Ithaca College. Our speech

made it into the finals and finished in 3rd place. The judges expressed enjoyment of the speech. This finish also qualified me for the state competition. With a few adjustments it should be a top finisher. I never suspected that your original article in Health magazine would manifest itself into such a great experience.

Since my retirement, I no longer teach in the classroom, but I still find time to lecture to various groups who request my services. These have included the Kiwanis Club of Ithaca, the Women's Club of Ithaca, the Ithaca College Biology Seminar, Cornell Food Science Club, and various church organizations concerning the application of my research to developing countries in Africa and Central and South America. Lectures have been presented to the International Division of the Cornell Campus Club and to the National Organization of Graduate Women in Science. As a part of the Faculty Fireside Series at Cornell University's student union, Willard Straight Hall, I was invited to lecture on fifty year's experience as a chemist. It was this lecture that inspired me to write this book.

I have found that for those who remain open to life's possibilities, their learning and teaching experiences never cease. Although I have retired and choose not to work at the same pace at which I worked as a full-time professor, I continue with my research and still enjoy addressing groups of people who are eager to hear the information I can provide.

Farmers

I have shared my research findings with the farmers of New York State through their publication in *Potato News* and to farmers in other states through *Spudman* Richard B. Amidon, Executive Secretary of the Empire State Potato Club and Editor of Potato News wrote:

> The Potato Growers of New York State have had a trying year. The potatoes bruised very easily and as a result, the gradeout was heavy and at times hard to make a No. 1 grade. We feel that there is a need for more research along the area of potato bruising—whether this should be for a more hardy variety that resists bruising or a variety that will mature at an earlier date or perhaps harvesting machines that tend to treat the potatoes more carefully.
>
> Nell Mondy, Associate Professor, has reported some of her findings in regards to the chemical nature of potatoes that cause darkening. We feel that her work has been real beneficial to the Potato Industry of New York State and that it should be continued. Since New York is favorably located close to large population centers and the soil and climate is conducive to growing potatoes, more research should be done in the above mentioned areas. Thank you for your consideration.

Farm and Home Week

This annual event for many years was an important link between Cornell and the rural population of New York and neighboring states. During Farm and Home Week, farm families from across the entire region visited Cornell to attend lectures, demonstrations, and workshops prepared by members of the Home Economics and Agriculture faculty.

I remember my own participation in various Farm and Home Week activities. I also remember the amount of preparation these activities inevitably required. For all the hard work it entailed, I have often found myself missing this annual event for it certainly brought Cornell to the attention of the public.

One year I participated in a session on international cookery. I worked with Professor Myrtle Ericson who was especially gifted in this area of special foods. Another year I worked on meat with Professor Wellington from the Department of Animal Science. He discussed the selection of certain cuts of meat, and I discussed issues involved in meat cookery. A third year I was involved in the making of yeast breads and rolls. These events established a bond between Cornell and the people of New York State. The university showed concern about issues affecting their lives and livelihoods.

Consulting for the Government

While on sabbatic leaves from Cornell, I also served as an consultant to the government. In 1960—61 I served as a Supervisory Food Specialist for the United States Department of Agriculture and in 1979—80, as a consultant to the Environmental Protection Agency.

Consulting for Food Companies—Another Way of Teaching

Over the years I have also consulted for Britannia Brands New Zealand Ltd. (New Zealand), General Mills (Minnesota), Endico Potatoes (New York), Frito-Lay (Wisconsin), Proctor and Gamble (Ohio), Nihon Kaken Co. (Japan), S & B Shokuhin Co., Ltd. (Japan), Holmen Brenderi (Norway), and R. T. French Company (New York).

Claude W. Bice, The R.T. French Company, Research Manager, 1974
I have known Dr. Nell Mondy since about 1953. At that time, I was Manager of the Technical Research activity at the R. T. French Company in Rochester, New York. Throughout this period I had frequent visits with Dr. Mondy at meetings of the Institute of Food Technologists and other food science conferences. On many occasions she was accompanied by several of her students, and it was

obvious that she had good rapport with them and was a real source of inspiration to them. She did an excellent job of introducing her students to the industrial scene and its opportunities for food research. As a result of these contacts, I hired quite a few of her students and all of them were exceptionally well trained and proved to be superb performers in research and product development. One of these young ladies, hired in 1954, is now a research manager. Dr. Mondy has done a good job of helping to bring the university and industry closer together.

R.T. Darragh, Manager, Food Division, Proctor & Gamble Company, 1978
Over the years I have found Dr. Mondy to be hard working, conscientious, and technically sound. She maintains high personal and professional standards and cares a great deal for her students. I have had the opportunity to interview and hire a number of people who have studied under her. By and large, these people stand out as well trained in basic sciences, well organized, hard working, and competent. Turning out good graduates, of course, is an important function of the University and its faculty.

Conclusion

During the course of my teaching career, I received several awards, such as the Danforth Award for a seminar teaching natural sciences in 1954, and another Danforth Award in 1958 for creative teaching. I also received the National Science Foundation Award for University Teachers of Chemistry in 1959 and the Cornell Higher Education Award in 1967. In 1997 I received the Elizabeth Fleming Stier Award from the Institute of Food Technologists for humanitarian ideals that resulted in a significant contribution to food industry, academia, students or the general public. However, I take the greatest pride in the kind words of the students I taught, who have kept me in their thoughts. Ultimately the greatest measure of a teacher is not awards received, but what the awards represent: the dedication and impact on former students.

Despite the constraints the food chemistry course imposed upon my schedule, I served on many college committees, including the Research Committee and the Committee on Academic Standing which involved recognizing the problems of students who were in danger of failing, determining what could be done, and making specific recommendations. While on this committee I suggested ways in which the college could honor our top students, something that had been overlooked previously.

I also spent many hours working with students as a member of the Student-Faculty committee, a position I was proud to hold. Serving on this committee was an honor, for it meant that I had earned the trust and respect of most undergraduates. A photograph taken during my tenure on this committee appears in the 1966 edition of the *Cornellian,* Cornell's yearbook. Other photographs in the *Cornellian* featured my laboratory teaching.

Perhaps the most significant honor given to me by the students of the School of Home Economics was their selection of me, from among all the home economics faculty, to represent them on the Ag-Domicon Council. The Council was an interesting entity, for it represented students from both the School of Agriculture and the School of Home Economics, working more closely together on certain issues of mutual concern. Students from the then predominantly male Agriculture School and students from the predominantly female School of Home Economics collaborated to form the Ag Domicon Council. One faculty adviser from each college was chosen by students to serve on this committee. Working with these students was a delightful experience.

I also worked with students in the various honorary societies, such as Sigma Delta Epsilon; Graduate Women in Science; Omicron Nu; (home economics honorary); and Phi Tau Sigma, (honorary for food science), which included both graduate and undergraduate students. The bright and enthusiastic students kept me alert.

The recognition of my students is a wonderful reward for my years of teaching. Producing good students is one way in which I can thank the teachers who have influenced me and played a valuable role in my education. Without good teachers, there could be no good students. I expected the best from each student and most students met these expectations. I am grateful for the opportunity to teach, and I am grateful to all the students who have contributed to my enjoyable career.

Summing It Up

When I look back to my beginnings, it is hard to believe how quickly the years have passed. As I trace my journey through the years, I realize how every part of my life, both the good and the bad, has made a significant contribution to my character. My years of growing up in Pocahontas, schooling at Ouachita, Texas U., and Cornell U. and various professional experiences have left me with wonderful memories and a sense of accomplishment. Without the constant help and support of family, friends, mentors, and especially students, I know that I would have accomplished very little. I am grateful for their company and encouragement along the way.

I am grateful to have made constructive changes in my environment. In the early years in Ithaca, N.Y. I was able to obtain the needed bus service on the Cornell campus; organize a "Friendship" class in the First Baptist Church; teach chemistry to NY World War II veterans; celebrate Cornell's Nobel Prize dinner in honor of Dr. J.B. Sumner; design new chemical experiments and equipment for teaching and research; help plan the first World Food Congress held in 1962; and participate in the "Food Revolution" following World War II. The latter transformed methods of food production, storage, processing, marketing and labeling. With other faculty we enlarged public awareness of nutrition, established the Institute of Food Science (1967) and the Institute of Toxicology (1981) at Cornell University. Serving as consultant to government agencies, EPA and USDA, and several food companies, I contributed to the general knowledge of food chemistry and nutrition. Information was shared with many countries including India, Nigeria, Ivory Coast, Peru, Bolivia, Chile, Indonesia, Singapore, Taiwan, Thailand, China, Korea, Japan, Ireland, Scotland, England, Finland, Sweden, and the Netherlands.

As a role model for young women in the hard sciences, and as national president of Graduate Women in Science (1983-84), I contributed to the status of women in science. Being a chemist in a changing world has been fun. I am not frightened by long chemical names used in newspapers, television, medicine, food and drug labels, and I enjoy observing and creating chemical changes around me. The world is made up of chemicals. Our body and our food are made of chemicals. Chemistry is defined as "the study of matter and the changes it undergoes" and I am happy to have studied such an interesting subject.

In 1997, the Institute of Food Technologists (IFT)—an organization of 28,000 members—honored me with the presentation of its first Elizabeth Fleming Stier Award. This award honors an IFT member for the pursuit of humanitarian ideals and unselfish dedication that resulted in significant contributions to the well being of the food industry, academia, students, or the general public. I was grateful to have been selected for the award and I especially appreciated the following kind statement made at the time of the presentation and later printed in *Food Technology* 51:108 (1997).

> The first Elizabeth Fleming Stier Award was presented to Dr. Nell I. Mondy, Professor Emerita of Food Science, Nutrition and Toxicology at Cornell University. After receiving her Ph.D. in biochemistry from Cornell, Mondy began her career when there were few women in the 'hard' sciences and served as role model for many who have come after her. Her thorough preparation, clear presentation, and skillful mentoring have earned her the admiration and respect of the more than 5,000 students to whom she taught chemistry, nutrition, food science, and toxicology. Her concern with her students' studies, personal lives, and postgraduate careers have earned her their lasting affection, as they speak of her 'warmth, sensitivity, and friendship,' her 'guidance and encouragement,' and the 'support and freedom to pursue projects divergent from her own interests.' She has lectured in 47 countries and is responsible for the introduction of a soybean diet for seriously malnourished children in Nigeria, a program that UNICEF has used as a model. She is a Fellow of the American Institute of Chemists, the American Association for the Advancement of Science, and was named an IFT Fellow in 1985. In honor of her many contributions to the potato industry, she was also made an Honorary Life Member of the Potato Association of America.

I am grateful for every single small success achieved throughout my lifetime, even grateful for the ones that did not turn out as I planned. However, I still look forward to more years of achievement. I have refused to allow retirement or growing older to interfere with my ideas, goals, and plans. Life constantly springs different challenges, and I want to be prepared to meet them as they occur. My motto, *"You Never Fail Until You Stop Trying"* still remains in my heart and mind each step of the way. I look forward to a future that is exciting and rewarding, and I plan to *"never stop trying."*

Mrs. F. Ethel Mondy
Mother of Nell I. Mondy
This book is dedicated to Mrs. Ethel Mondy, my mother.

Dr. Mondy teaching food chemistry to undergraduates in College Home Economics and School Hotel Administration, Cornell University.

Dr. Mondy presents lecture at Fifth International Congress of
Food Science and Technology.
Kyoto, Japan (1978)

Dr. Mondy accepts gavel as she is installed as
National President of Graduate Women in Science.
Detroit, Michigan (1983)

Dr. Mondy—guest of Faculty Institute of Food Industry.
Moscow, USSR (1987)

Dr. Mondy with students at Singapore World Food Congress.
Dr. Mondy was a speaker at the 1987 Congress.

Dr. Mondy in a potato field at Alaska Experiment Station.
Palmer, Alaska (1989)

Dr. Mondy consulting with a female potato farmer (Mrs. Jane Bourne) in Adalaide, Australia (1991).

Dr. Nell Mondy, Mrs. Harvey Jones, Dr. Ben Elrod (President Ouachita Baptist University) at the Dedication of *Nell I. Mondy Organic Chemistry Laboratory* located in Harvey Jones Science Center. Ouachita Baptist University, Arkadelphia, AR (1997)

Dr. Mondy—recipient of the Elizabeth Steir Award at Institute of Food Technologist Meeting in Orlando, Florida 1997.

Dr. Mondy—honored for her research accomplishments by College Human Ecology and College of Agriculture, Cornell University, Ithaca, NY. (1998-99) Life size photo in foyer of Human Ecology Building, Cornell University.